Lal Bahadur Shastri

Lal Bahadur Shastri

Series Editor
Dr. M.H. Syed

Editor
R.K. Singh **P.K. Choudhry**

Himalaya Books Pvt. Ltd.

'Ramdoot', Dr. Bhalerao Marg, Girgaon, Mumbai - 400 004
Tel : (022) 23863863. Fax : (022) 23877178
Email : himpub@vsnl.com

Edition : 2013

Published by : **H.B.P.L.**
"Pooja Apartments", 4-B, Murari Lal Street, Ansari Road,
Darya Ganj, New Delhi-110 002
Phones : 23270392, 23278631 Reliance : 30180392 to 396
Fax : 011-23256286 Email : hphdel@vsnl.com

Sole Distributers : HIMALAYA PUBLISHING HOUSE PVT. LTD.

Branch Offices

Mumbai : "Ramdoot", Dr. Bhalerao Marg, Girgaon, Mumbai-400 004.
Phones : 23860170/23863863 Fax : 022-23877178
Email : himpub@vsnl.com
Website : www.himpub.com

Nagpur : Kundanlal Chandak Industrial Estate, Ghat Road, **Nagpur - 440 018.**
Phone: 2738731, 3296733 Telefax : 0712-2721215

Bengaluru : No. 16/1 (Old 12/1), 1st Floor, Next to Hotel Highlands,
Madhava Nagar, Race Course Road, **Bengaluru - 560 001.**
Phone : 22281541, 22385461, Telefax: 080-22286611

Hyderabad : No. 3-4-184, Lingampally, Besides Raghavendra Swamy Matham,
Kachiguda, **Hyderabad - 500 027.** Phone: 040-27560041, 27550139,
Mobile:- 09848130433 Telefax: 040-27560041

Chennai : No. 85/50, Bazullah Road, T. Nagar, **Chennai - 600 017.**
Phone: 044-28344020, 32463737, 42124860

Pune : No. 527, "Laksha" Apartment, First Floor, Mehunpura, Shaniwarpeth,
(Near Prabhat Theatre), **Pune - 411 030.**
Phone: 020-24496323/24496333/32326733

Lucknow : House No. 731, Sehkhupura Colony, Near B.D. Convent School,
Lucknow - 226 024. Mobile : 09307501549

Ahmedabad : No. 114, "SHAIL", 1st Floor, Opp. Madhu Sudan House, C.G.Road,
Navrang Pura, **Ahmedabad – 380 009.**
Phone: 079-26560126, Mobiles: 09327324149,09314679413

Ernakulam : No. 39/104 A, Lakshmi Apartment, Karikkamuri Cross Rd.,
Ernakulam, **Cochin – 682011**, Kerala.
Phone: 0484-2378012, 2378016, Mob.: 09344199799

Bhubaneswar : 5 Station Square, **Bhubaneswar (Orissa) - 751 001.**
Mobile: 9861046007, E-mail:- orissa@himpub.com

Indore : Kesardeep Avenue Extension, 73, Narayan Bagh.Flat No. 302,
IIIrd Floor, Near Humpty Dumpty School, Narayan Bagh,
Indore (M.P.) 452 007 Mobile: 09301386468

Kolkata : 108/4, Beliaghata, Main Road, Near ID Hospital, Opp. SBI Bank
Kolkata - 700 010.
Mobile: 09910440956, E-mail:- nkmitra@himpub.com

Guwahati : House No. 15, Behind Prajjyotish College, Near Sharma
Printing Press, P.O. Bharalumukh, Guwahati - 781009 (Assam)
Mobile: 07439040301; 07439040302

Printed by : Sri Prints & Sales, Delhi

Preface

Biography, is now a form of literature, very much in vogue. In fact, biography is a description or account of someone's life and the times, which is usually published in the form of a book. A biography is more than a mention of personal facts (life, education, work, relationships and death), it also portrays the subject's experience of events. Technically speaking, a work is biographical, if it covers, all of a person's life. Biography writing has a long history. A biography is real. Ancient Greeks developed the biographical tradition, which we have inherited, although until the 5th century AD, when the word 'biographia' first appeared, in Damascius' "Life of Isodorus," biographical pieces were called simply "lives". It is quite likely that the Greeks were drawing on a pre-existing eastern tradition. Certainly Herodotus' "Histories" contains more detailed biographical information on Persian kings and subjects. The earliest surviving pieces, which we would identify as biographical are Isocrates' "Life of Evagoras" and Xenophon's "Life of Agesilaos," both from the fifth century BC. "Parallel Lives" by Plutarch, a Greek writing under the Roman empire, is a series of short biographies of eminent men.

The Golden Age of English biography emerged in late eighteenth century, the century in which the terms "biography" and "autobiography" entered English lexicon. The classic works of the period were Samuel Johnson's "Critical Lives of the Poets" and James Boswell's "Massive Life of Johnson". Generally American biography followed English model. By World War I, cheap hardcover reprints had become popular. The decade of the 1920s witnessed a biographical 'boom'. Later, biographical writings developed a lot and today biographies are written and compiled in the finest form of the genre. In India too, biography, as a form of literature has been evolved, cultivated and polished over the years. Here is an effort to promote this tradition further.

This series of biographies of great men, great women and celebrities in all walks of life is an adventurous academic endeavour, in its own right. A team of researchers and compilers has worked for a good period of time to accomplish the project. For this purpose, hundreds of books by eminent authors and editors have been consulted and referred to. We have benefited from various works, liberally, in order to illustrate and enrich this effort of ours. Present book is devoted to the great personality of Lal Bahadur Shastri.

Lal Bahadur Shastri, former Prime Minister of India, devoted his life for the pride and honour of the country. He was regarded as man of principles. He laid the foundation stones of the well-productive schemes like Green Revolution and White Revolution. Shastri was against the prevailing caste system and therefore decided to drop his surname. The title "Shastri" was given after the completion of his graduation at Kashi Vidyapeeth, Varanasi. This title refers to a "scholar" or a person, adept in the "Holy Scriptures". He was one of the leading and prominent faces that ran the Quit India movement, called by Mahatma Gandhi. Lal Bahadur Shastri had served in various positions before being elected as the Prime Minister. Nehru, had once said, "No one could wish for a better comrade than Lal Bahadur, a man of the highest integrity and devoted to ideas". Lal Bahadur Shastri was the first person to be posthumously awarded the Bharat Ratna, India's highest civilian award.

This is a compact and comprehensive account of the above mentioned great life, which is bound to attract the attention of scholars, researchers, students and the general readers alike. Let's hope this humble effort would receive a warm welcome and due applause.

— ***Editors***

Contents

1

An Illustrious Life

Birth and Early Days

India's second Prime Minister Lal Bahadur Shastri popularly known as Shastriji was born on October 2, 1904 in Uttar Pradesh at a place known as Mughal Sarai, a very well known city. Lal Bahadur's father, Shri Sharda Prasad Shrivastva was a school teacher. His mother Ram Dulari Devi was the proud daughter of this country, who gave birth to this great son who rose to the highest position and led the country on the principles cherished by Gandhiji and Jawaharlal Nehru. Interestingly, Lal Bahadur's birthday falls on the same day as that of his mentor Mahatma Gandhi. Unfortunately, Lal Bahadur could not have the love and affection of his father since he died prematurely when Lal Bahadur was only one and a half years old.

Fatherless Child

His parents Sharda Prasad and Ram Dulari Devi were agriculturists. Shrivastava was part of Lal Bahadur's name. He dropped that part indicating his caste, when he grew up. He did not like such indications of caste. Lal Bahadur's father, a poor teacher at first, became a clerk in the Revenue Office at Allahabad. Here, too, he earned very little. But, even though he was poor, he never accepted bribes. He lived a life of honesty and integrity. Sharda Prasad died when Lal Bahadur was only a year old. Ram Dulari Devi felt as though the skies had come down on her. Her father gave shelter to her and her three children, a boy and two girls.

Loving Grandfather

Lal Bahadur's grandfather Hazari Lal's family was very large. His brothers, their wives and children, besides his own children and grand children, lived under the same roof. It was a small world in itself and Hazari Lal was the fountain of love and affection to all of them. He looked after every one in the family with love. He was especially fond of little Lal Bahadur. He always affectionately called him 'Nanhe' which means 'tiny'.

An interesting incident took place when Lal Bahadur was only three months old. The mother went to bathe in the holy Ganga with her child. In the milling crowd at the bathing ghat she lost her child. The child had slipped from his mother's arms into a cowherd's basket. The cowherd had no children, So he took the child as a gift from God and celebrated the event with great joy.

The mother was lost in grief. A complaint was lodged with the police. They traced the child. The foster parents wept bitterly to give back the child. Lal Bahadur, who was destined to govern the country, narrowly missed the 'good fortune' of becoming a cowherd.

Lal Bahadur stayed at his grandfather's house till he was ten. By that time he had passed the sixth standard examination. There was no high school in that place. They sent him to Kashi for further education.

Early Childhood

Lal Bahadur's surname "Shastri" did not indicate his caste or community. It was an honorific surname referring to the Shastri course he pursued at the Kashi Vidyapeeth (Varanasi) where he studied. He was born in a Shrivastava (Kayastha) family of minor government officials on 2 October, 1904 at Mughal Sarai, a railway colony about 10 kilometres from Varanasi. His father was a school teacher who died when Lal Bahadur was about two years old so that he and his two sisters were brought up by his maternal grandfather. At Varanasi, he joined the Harish Chandra High School in 1914 which he left in 1920 to join the non-cooperation movement started by Gandhi, Krishna, Hutheesingh records an incident of 1920:

At that time he looked about twelve years old with his small frame and round innocent face, but he was full of spirit. Once, when the municipal authorities of Allahabad refused to let us fly our national flag from the pole atop the court house. Shastri dressed himself up in the tent-like robes and hood of a Muslim woman and got through the guards. Then throwing off his disguise, he bounded up the stairs like a chamois and hoisted the flag before any one knew what he was doing.

Shortly after, he joined the Kashi Vidyapeeth in 1922 and passed the Shastri Examination. At Varanasi he came in contact with one Pandit Niskameshwar Mishra who taught him mathematics and roused his interest in philosophy, religion and teachings of Ram Krishna Paramhansa, Vivekananda, and Ram Tirth. He also read some literature on Bertrand Russell, Hegel, Kant and Huxley.

The principal of the Kashi Vidyapeeth, Bhagwan Das imparted to him the principles of humanism. But his personal contacts remained confined to persons such as Kripalani, Sri Prakash and Sampurnanand. Nehru and Gandhi were rather remote, at the time. In 1925, he met Lala Lajpat Rai and joined the Servants of India Society. On his death in 1928 AD. Tandon took over the Society and he shifted to Allahabad, where he got in touch with Nehru and became a Congress worker.

In 1927, he married Lalita Devi of Mirzapur, then 18 years old. They had four sons and two daughters, which he admitted was "not a good example of family planning". His wife rarely appeared in public and never attended official functions. On her husband's tragic death at Tashkent in January 1966, she insisted on visiting the spot where he died seeking Soviet hospitality, to the embarrassment of Mrs. Gandhi. Three years later she issued the fantastic, attention-catching statement that her husband had been poisoned'. By whom and for what reason she never specified but she went to repeating purposefully that there were discrepancies in the accounts of several of those present when he died of massive heart attack. These statements sounded eccentric. Nevertheless "a curious if minute coterie has formed which believes that Shastri was murdered, not by the Russians, who had no reasons to kill him nor by the Pakistanis, who had come to terms with him but at the instigation of his Indian political opponents" which is a reminder of a racial memory in India today of a time when the stealthy annihilation by poison of political enemy was more or less commonplace."

The following account of his death is given by the oldest of India's politicians then, Morarji Desai.

During the negotiations that took place at Tashkent, he agreed to return the areas that we had recovered from Pakistan during the war. This created a very bad impression in India and Lal Bahadurji, who had become very popular during the war, became very unpopular as a result. I was told that he talked over the telephone with the members of his family before he got the heart attack. He was informed about the opposition to the Tashkent decision. This information perhaps gave him a shock and he died within an hour and a half after this talk.

Contact with Nehru

His stay at Allahabad deepened his contacts with Nehru. On December 31, 1929 he joined Nehru and his followers who demanded unconditional independence. In 1930, he joined the Civil Disobedience Movement and was arrested for the first time. He got two and half years' sentence.

Thereafter, he went to jail in 1932, 1941, and 1942, altogether 6 terms in prison totalling seven years. At Allahabad, he was in the same prison with Nehru but they were kept in separate barracks. "We couldn't meet", Shastri said: "but Nehru was very kind about sending books to us." In prison, he spent time in reading, and translated the biography of Madame Curie in Hindi.

In 1930, he became secretary of the Allahabad District Congress Committee and organised the No Rent Campaign in Allahabad district under the guidance of Nehru. In 1935, he was elevated to the position of the general secretary to the U.P. Congress Committee, then dominated by the Congress heavyweight Pandit G.B. Pant in the 1937 elections, he got elected to the U.P. Assembly. In 1940, he participated in the individual satyagraha of Gandhi and got arrested.

In August 1942 came the Quit India movement. The U.P. leaders wanted him to avoid arrest so that he could supervise the agitation.

Mohammad Yunus says:

Someone suddenly got a brain wave that the best way would be to dress him up like a sweeper woman and station him in Anand Bhawan itself. So he wore a skirt, earned a broom and a dupatta to hide his face in the typical style in case the police came for a surprise check. The outfit was replete with a few bangles as well. The memory of that feminine disguise, its low-caste associations, allied above all with memories of the splendour of Anand Bhawan perhaps left a stigma of shame and humiliation on Lal Bahadur's mind. It could partly explain some of his later complexes.

After the war he was re-elected to the U.P. Assembly and was named secretary to the U.P. Parliamentary Board. Alongwith C.B. Gupta whom Galbraith described as "a politician of minute stature-some of five feet high." (same as Shastri), Shastri was appointed as Pant's Parliamentary secretary. It was, therefore, largely to Pant that Shastri owed his entry into the upper echelons of the Congress.

Pant had picked up Shastri because "he was likeable, hardworking, devoted and trustworthy. He was also non-controversial." Pant relied on him to assess the political impact of measures the state government proposed to take. In 1947, he was given charge of public security in U.P. and became the home minister in charge of police and transport. As the police minister, he asked them that instead of lathis, they should use water-hose to disperse a demonstrating mob.

Following the Tandon-Nehru controversy of 1950-51. Nehru became the Congress president and he called Shastri to Delhi, to organise the Congress campaign in India's first general elections.

He became the Congress general secretary. Throughout the elections, he stayed at Teen Murti House, Nehru's residence, and used the period for cultivating Nehru in order to realise his political ambitions. The landslide Congress victory produced his reward in the form of election to the Rajya Sabha and his appointment as the Union minister for transport and railways (1952). Following the railway accident at Ariyalur in 1956, killing 144 persons, injuring 115, in a show of righteousness, he resigned, a major politically motivated act calculated to earn him a halo.

Witness the observations made by Morarji Desai: At the end of 1956 before Shri Krishna Menon joined the Cabinet Shri Lal Bahadur Shastri had resigned his railway ministership as several accidents had taken place on the railways at that time. Such accidents had occurred before and have occurred again since, not only in India, but in all countries.

But Shri Lal Bahadur Shastri felt that the railway ministry must accept the blame for not preventing the accidents and that he must resign as the minister in charge Jawaharlalji accepted his resignation.

It did increase the reputation of Shri Lal Bahadur Shastri and I felt at that time that he took this step only to enhance his reputation and prestige. Shri Lal Bahadur Shastri was a *skilled political tactician,* and I, therefore, felt that he had taken this step to enhance his political prestige".

> "After the second general elections, everything about the railway accidents was forgotten and Shastri was elected to the Lok Sabha from Allahabad and served as minister of transport and communications until March 1958. This was the reward for the fashion in which he did the selection of candidates, following Nehru's wishes. In 1958, following the Mundhra Deal scandal and the resignation of T.T. Krishnamachari (TTK) as finance minister. Shastri in a Cabinet reshuffle got into the important ministry of commerce and industry in which capacity he proved a flop. He demonstrated almost a total lack of initiative and in everything he did or did not do he followed Nehru."

Home Minister

By February 1961, Pant's health began to deteriorate and Shastri became acting home minister On March 7, Pant died and bypassing Morarji Desai, Shastri became the home minister.

Desai has this to say about the event: Some people had felt, after the passing away of Panditji in 1961, that the home ministry should be entrusted to me but I did not think that Jawaharlalji would accept such an arrangement I felt that he was afraid that if the home ministry was entrusted to me, it would increase my political importance a great deal. Ultimately it was entrusted to Shri Lal Bahadur Shastri who always carried out Jawaharlalji's wishes and did not do anything which he did not like.

"Here also the contrast between Shastri and Pant whom he replaced was sharp." Shastri seemed furtive as he slipped unnoticed on to the government front bench Pant's entrances always sent a stir through the huge hall. The Emperor Akbar could not have commanded more deference. The contrast was even more marked when Shastri rose to speak in a small monotone. The words were lost in the hubbub of heedless legislators. Pant, on the other hand, always held Parliament spell-bound. It seemed as if Oliver Wendell Holmes had been replaced by the Clerk of the Court."

As home minister, Shastri never rose to the challenge the job posed. His performance was lacklustre and he displayed lack of initiative in moments of crisis. In November 1962, he became panicky and is reported to have told a colleague that NEFA, Assam, and northern Bengal would all be occupied by the Chinese and that he was preparing to have the oil Walls in Assam blown up. He had to took after law and order, internal security, the central reserve police, the political department, the intelligence bureau, the language question, the centre-states relations, the All-India Services, major appointments in the high courts and the supreme court as also in the union public service commission, the minorities problem, and a hundred other vitally important issues.

Either he followed the orders or instructions given to him by Nehru whose mere wish was a command to him, or he was overawed by the old ICS bureaucrats— V. Vishwanathan, L.P. Singh and Hari Sharma. Vishwanathan was "the *de facto* home minister except on the rare occasions when Shastri intervened to overrule his lieutenant." L.P. Singh looked after the administrative services while Hari Sharma was charged with the government of the Union Territories This triumvirate ran the home ministry but it was Vishwanathan, the home secretary, who was "the uncrowned King of India."

As for Shastri, he rarefy visited the home ministry until 5 or even 5.30 p.m. and that only to sign on the dotted lines or to meet visitors upto 11 p.m. in the South Block labyrinth. Normally, he got up at 5.30 a.m. did some yoga exercises which he gave up after his first heart attack in October, 1959 and then met the visitors at his residence, at 1 Motilal Nehru Place which, long before he woke up resembled "a metropolitan railway station at rush hour." As one observer put it Waiting there, you feel as if you were at the crossroads of India. Turbaned Sikhs, dhoti-wearing Congressmen, and half-naked sadhus are among the flood of audience-seekers who fill his sitting rooms and spill out into the garden.

When Shastri is ready, he receives each caller individually rather than having them come in delegation as Pant used to do. He rises to greet each visitor, he would not dream of lying on his couch, let alone allowing petitioners to kiss his feet. Despite the milling throng outside and the other pressures on him (he is) always calm, courteous, and seemingly unhurried."

But despite the trying time he had with the visitors, he never lost his cool. He was always anxious to appear fair and very humane and tended to treat an individual as an individual rather than part of the mass By this technique, he rose from the position of nobody in the Congress to fourth rank in the hierarchy by 1960, immediately after Desai. Just because he entirely depended on the able and experienced ICS officers, he avoided all controversies which attend a decision taken by a minister independently and at his own.

Shastri preferred to be non-controversial and "to stand in the wings of the party leaving the centre of the stage to Nehru." His admirers and kinsmen built up the legend of his administrative ability, he himself remaining "a middle-of the-roader ideologically" and building up "a growing following among the rank and file." Gradually, he gained the reputation of being "a man of the people" and "a pure man".

Before he became the home minister, on the question of Nagaland to be declared a state within the Indian Union, Shastri as also Pant had supported Nehru. In 1959-60, Phizo-had come out with the demand of an independent Nagaland and the Nagas began to set up an independent rebel government. The Naga rebels were getting sympathy from other Nagas and the Indian army was not given full freedom to suppress the rebellion by means of force.

In 1960, Nehru called a conference of the representatives of the Assam Government in which the views of Assamese and Naga people were presented. Nehru suggested the separation of Nagaland from Assam and making it a separate state. Desai opposed it on the ground that giving separate statehood to such a small population would lead to demands for separate states from different parts of the country and the unity of India would be endangered Both Pant and Shastri kept quiet.

Nehru told Desai that if there were demands from other parts for separate states, those could also be considered Nehru had his way. Desai writes: This convinced me that Jawaharlalji had prior discussions with them and had taken their consent."

As home minister, Shastri's astuteness came into full display on the question of language dispute in the Cachar district of Assam. In late June and early July of 1960, language issue ignited the long-smouldering economic jealousies in Assam. The backward Assamese-speaking majority had always resented the fact that the Bengali-speaking minority held the best jobs and also dominated trade and commerce.

The Bengali resistance to the Assamese language being declared as the sole official language of the state was used as a pretext for a wholesale assault on the Bengali community About 45,000 Bengalis became refugees of whom about 40,000 went to West Bengal. On July 4, the police opened fire on a crowd in

Gauhati killing one student and injuring six others. This made the anti-Bengali frenzy "a hurricane of violence'. At least 500 Bengalis were killed in cold blood and many more hundreds injured. An ashen-faced Nehru walked among the hordes of the homeless during a tour of stricken villages After the death of Pant eight months later, violence erupted again on 19 May, 1961 when the Bengalis agitating for the recognition of Bengali as an additional state language of Assam clashed with the police so that 15 persons were killed and 80 injured.

When the police opened fire on a crowd of 2000 Bengalis in Cachar district the result was hartals in the Bengali areas in Assam. On May 24, hartal was observed in Calcutta and other West Bengal cities. Shastri flew to Cachar. He "Went on probing and pursuing this thing until people started thinking in terms of human tolerance and their obligations to the country. It required tremendous patience: he to convince all groups of his own deep sincerity and firmness".

Shastri listened to different view points As he put it "I have the capacity of understanding different view points. I kept an open mind. I talked to different sets of people." Shastri returned with a permanent solution acceptable to all. It was based on the use of English, Assamese, and Bengali languages for different purposes. Correspondence between Cachar district and Assam Government headquarters began to be conducted in English and both Assamese and Bengal were now used in Cachar government offices and schools with preference for Bengali as the language of the local majority. This 'Shastri formula' ensured communal harmony in Assam. Cachar district was now represented in the Assamese Cabinet.

Strong and Self-respecting

Courage and self-respect were two virtues, which took deep root in him from his childhood. While in Kashi, he went with his friends to see a fair on the other bank of the Ganga. On the way back he had no money for the boat fare. His self-respect did not allow him to ask his friends for money. He slipped from their company without their knowledge. His friends forgot him in their talk and boarded the boat. When the boat had moved away,

Lal Bahadur jumped into the river; as his friends watched breathlessly he swam to the other bank safely.

Though Lal Bahadur was, a man of small build, he was unusually strong. His moral strength was even greater. As in water so in life he swam quite successfully. Twice he was about to be drowned but was saved. It is said that when he was saved the second time, he had his teacher's three-year-old baby on his shoulders.

Lal Bahadur acquired virtues like boldness, love of adventure, patience, self-control, courtesy and selflessness in his childhood.

Even as a boy he loved to read books. He read whatever books he came across, whether he understood them or not. He was fond of Guru Nanak's verses.

He used to repeat the following lines often:

> "O Nanak! Be tiny like grass, For other plants will whither away, but grass will remain ever green."

Education

Lal Bahadur was only ten years old when he came to Banaras for his studies. The maternal uncle of Shastriji had been living at Banaras and that was what made him shift there for his schooling. He studied at Harin Chandra High School, Banaras and Kashi Vidyapeeth.

In the year 1926, Shastriji secured a first class degree of Shastri in Philosophy. Shastriji was very much impressed by the personality and spiritual greatness of the Principal of the Vidyapeeth. It had a lasting impact on the personality of Shastriji for all times to come.

In fact, if we may say so, Dr. Bhagwan Das, the great Principal moulded the personality of Shastriji through his own example of high class morality and spirituality. The giants like Acharya Narendra Dev, Acharya J.B. Kriplani, Sri Prakasa and Dr. Sampurnanand were the teachers in the Kashi Vidyapeeth. Shastriji was thus one of the luckiest persons to have his education, academic or otherwise, under the charge of these great personalities. Shastriji was born and brought up in the holy cities of Banaras and Allahabad which shaped his mind and personality into an orthodox, moral purity and humility.

Marriage

In the year 1927, Shastriji was married to a great lady by the name Lal Mony (Lalita Devi) of a famous town Mirzapur (U.P.). The only thing which Shastriji accepted as dowry in his marriage was a charkha and a little yam. It is a historical fact that Jawaharlal had been a very close associate of Lal Bahadur Shastri. Lal Bahadur had the good fortune of watching Jawaharlal Nehru unfurling the flag of independence on the banks of Ravi in the year 1929.

In the thirties, Shastriji joined service in *the* Municipal Board at Allahabad. Shastriji could remain there only for a short span. In the year 1930, at Gandhiji's call, Shastriji participated in the Salt Satyagraha and was arrested and sentenced for two and a half years. He utilised his period of detention in as best a manner as possible and had gone through the biographies of great leaders as also the political philosophies of Kant, Hegal, Laski, Marx, Lenin, etc. He also translated into Hindi the autobiography of Madam Curie.

The Lesson

An incident, which took place when he was six years old, seems to have left a deep mark on his mind. Once he went to an orchard with his friends. He was standing below while his friends climbed the trees. He plucked a flower from a bush.

The gardener came in the meantime and saw Lal Bahadur. The boys on the trees climbed down and ran away. The gardener caught Lal Bahadur. He beat him severely.

Lal Bahadur wept and said, "I am orphan. Do not beat me."

The gardener smiled with pity and said, "Because you are an orphan, you must learn better behaviour, my boy."

The words of the gardener had a great effect on him. He swore to him, "I shall behave better in future. Because I am an orphan I must learn good behaviour."

Though short he was not timid at school. All boys were friendly with him. Like the grass he always looked fresh and smiling. Not only during his school days but also in his later life he did not hate anyone. It seems he used to act in plays at school. He played the role of Kripacharya in the play 'Mahabharatha'. Kripacharya was in the court of Duryodhana and yet was loved by the Pandavas. Lal Bahadur Shastri had acquired the same worth.

Death

Lal Bahadur Shastri, who had earlier suffered two heart attacks, died of the third cardiac arrest on 11 January, 1966. He is the only Indian Prime Minister, to have died in office, overseas. Lal Bahadur Shastri was the first person to be posthumously awarded the Bharat Ratna, (India's highest civilian award).

Great Moral Character

On his early life he need not dwell much, because it has already been touched upon by those who have written about him, specially the swimming of the Ganga incident. Having lost his father as an infant, his mother's influence was strong upon him and to the very end he faithfully followed the advice she had given him when he had announced his intention of joining the freedom struggle: "Think well and decide, but once having decided, never turn back."

From an early age he was involved in the National Movement, and to the end of his life he remained a member of the Servants of the People Society founded by Lala Lajpat Rai. This member-ship had a deep influence on him and instilled the spirit of service which was so characteristic of him.

Like others who took part in the freedom struggle, he had his share of suffering and sacrifice. But, as will be mentioned in his letter to me, the help and cooperation of his wife went a long way to make the burden bearable. Of his prison days Shastriji used to say that some of his fellow prisoners had begun to almost dread the days when their family members were permitted to visit them. Very often there used to be reproaches to the effect that you are sitting comfortably in jail getting two square meals a day, while the family and children are almost starving, and having a bitter struggle for even bare necessities. But Shastriji said that on such occasions whenever he asked his wife whether she was facing any difficulty she used to smile broadly and say "None at all. There is now one person less to eat".

But of suffering there was no dearth, which can be illustrated by just one instance, which Smt. Shastri once related. Shastriji was in jail when his little daughter fell seriously ill. The doctors said it was typhoid, and the child was unlikely to survive. Even so, Shastriji was unwilling to apply for parole; but at the intervention of some persons the jail authorities permitted him to visit his dying daughter.

Perhaps happiness at her father's presence made the child linger on and on and delayed the inevitable end. Came the last night, when the next morning Shastriji had to return to prison. Smt. Lalita Shastri was faced with the terrible prospect of having to arrange herself for the funeral rites of her child. As she said' "All that night I kept praying to my God. Other mothers pray for the long life of their children; I was praying for the death of mine. God heard my prayers, and the child passed away in the early hours of the morning, and Shastriji was able to perform the last rites before going back to prison".

However, to come to Shastriji himself, the lasting impression one has of him is his essential goodness. He was in every sense of the word one of God's good men, full of compassion and the milk of human kindness. Never did he wish ill to others, and he always recoiled from giving pain.

For one who was the Home Minister and Prime Minister of India he could not always avoid doing so, but never did he consciously desire it. And whenever he did come to know of any hurt caused to somebody by any action of his, he agonised over it, sometimes to the extent of making himself miserable. Always, and to all matters, he sought to bring the healing touch.

His goodness found its base in his gentleness and humility, his simplicity and shining integrity. The last few years of his life were those of constant rise, but the pleasures and privileges of office sat lightly on him. One is reminded of the Roman farmer,

Cincinnatus who, when the enemies of Rome were at its gates, answered the call of duty and led the armies of Rome to victory, and thereafter returned to the quiet and anonymity of his fields. Like Cincinnatus of old, Shastriji would have been glad to return to his role of a quiet, constructive worker.

In his own quiet, humorous way he put it very nicely when after laying the foundation of Mangalore Port as Minister without Portfolio in early 1964, he visited Bangalore. He was presented with a Civic Address by the Bangalore Corporation, on which occasion the Congress President, Shri Kamaraj Nadar, was seated by his side. In the Address, after the usual complimentary sentiments and phrases, there was a reference to Bangalore's problems—the need for more roads, housing, water, civic amenities, etc. and above all the need for more funds for which the Minister's help was solicited.

When it came to Shastriji's turn to reply, he thanked them for the honour done to him. Then he went on to say: "You have referred to some of your problems, with which I am in full sympathy. But why have you addressed them to me, because I am only a Minister without Portfolio.? At one time I was the Home Minister of India, and I thought I was a big and powerful man. But, along came a man called Mr. Kamaraj, and he said, 'I have a Plan'. As a result of that Kamaraj Plan, I found office and power vanishing away from me.

However, constituted as I am, accepted this change without getting upset, and was settling down to my befitting role of a quiet, constructive worker. But suddenly Panditji fell gravely ill at Bhubaneshwar, and then along came this man, Mr. Kamaraj, once again and told me. "You have got to help Panditji". So he took me by the ear and brought me back into the Cabinet, though this time as a Minister without Portfolio. So you see (pointing to Shri Kamaraj), this is where the real power resides. So why not address your problems to him?"

More seriously however, he outlined his philosophy and approach to life in a letter dated 6th October 1963 sent to me in London. After four and half gruelling years with him I had managed to get away to the UK on a Nuffied Foundation

Fellowship in May 1963. Shortly thereafter came his resignation from the post of Home Minister under the Kamaraj Plan. Knowing full well his family circumstances and the difficulties he must have been facing. I had written a very feeling letter to him. In reply to that came this intensely moving letter of October 1963, which, so far as I know, is the only expression in writing he ever made of his general philosophy and approach to life.

Lal Bahadur Shastri

I, York Place

New Delhi October 6, 1963

My dear Rajeshwar Prasadji Namaskar,

I had received your letter of the 2nd September, and yesterday I also received your letter of the 28th September. I am sorry I could not write to you earlier. I have been extremely busy during the last one month. There was the election of the new Chief Ministers and the formation of their Cabinets, etc. and these took a great deal of time. We have not yet been able to resolve the disputes in Uttar Pradesh. The situation there is causing concern. Our colleagues in U.P. do not seem to realise how much harm they are causing to the State. They are so preoccupied with their individual rivalries.

Panditji wanted very much that I should continue on my post. He mentioned this several times, but I myself wished to leave office. I had always been feeling uncomfortable in my mind about giving advice to others and not acting upon it myself. The speed with which we in the Congress are going down is sometimes frightening. Government administration in the districts is rapidly reaching a low level. No strong opposition party has been able to emerge. In these circumstances if some of us in Government come out and do something, then this relinquishing of office should be welcomed.

So far the signs are not very favourable. But it is hardly surprising that such a big step should give rise to some doubts and hesitations in the beginning. For those of us who are regarded as experienced and elders, this is a testing time. I feel that the fault is ours and not that of our Congress workers in the states or the districts. The next few months will show just how much utility we will have outside. I am not without hope.

Difficulties and hardships in the household will have to be put up with. A person learns to adjust himself. I have not yet shifted from my house but I shall be going to a smaller house. We have reduced one vegetable dish, as well as milk, and have started washing some of our clothes ourselves. I am using Ramji's car and shall put in the petrol myself. We shall have to be careful in respect of other things also. I have left office twice before also and this is the third time. This time there are a few more facilities than on the previous occasions. Hari is also now employed. There is also the Parliament allowance. It is, however, a fact that the burden of expenditure has greatly increased. The truth is that the help and cooperation of my wife is most sincere and without parallel, and I get great strength and support from her. So we shall manage somehow. It is natural for you to be concerned. It is perhaps better not to think too much about what may come. I believe that whatever he does, we should accept cheerfully.

> *Hariye na himmat, bisariye na Ram ko Jahi vidhi rakhen Ram, Tahi vidhi rahiye*

Do not lose heart and forsake Ram.

In whatever manner he chooses to keep you

in that manner should you learn to live.

On the 2nd of October, all of us went to Rajghat. It was the same familiar scene except the new constructions which had come up around the Samadhi. The memory of Gandhiji brings one close to tears. All of us are consumed by the desire for comfort and office. The feeling of service and dedication is so much less evident in office. Gandhiji's renunciation was utter and complete. The story of his life is summed up in the beautiful verse of Kabir:

> *Das Kabir jatan se odhi, Jyon ki tyon dhar deeni Chadariya*

> Thy servant Kabir used this coverlet with care and left it just as he found it

At Rajghat Panditji recollected that it was my birthday also. The conversation which took place has been reported in *Navbharat as* follows: Gandhi's birthday is everyone's birthday

New Delhi, 2nd October: This morning at Rajghat, Shri Nehru asked Shastriji "I hear that today is your birthday?" Shastriji, who does not ordinarily make any mention of this fact, replied, "Today is the birthday of Gandhiji, and hence it is not only mine but everyone's birthday."

I am glad to know that you and your wife are keeping good health and are happy. You will come back with new experience and new knowledge. You will be of even greater utility to Government and to the country. I am sure that you would have put every moment to the best possible use. I would like to convey, even at this stage, the congratulations and felicitations of all of us.

Ajay, Alok, Ravi and Anshu are all well. They came here and had their meals with us on two occasions. We also met them when we went to Maheshwar Prasadji's house for dinner. They are all living happily, although they must be missing you both and looking eagerly forward to your return. You and perhaps more than you, your wife, must also be longing to see them again. She must be wondering why the date for return does not come sooner.

I met your elder brother also. Maheshwar Prasadji is still in the Home Ministry.

Ail else is well.

Yours

(Sd.) Lal Bahadur

Shri Rajeshwar Prasad, IAS 7, Prince Albert Road, London, NW-I

Endearing Qualities

An Interesting Account

One of Lal Bahadurji's most endearing characteristics was his utter simplicity—simplicity in thought, word and deed. This used to be exemplified in his dress itself. There is a humorous and endearing example of this. Once the closed collar black coat of 'pattu' that he used to wear on formal occasions had got so worn out that even the weave was becoming visible. To replace it the family got a black pashmina coat made to the measure of the old coat. But when Shastriji was shown this, he reacted sharply and firmly refused to wear anything so bright and shining. Since he was going to Calcutta to attend an important dinner where the Prime Minister (Pt. Nehru) would be present, the old pattu coat, all mussed up at the tailor's, was hurriedly got dry-cleaned, and both the coats were put into his suitcase and sent off to Calcutta. When the time for the dinner came, Shastriji put on his old coat, but having just come from the dry cleaner's it had a very strong, almost unbearable odour.

Seeing his desperation we persuaded him to lay it aside, and put on the new black pashmina coat for just this once, which he reluctantly did. But all the way in the car he kept saying. "These people (the home people) act so thoughtlessly *(Nasamjhi se)* and get this son of coat prepared for me. What will people say when they see me wearing this *chamkili bharkili* (shining, exotic) dress. So I will go quietly to some corner of the hall and try to be as inconspicuous as possible." But the moment he entered the hall, the first person he ran into was none other than Pt. Jawaharlalji himself. Panditji took a good look at him, and then placing his hands on both shoulders brought Shastriji into the light, and then gave him a big whack on the back and said, "Lal Bahadur, you are wearing pashmina.

Now you are becoming fashionable." Shastriji, who looked as if he was praying that the earth would open up and swallow him, was just able to mumble: "Ji, I did not wear it. She (meaning Smt. Shastri) put it in my suitcase." Upon which Panditji gave him another whack on the back and said: "Well, one day she will put a pair of *paijamas* in your suitcase, and then you can start wearing *paijamas also"*.

But Shastriji would never agree to wear *paijamas,* so wedded was he to his *dhoti* The only occasion when he did wear them was at the Rashtrapati Bhavan dinner in honour of the Queen of England in 1961, when his daughters, who were keen on getting a first-hand account of the glamorous young Queen, virtually lifted and put him into a pair of *churidar paijamas* to attend the Rashtrapati Bhavan formal dinner.

As per an Account: Even when he was the Minister for Commerce and Industry, when there was not only the opportunity but also the necessity for the Minister to go abroad. Shastriji would avoid going, because he did not want to wear anything other than the dhoti. It was in vain that I kept trying to persuade him to make some foreign visits, because if he went then I could go loo.

But Shastriji used to say that it would be difficult to manage abroad wearing a dhoti, and he would not wear anything else. When I pointed out that Gandhiji used to go abroad in a loin cloth, he said that Gandhiji's case was quite different, he was in a class by himself; but he himself would rather forego the foreign visits than give up his *dhoti* And so in the giant Ministry of Commerce and Industry with unlimited opportunities for foreign travel, I used to gnash my teeth in impotent rage and keep putting up to the Minister almost daily files for clearance of officers going abroad to all the five continents and seven seas, while the head of the Ministry himself was unwilling to stir a foot outside India. It was only much later, after he became Prime Minister and could go anywhere in his *dhoti* that Shastriji began to experience the pleasures of travel abroad.

"This simplicity in dress used to communicate itself to us, who worked in close proximity to him. One felt very uncomfortable wearing a suit and tie before him. Not that he would ever say anything, unlike some others, for instance Pt. Govind Ballabh Pant. When Panditji was Chief Minister, U.P. after Independence he had been invited by the U.P. ICS-IAS Association to address their annual gathering. Panditji, his head and hand shaking owing to his ailment, looked around the room with all the officers in their best suits and colourful ties, and his first remark was: *"Desh ke sare bandhan khul gaye, kintu aap logon ke gale ka bandhan nahin khulpaya"*. (The country has been freed of all its bonds, but the bond around your necks still remains.) Shastriji would never dream of making any such remark, but his love of utter simplicity spoke for itself. I still remember one particular occasion when I felt acutely embarrassed. My wife, Aruna, who until that time had not given up her hopes of making a colourful personality out of so colourless a person as myself, thought that what I lacked in internal sparkle could be made up by external colouring. Amongst some clothes she had got prepared for me was a very bright blue dressing gown with some striking motif on it, which may have resembled flowers or even stars. So eye-catching was it that I was careful never to wear it in Shastriji's presence. But once when on tour with him, I was woken up around midnight by the Minister's PA who said that the Minister was working in the next room and wanted me in connection with a certain file. I was wearing a *paijama* suit, and it would have taken too much time to get dressed all over again; so rather reluctantly I put on my bright blue dressing gown, flowers and all, and went into his room. He was looking towards the door, and at the sight of the apparition which entered, he gave a start as if something had struck him between the eyes. Yet, thereafter, he said not a word: but whenever he looked at me, a faint smile kept playing on his lips, and I could hardly have felt more embarrassed had I gone there in the nude.

"Another of his lovable characteristics was his courtesy and consideration for others. This is something that knew no bounds, and the greatest as well as the humblest felt completely at home with him. One had only to meet him to succumb to his charm.

"I recall my own first meeting with him on the 11th January 1959, when he was the Minister in charge of the then giant Ministry of Commerce and Industry, and I had come to take over as his Private Secretary. I hardly knew him at all, because the only occasion I had come into contact with him was when I was District Magistrate, Etawah in U.P. in 1955-56, and he had come on a brief one-day unofficial visit as Railway Minister. I had just received him at the Railway Station in the morning and seen him off at night. And now, at the instance of the then Chief Secretary, U.P., Shri Govind Narain, I was coming to work in such close proximity to him. Shri Govind Narain as Home Secretary, U.P. had worked closely with Shastriji when he was the Police Minister, and at the latter's request to send him an officer in whom he could have the utmost confidence, he (Shri Govind Narain) overcame my reluctance and persuaded me to go. Shastriji was already one of the big names in the Congress and the Government and I could not help feeling a little nervous and wondering how I should conduct myself, and how I should thank him for reposing so much confidence in me, and so on. But the moment I entered his spacious room in Udyog Bhavan, the Minister rose from his seat, walked round the table and came up to me, and shook hands warmly. Before I could get in a word to thank him, he thanked me for having agreed to work with him. I was left dumbfounded at the transparent modesty and innate courtesy of so big a man.

"That this was not a one-time show, but was something deeply inherent in his character and personality, I saw for myself times without number during the seven years that I worked with him. In all that period I can scarcely recall an abrupt or peremptory order from him like "Do this" or "Don't do that". It was generally in a question form, or a gentle hint upon which you had to act. For instance, when going on tour he used to say something like: "I am going next week to Calcutta, would you like to come along?" Now the relationship of the Minister and his Special Assistant is like the relationship of Mary and her little lamb: "Everywhere that Mary went the lamb was sure to go". So there was never any question of liking or disliking; it was just the Minister's gentle way of putting it. But lest there be any misunderstanding that this was an indication of softness on his part, I shall recount later how this gentle phrase was more in the nature of a commandment written on stone.

"Likewise, whenever he had to call me to his residence late at night or very early in the morning, the phraseology used to be something like this: if it is not too much trouble, could you come over at 6 a.m. or "If it is not inconvenient, could you stay on a little late and finish the draft". Most of the time the remark was in question form, and the burden of proof was entirely on you, to say that it was no trouble at all, or that there was no question of any inconvenience. Once, when I had worked on an important draft speech at his residence till about 2 a.m., I completed it and laid it on his table, and coming home I told my wife that the meeting in Vigyan Bhavan is only at 10 a.m. So please do not wake me before 9 a.m. But the next morning she shook me awake at 6 a.m. and when I protested, she whispered: "What am I to do? The Minister is sitting just outside in the verandah". This was one of those small D-II Meena Bagh flats where the bedroom door opened out into the small front verandah. I jumped out of bed and rushed out—albeit this time without my blue-flowered dressing gown—to see the Minister sitting patiently in the verandah. On seeing me, he remarked: "I am sorry to disturb you again so early in the morning when you were sitting up till so late last night. But there are one or two important points that I wanted to clarify. Since it would have been too much trouble for you to come again so early, I have come over myself." What could one say to a man like that?

"When he was Home Minister he used to sit at his semicircular table in South Block, where there was room at the table for only one chair—his own. I used to stand alongside and help him with the files. Generally, this used to be quite late at night, after 10 p.m. or so. After sometime he used to say: "You also sit down". Where was I to squeeze in a chair for myself at that semicircular table? So I would say: I have been sitting all day and am tired of sitting. I would like to stand for a while". He would resume his perusal of the files, and then suddenly he would push back his chair and say: "I am also tired of sitting. Let me also stand for a while". And so with both of us standing at the Home Minister's table, we would continue looking through the files.

"This same extraordinary courtesy and consideration was displayed when we went on tour. On reaching the Raj Bhavan concerned I would go to his room to see whether everything was as he would like it. And then to my amazement I would find that he had gone to my room to have a look at it. He would tell the Raj Bhavan staff. "Please do not mistake him for a PA. He is a senior IAS Officer of U.P. who has done me a favour by coming to work with me" *(Mere' yahan aakar mujh par inayat ki hai).* The richness of the Urdu word can scarcely be matched in English. He used to keep telling his PAs: "I am a Minister and there are so many people to look after me. You should take care of the SA. *"Voh bahut sankochi jeev hain, muh se kuch bolle nahin par mahsoos bahut karte hain"* (he is a somewhat shy and reticent being who does not speak out hut feels things deeply)—which is perhaps correct. Thus, even on these tours I would sometimes ask myself in bewilderment whether I was supposed to look after him or he was supposed to look after me.

"Another instance of his extreme consideration is that which he extended to my wife Aruna. In 1960 she and I had gone on a pilgrimage to Gangotri, which included several days of trekking on foot, and I had also managed to cover the difficult and at that time dangerous route to Gomukh the real source of the Ganga, from where I had brought back a little of the sacred water. Shastriji had been camping at that time in Dehra Dun, which is my home, and had seen us off at the start of the trek. When we returned Aruna brought some of the holy Ganga water of Gangotri and Gomukh to Smt. Lalita Shastri. She also mentioned in Shastriji's presence that now her dearest wish was to offer some of these sacred waters from the high Himalayas at the shrine of Rameshwaram washed by the southern seas. Shastriji remarked that when she had already covered the difficult part where no road or proper communication facilities existed, going to Rameshwaram, which was well connected by rail and road, should be a much simpler matter. But in view of the extreme distance involved. Aruna did not cherish much hope of being able to fulfil her ambition early. Imagine her surprise and joy, when a few months later Shastriji sent word to her that he was flying to Madurai to attend the Southern Zonal Council Meeting at Kanya Kumari and she should come along with him in the special plane to Madurai from where he would arrange for her onward journey to Rameshwaram. Hers had been a chance remark about offering the water of these Himalayan shrines in the great temple of the far South, but Shastriji had kept it in mind and at the first opportunity, he took the initiative in helping her to bring her dream to fruition.

"One of the qualities Shastriji will always be remembered for was his humility. He was in every sense of the word an Apostle of Humility, and he remained so till the end even as Prime Minister. There is a great sweetness as well as strength in humility, and Shastriji's humility was one of the sources of his strength. He used to say that from childhood he was attracted by one of the verses of Guru Nanak Dev: *"Nanak, nanhe hi raho, jaise nanhi doob, Aur rukh sookh jayenge, doob khoob ki khoob"* (Nanak, be small like the little blade of grass: When the other trees wither and die the grass will continue to remain green).

"I could cite innumerable instances of his humility, but perhaps just one or two will suffice. Once as Home Minister he was in Calcutta and had to catch the flight back to Delhi. It was the evening rush hour, and there was little hope of his completing the long drive to Dum Dum Airport in time to catch the plane to Delhi. The Commissioner of Police said that he would send a pilot car with a siren ahead, so that the Minister could have a clear road. But Shastriji immediately and firmly declined. When some one expostulated, Shastriji said that the Police car would go ahead making a loud noise with the siren, and everyone would think that some big man was driving down, and then they would feel let down to see what "thing" had come along—*Kya cheez chali aiyee hai.*

"On another occasion, as Prime Minister, he was to visit one of the States, but at the last minute he found it difficult to get away. So he rang up the Chief Minister and begged of him to excuse him (PM). But the Chief Minister was naturally cut up and he pleaded with Shastriji: "Please do not disappoint us. I have made really first class arrangements for your visit". To which Shastriji's instinctive response on the spur of the moment was: "Why do you make first class arrangements for a third class person"?

"Perhaps the most touching tribute of all to his humility was by the guard at the gate when his dead body lay in State at 10, Janpath on that cruel night of 11th January 1966. Thousands of people were filing past in silent and tearful tribute, and the guards at the gate had been instructed to see that everyone came in line in single file. But it was observed that people were breaking the line and coming out of turn, and that was causing commotion and confusion. So I went along with the PM's security-in-charge, Shri G.C. Dutt, a Joint Director of the Intelligence Bureau, to the gate, and the Security Chief pulled up the guard for allowing people to come out of turn and break the line. I still remember his reply: "Sir, what can I do? ! keep begging them with folded hands not to break the line, but they keep saying 'Who are you to stop me? Don't you know. I am so and so, and insist on going in then and there. The only thing I know is that he whom they have all come to see if he had come here I would have had no hesitation in stopping him and I know that he would have had no hesitation in listening to me." That tribute from the guard at the gate while Shastriji's dead body lay in State was perhaps the most touching tribute of all.

"Those of us who worked closely with him will always remember his forgiveness and magnanimity. There were times when we could not help playing truant. On tours with the Minister, one would accompany him in a car to a function. The moment he got out he would be garlanded and photographed, while we slunk out of the other door. On entering the hall there would be more clapping, more garlanding, more photographing, while the Minister was led to the seat of honour on the dais. But since the Minister was the last to arrive, by the time we entered with him every single scat would be occupied, and there was no place to seat ourselves. And while we were circling round and round, trying desperately to find some place to park ourselves, we would see businessmen jump up when they saw some local officer such as the Deputy Chief Controller, Imports and Exports, and rush to offer him their seals, at the same time shouting for paan and cigarettes and cold drinks for the Deputy Chief Sahib. After sometime, all this used to get on our nerves, and when we felt we had enough we would just take a car and vanish from the scene and proceed on some outing. Later at night we would tiptoe to his room. If he was in good humour he would smile and ask whether we had been able to see everything *(Aap log sab kuch dekh dakh aye)—a*nd then we knew we were forgiven, and we would launch into enthusiastic descriptions of the places we had visited, and urge him to find some time to go there himself (which seldom was the case). But at other times when he was not in so good a mood, he would lake a deep breach and say *"Accha aap log ghoom gham aye hain"* (so you have been roaming about). Not a word more would he utter in reproach or recrimination, but we used to slink away with our tails between our legs."

2

In Political Arena

Joining Gandhiji's Movement

It is a known fact that Mahatma Gandhi, the Father of the Nation was a model for Lal Bahadur Shastri. In the year 1921, Shastriji responded to Gandhiji's call for joining the independence struggle. He, therefore, gave up his studies to take part in the Non-cooperation Movement and courted imprisonment. Shastriji was influenced by the speeches of Lokmanya Bal Gangadhar Tilak, Bipin Chandra Pal, Lala Lajpat Rat, Gopal Krishana Gokhle and many other leaders who were spearheading the movement. The atmosphere at that time was charged with the rousing feeling of nationalism among the masses.

Lala Lajpat Rai founded a society known as the Servants of the People Society in the year 1921. The said society was inaugurated by Mahatma Gandhi. In the year 1926, Shastriji became the life member of the said society and he started working among the Harijans in Allahabad.

Member Legislative Assembly

By the dint of his hard work, dedication and devotion, he went on higher and higher and attained the highest office of responsibility. In the year 1930, Shastriji became the General

Secretary of the Allahabad District Congress Committee and he was the General Secretary of the U.P. Congress Committee from 1935 to 1937.

In the year 1937, he was elected as a member of the U.P. Legislative Assembly.

Lal Bahadur's First Arrest

Lal Bahadur, went to jail for the first time in the year 1930. He served seven terms totalling about nine years in a span of twelve years. The heart moving scene of the first arrest of Lal Bahadur had been aptly described by Dr. Mankekar in his book—*Lal Bahadur Shastri* (pp. 46-48). To quote:

> "In Allahabad as elsewhere in the country. Congressmen were arrested in hundreds and put in jail in anticipation of their participation in the Civil Disobedience Movement None could be certain if he would remain a free person the next day, may be the next hour.."

Until he himself was arrested, Lal Bahadur kept himself fully occupied carrying out his duties and looking after the affairs of his colleagues. The only time he could give to his family was during meals, when his wife prepared hot chapaties and his mother served him the food. One day eating his food he casually remarked that one of these days he too might be arrested, he could not say when but, he said he would feel very unhappy if the members of his family cried or created a fuss over his arrest.

Those who love me should show their affection by facing whatever comes with a smile and not by crying like cowards" he said.

One day Ammaji (Shastriji's mother) and his two sisters went to a shrine outside the city. They were not expected back before night-fall. After his meals, when Lal Bahadur was going out, Lalita Devi enquired casually when he would return. "Soon" was his reply. He said he was going to Meja, one of the tehsils of Allahabad District, for some work.

Lalita Devi was then expecting a child, Kusum, and was not keeping too well..

While Lalita Devi was resting in the room upstairs, she heard shouts of *"Mahatma Gandhi Ki Jai"* and *"Inqlab Zindabad"*. She rushed to the window and looked into the street. She saw a police van full of khadi clad people passing by her house and she saw a person waving at her. It was her husband sitting near the window in the police van along with the other arrested Congress workers. Lalita Devi received a jolt. There was no one else in the house.

She felt like crying. But then she remembered the words of her husband: Those who really love me should not cry when I am arrested. She gritted her teeth and wiped her tears off with the back of her hand.

Lal Bahadur was sent to Malaka Jail situated in the suburbs of Allahabad. His mother, sisters and wife came to meet him in the jail. In the presence of his mother and sisters. Lal Bahadur could hardly talk to his wife. He asked the jail official on duty to let his wife stay on for another minute. When they were alone he put his hand on her shoulder reassuringly and said. "Don't worry, every-thing will be all right. Separation only strengthens the bonds of affection. Try to serve the elders at Ram Nagar but don't neglect your own health."

Another Arrest

"In an article in "Women on the March", Indira Gandhi describes the circumstances in which she and Shastriji were arrested. To quote the relevant paragraph:

"There was a warrant for Shastriji's arrest. Acting on the assumption that no one would ever guess that he could be rash enough to stay in Anand Bhawan, he did just that and remained with us incognito until he could make full arrangements for the work of the movement to go on. He could not come out of his room until after dark and food was taken up to him surreptitiously. We pretended we had an ailing relative. This situation could hardly be maintained for long without the news leaking out. Besides, there was always the danger of a search. So, Shastriji had to move and was arrested within a short time. We were hedged in on all sides and it was well nigh impossible for workers to treat together.

"My husband became one of the links through whom I could pass on money and political literature to other underground workers and we had to arrange to meet briefly and late at night in the houses of different non-political friends."

In the Cabinet of Pandit G.B. Pant

In the year 1946, Shastriji was elected again as a Member of the Legislative Assembly. Pandit Pant, who was then Chief Minister of Uttar Pradesh initially appointed Shastriji as the Parliamentary Secretary, but later in the year 1947, made him full fledged minister giving him the portfolio of Police and Transport. He was in fact a true Gandhian having simple habits and utmost modesty in his general behaviour towards all who came in his contact in one way or the other.

In U.P. politics, Lal Bahadur became very popular and worked with full zeal in the party work as well as in the Government under the Chief Ministership of Pandit G.B. Pant. He rose to these heights sheerly by dint of his simplicity, devotion, dedication and by gaining popularity right upto the grass root workers. He was a pure Indian, nursed and nurtured in the Indian culture.

Impact of Tilak and Gandhi

Even when Lal Bahadur was a student of Harishchandra. High School at Varanasi a whirlwind had disturbed India.

Everywhere there was the cry of 'Freedom'! "Swaraj is our birth right" - Bal Gangadhar Tilak had declared. This had become the nation's battle cry.

Lal Bahadur reverenced Tilak. He longed to see him and hear his speech. Once Tilak visited Varanasi. Lal Bahadur was away in a village fifty miles from Varanasi. He borrowed money and travelled in a train to see and hear Tilak. He saw him and heard his speech. It reverberated in his ears like Krishna's conch, the Panchajanya. Like Bharata, carrying Rama's sandals on his head,

Lal Bahadur carried Tilak's message in his heart. This message guided him all through his life. The greatest influence on Lal Bahadur was that of Mahatma Gandhi. Lal Bahadur was electrified when he heard a speech of Gandhi at Varanasi in 1915. Then and there he dedicated his life to the service of the country.

Young Satyagrahi

In 1921, Mahatma Gandhi launched the non-cooperation movement against British Government and declared that the country would not cooperate with the Government in its unjust rule. Lal Bahadur was then only seventeen years. When Mahatma Gandhi gave a call to the youth to come out of Government schools and colleges, offices and courts and to sacrifice everything for the sake of freedom, Lal Bahadur came out of his school.

His mother and other relatives advised him not to give up his studies. But Lal Bahadur was firm in his decision — Lal Bahadur joined the procession, which disobeyed the prohibitory order. The police arrested him. But as he was too young, he was let off.

Lal Bahadur did not go back to his school. He became a student of Kashi Vidyapeeth. During his four years' stay there, he made excellent progress. Dr. Bhagawandas's lectures on philosophy went straight to his heart. In later life Lal Bahadur displayed surprising poise in the midst of conflict and confusion. This he learnt from his teacher, Bhagawandas.

Servants of the People Society

It was in 1926 that Lal Bahadur got the degree of 'Shastri' and left the Kashi Vidyapeeth. The whole country became the arena of his activity. He became the life- member of The Servants of the People Society, which Lala Lajpat Rai had started in 1921. The aim of the Society was to train youths that were prepared to dedicate their lives to the service of the country.

One of the rules of the Society required the members to take an oath to serve the Society at least for twenty years and to lead a simple and honest life till the end. Lal Bahadur earned the love and affection of Lajpat Rai by his earnestness and hard work. Later he became the President of the Society.

Shastriji married in 1927. Lalitha Devi, his bride, came from Mirzapur. The wedding was celebrated in the simplest way. All that the bridegroom took as a gift from father-in-law was a charakha and a few yards of Khadi.

Freedom's Soldier

The struggle for freedom was intensifield all over the country in 1930. Mahatma Gandhi started the 'Salt Satyagraha'. Lal Bahadur took a leading role in it.

At the age of seventeen Lal Bahadur had participated in a procession against the British Government. The government had arrested him and then freed him. But this time it did not let him off easily. He had been calling on people not to pay land revenue and taxes to the government and the government had been keeping a wary eye on him. Now he was sent to prison for two and a half years.

From this time onwards prison became his second home. He was sent to prison seven times and was forced to spend nine long years in various prisons on different occasions.

His going to prison was a blessing in disguise. He had time to read a number of good books. He became familiar with the works of western philosophers, revolutionaries and social reformers. He translated the autobiography of Madam Curie (a French scientist who discovered radium) into Hindi.

Lal Bahadur's virtues shone even in the prison. He was a ideal prisoner. 'He was a model to others in discipline and restraint. Many political prisoners used to quarrel among themselves for small things. They used to cringe for small favours before the officials of the prison. But Lal Bahadur used to give up his comforts for others.

Sense of Honour

The greatness of Lal Bahadur was that he maintained his self-respect 'even in prison. Once when he was in prison, one of his daughters fell seriously ill. The officers agreed to let him out for a short time but on condition that he should agree in writing not to take part in the freedom 'movement during this period. Lal Bahadur did not wish to participate in the freedom movement during his temporary release from prison; but he said that he would not give it in writing. He thought that it was against his self-respect to give it in writing. The officers knew that he was truthful. Therefore, they did not insist. Lal Bahadur was released for fifteen days.

But his daughter died before he, reached home. After performing the obsequies he returned to his prison even before the expiry of the period.

A year passed. His son was laid up with influenza this time. Lal Bahadur was permitted unconditionally to go home for a week. But the fever did not come down in a week. Lal Bahadur got ready to go back to prison.

The boy pleaded dumbly with his tearful eyes. In a weak voice he urged his father to stay. For a moment the father's mind was shaken. Tears rolled down from his eyes. But the next moment his decision was made. He bade good bye to all and left his home for prison. His son survived.

Two qualities, which the leader of any nation must have, are devotion and efficiency. Lal Bahadur had both the qualities in a large measure. He would not swerve from his aim, come what may. When the people of India.

Were fighting for freedom he brushed aside all thought of personal happiness and plunged into the freedom struggle. His daughter's death, his son's illness, poverty - none of these made him swerve from his selection path. Even when he became a minister and, later, the Prime Minister he was never attracted to a life of luxury and comfort.

In Prison Again

When the Second World War broke out in 1939, the leaders of our country were in a dilemma. When the people of India were slaves how could they support the cause of Britain?

In the end they decided to launch a 'Satyagraha' against the British Government for the freedom of the country (1940).

Satyagraha means opposition based on Truth. Lal Bahadur was one of those who offered individual Satyagraha. He was sent to prison for one year for this.

The freedom struggle became more widespread and intense. The prisons were bursting with political prisoners.

On 8th August 1942, the Indian National Congress which led the fight for freedom decided at its historic meeting in Bombay to sound the trumpet for the final struggle against the British in India. It called on the British to 'Quit India'. The people were determined to 'do or die'.

The government reacted sharply to these calls and arrested many leaders. Prisons became overcrowded. The government used all cruel methods of suppression to nip the movement in the bud.

Lal Bahadur, who had just then come out after a year in prison, travelled from Bombay to Allahabad by train. He got off at a station, unknown to the police. For a whole week he used to send instructions to the freedom fighters from Anand Bhavan, Jawaharlal Nehru's home in Allahabad.

Vijayalakshmi Pandit, the sister of Nehru, lived in Anand Bhavan at the time. The police came there to arrest her and to take possession of the house. Lal Bahadur destroyed all-important documents. Luckily, the police arrested only Vijayalakshmi Pandit and went away.

A few days later Lal Bahadur who was underground came out and shouted slogans against the government. The police arrested him then.

A New Arena

India got freedom in 1947, Lal Bahadur's administrative ability and skill in organisation came to light in the days following India's freedom. He was an expert in the art of bringing together people and winning their hearts. Pandit Govind Vallabh Pant, the leader of Uttar Pradesh, was the first to recognise this talent of Shastriji and to encourage him. He earned the love of Pant by his hard work during the elections of 1946 in the provinces. The

Congress Office had become Shastriji's home during that period. The Congress won a resounding victory in the elections.

When Govind Vallabh Pant became the Chief Minister of Uttar Pradesh, he wished to train able young men to run the government. But it was not easy to please him. Lal Bahadur did not want any office; yet he was appointed as Parliamentary Secretary to Pant. Pant praised him as 'likable, hard-working, devoted, trustworthy and non-controversial'.

Responsibility of Freedom

Later, in 1947, Lal Bahadur became the Minister of Police and Transport in Pant's Ministry. He took many steps to bring discipline into the administration. As Transport Minister he subjected government buses to discipline. He was the first to appoint women conductors. Usually the minister in charge of the Police Department will not remain popular for long. But Lal Bahadur Shastri never allowed the police to resort to lathi charge and firing. He ordered that using jets of water instead of lathis should disperse unruly crowds. Though there were many strikes in Uttar Pradesh when he was in office, there was not a single occasion when people shouted slogans against him.

Lal Bahadur was a lover of cricket. Once he was watching a match at Kanpur. Trouble broke out among the spectators. The Police and young men came to blows. Since Shastriji was on the spot the situation did not go out of control.

The young men demanded that the red turbans' (the police) should not be found on the cricket ground and Lal Bahadur agreed. But the police were there the next day. The young men became angry with Shastriji and protested. Lal Bahadur laughed and said, "I fulfilled my promise to you faithfully. You did not want red turbans to be here. You see the police are now wearing khaki turbans." The spectators laughed and dropped the matter.

Coming onto the National Scene

Right upto the year 1950-51, Lal Bahadur was at the political scene in the Uttar Pradesh politics and held various positions. He was a Minister of Transport. After having worked in the Uttar

Pradesh Ministry, Lal Bahadur Shastri resigned in the year 1951 and was appointed as General Secretary of the All India Congress Committee at New Delhi. Jawaharlal Nehru was at that time the Prime Minister as well as the President of the Indian National Congress. Since Nehru was in search of a General Secretary who should not only be loyal but a man with dedication, devotion and great zeal, the choice, therefore, fell for Shastriji who had both the qualities in him.

In the year 1952, Shastriji was elected as Member of Parliament in the Rajya Sabha from Uttar Pradesh. Soon after that, Jawaharlal inducted Lal Bahadur in the Union Cabinet as a Minister of Rail-ways and Transport. He was a very successful minister and was very popular because of his simplicity, straightforwardness, dedication and devotion for the office he held.

Unfortunately, late in the year 1956, a major railway accident took place at Aliyalur. Lal Bahadur was very much upset to learn of this major railway accident and his conscience pricked him to own a moral responsibility, being the head of the Railway Ministry. He, therefore, tendered his resignation forthwith.

The people of our country very much appreciated the step taken by Shastriji owning complete responsibility of the accident upon himself. But Shastriji's rare example became a headache and problem for several of his successors. Even Jawaharlal Nehru was not of the view that Shastri should resign, but he was certainly very much satisfied and happy with the principle stand taken by Shastriji.

It is a known fact that even after tendering his resignation, Shastriji continued with Panditji like an adviser for a long time. By doing so, he came more close to Panditji during this period and earned funds of goodwill at the hands of Panditji. During this period, Jawaharlal used the services of Shastriji for party affairs and other miscellaneous works and confided in him on many important matters.

In the year 1957, Lal Bahadur Shastri was again inducted in the Union Cabinet and held several important portfolios such as Transport and Communication, Commerce and Industry. Not only this, Shastriji also held the portfolio of Home Affairs under the Premiership of Jawaharlal Nehru.

In the year 1952, 1957 and 1962, for the parliamentary elections, Lal Bahadur Shastri organised the party campaigns marvellously and was thus instrumental in the selection of candidates which was, of course, a neck-breaking job. It is a fact that in all these elections, Congress achieved brilliant results and victories.

In the year 1963, there was a Kamaraj Plan. Under the Kamraj Plan, Lal Bahadur Shastri voluntarily tendered his resignation from the Union Council of Ministers. Lal Bahadur was a very tactful negotiator also and he would not allow the talks to be deadlocked. In March 1963 he made a trip to Nepal.

Since Lal Bahadur Shastri was the most favourite and confidant of Jawaharlal Nehru, his services had always been utilised in one assignment or the other. On January 24, 1964, Jawaharlal inducted him in his Cabinet as a Minister without portfolio. He was particularly inducted in the Cabinet and was given no portfolio because Nehru wanted some loyal and confidant colleague who should assist him in his day-to-day work as his health started failing after the Chinese Aggression.

Post-independence Activities

Lal Bahadur Shastri had served in various positions before being elected as the Prime Minister. After Independence, he became the Minister of police in the Ministry of Govind Vallabh Pant in Uttar Pradesh. His recommendations included the introduction of "water-jets" instead of sticks to disperse the unruly mob. Impressed with his efforts in reforming the state police department, Jawaharlal Nehru, invited Shastri to join the Union Cabinet as a Minister for railways.

He was a responsible man and known for his ethics and morality. In 1956, Lal Bahadur Shastri resigned from his post, following a train accident that killed around 150 passengers near Ariyalur in Tamil Nadu. Nehru, had once said, "No one could wish for a better comrade than Lal Bahadur, a man of the highest integrity and devoted to ideas".

Lal Bahadur Shastri returned to the Cabinet in 1957, first as the Minister for Transport and Communications, and then as the Minister of Commerce and Industry. In 1961, he became Minister for Home and formed the "Committee on Prevention of Corruption" headed by of K. Santhanam.

Minister for Railways

In the first General Elections after India became a Republic, the Congress Party returned to power with a huge majority. Lal Bahadur Shastri worked hard for this success. He was the General Secretary of the Congress at the General Secretary of the Congress at the time.

The selection of candidates and the direction of publicity and electioneering were under the direct guidance of Shastriji. But he did not contest the elections. However, Nehru did not wish to leave such an able and honest man outside the government. He persuaded him to seek election to the Rajya Sabha. He was elected to the Rajya Sabha. He was appointed as the Railways and Transport Minister in the Central Cabinet (1952).

The railways are among the biggest Central Government undertakings, transport plays a vital role in the progress of any country. The railways in India had been badly disrupted after the division of the country. Lal Bahadur strove hard to set right and regulate the railways. It is not easy to organise movement of passengers and good from place to place without waste of time and without inconvenience.

Lal Bahadur succeeded in this to a large extent. There were four classes- first, second, intermediate and third in the railways then. First class compartments offered extreme luxury and were almost heavenly. But the discomfort of passengers in the third class compartments was beyond description. They did not have even minimum comforts. Lal Bahadur's efforts to reduce the vast disparity between the first and the last classes cannot be forgotten. The first class that offered royal comfort was abolished.

The old second came to be known as the first class and the intermediate class as the second class. His idea was to have only two classes of compartments in course of time - the first and the second. It was he who provided more facilities to travellers in third class compartments. It was during his time that fans were provided in the third class compartments. He also worked hard to improve the administration of Railways and to eliminate thefts in the trains.

I am Responsible

Lal Bahadur identified himself with the Railways so much that he felt he was responsible if anything went wrong in his department. When he was the Railway Minister in 1956, 144 passengers died in an accident that took place near Ariyalur in Tamil Nadu. Just three months before this, an accident that took place near Ariyalur in Tamil Nadu. Just three months before this, an accident had occurred at Mehboob Nagar in which 112 people died. Lal Bahadur was in no way responsible for these accidents. Yet he was very much pained. He felt he could not escape the moral responsibility for them. He had submitted his resignation letter to Pandit Nehru when the Mehboob Nagar accident took place. But Nehru had not accepted it. But when the Ariyalur accident took place Shastriji said, 'I must do penance for this. Let me go.' So strong was his sense of responsibility.

Homeless Home Minister

Lal Bahadur Shastri's exit from the Central Cabinet was a blessing for the ruling party. He worked for the party during the General Elections next year. Then, he became the Minister for Transport and Communications and later the Minister for Commerce and Industry. He became the Home Minister in 1961, after the death of Govind Vallabh Pant.

People used to call him the homeless Home Minister because he did not have a house of his own. He had rented a small house in Allahabad. Even when he was a minister, he used to stay in that house when he went to Allahabad. After a few days the owner of the house let it out to another family. When Shastriji resigned as minister he vacated the government quarters and he did not have a place to line in!

Not a Slave to Position

The greatest danger that India had to face at the time was China's aggression (1962). The Chinese army crossed the

Himalayan border and moved forward in wave after wave and occupied Indian territory in the north. But India stood up like one man against China. The Chinese moved back. But they did not return the areas they had occupied. China stabbed India in the back and lost the friendship of India.

This was the time when China in the north and Pakistan both in the east and the west started giving trouble to India. It was absolutely necessary that the people of India should forget internal quarrels and that they should unite like brothers and sisters. Lal Bahadur Shastri strove hard to make the people feel that they were all one.

People who clung to power sometimes showed their pettiness. To some people clinging to the minister's seat, rather than uniting the people, is the aim of life. At this time a plan was carried out to purify the ruling arty. The Chief Ministers of all states and the senior Ministers at the Centre had to hand over their resignations to the Prime Minister Nehru he was to decide who should come out of office and work for the party and who should remain in office. Accordingly they all tendered resignations.

Active Nationalist

In 1930, Lal Bahadur Shastri became the secretary of the Congress party and later the president of the Allahabad Congress Committee. He played a crucial role during the "Salt Movement". Lal Bahadur lead a door-to-door campaign, urging people not to pay land revenue and taxes to the British authority. The leader was also sent to jail for the campaign. During the long span of nine years he spent in jails, Lal Bahadur utilised the time in reading the social reformers and western philosophers. He was one of the leading and prominent faces that continued the Quit India movement, called by Mahatma Gandhi. Lal Bahadur, in 1937, was elected to the U.P. Legislative Assembly.

3

Rise in Politics

Shastri as Home Minister

In 1961, the fast unto death' by Master Tara Singh to secure a Sikh-controlled Punjabi-speaking state in Punjab proved to be more intractable for Shastri, for here the demand for a Punjabi-speaking state was used as a cover for a Sikh state. The motive was religious; the justification was linguistic. Nehru saw through the game and refused to accord full official status to the Punjabi tongue in the Gurumukhi script. Tara Singh realising the futility of it all gave up the fast.

In the domain of administration, Shastri as the home minister addressed himself to the twin problem of delayed disposal of papers and corruption at different levels He himself was honest and simple He lived austerely and his wife cooked for him.

As S.K. Patil put it: "When he died, he left nothing behind. Even some of the instalments on his Fiat car had remained unpaid Some friends arranged to have the dues paid in order that the car should remain with his family Although, he was very fond of his wife, he never took advantage of his position even for her." With a few exceptions, he did not trust the bureaucrats who "can quote things admirably well" without making any change in the existing situation. He was convinced that "they are not able to think in advance and they only think when the situation is almost out of control. Although I am a mediocre, yet I find that a mediocre like me is able to produce something new and original, not in a very high sense but whatever new things are suggested in the ministry, well, they generally come from me and not from officers who are with their routine way of thinking and.. working." This, however, was an exaggeration.

Among the very few innovations that Shastri made in the home ministry was the experiment of taking up all "important matters" at the higher level, right from the start To shorten the time consumed in holding consultations with the states, on the issue of the status of Scheduled Castes and Tribes, he called a conference in Delhi in July 1962 where all the chief ministers and their principal assistants and the senior central officers took part. On the issue of eliminating corruption, he could not make any headway.

Ideologically, Shastri was a centrist with a rightist bias. He never felt dismay at the emergence of right wing obscurantism, although he was alarmed at "the communist menace which could destroy India's infant democracy and her parliamentary institutions". As long as Nehru lived whatever Shastri did, he did with 'Nehru's permission and in his shadows. After his death, he was for further diluting Nehru's own diluted socialism "We should try as far as possible", he said, "to have equitable distribution of wealth. We should decentralise wealth although this doesn't mean the same salary and the same house for everyone Every person should have enough to live on, to clothe himself and to educate his children. "Ideologically, he was much less biased against private enterprise than Nehru was, and much less biased against private enterprise than Nehru was, and much less sympathetic to big business than Desai or Patil were. "I feel, he said, "India is an example to world that the public and private sectors can work together for the growth and expansion of the country."

Shastri is reported to have fen the need of a Deputy Leader (DL) of the Congress parliamentary party; and presumably he put it to Nehru. Nehru never wanted to make Desai the DL for that would have opened the gate of succession to Desai. Nehru wanted Shastri or Jagjivan Ram to be the DL but that he found difficult to manipulate. From 1946 to 1950 Sardar Patel as number two was the DL followed by Azad from 1951 to 1958 on his death. Pant became number two in the Cabinet and was DL from 1958 to 1961, when he died.

In 1956, Desai had entered the Cabinet and was put at number four On the death of Azad in 1958 and Pant in 1961, he became number two and if Nehru had so wanted Desai could then easily become the Deputy Leader. But Nehru had different ideas Desai opposed Jagjivan Ram's candidature. The name of Shastri was never formally mentioned but he was very much in the picture. Nehru, to counter Desai, proposed two DLs-one from each house. Desai opposed this also.

He also did not accept the idea of a contest for the Post of Deputy Leader and threatened resignation from the Cabinet in the event of election. Later, he resiled from that stand and agreed to contest saying that he would resign from the Cabinet in case he lost the election for DL. Thereupon, Nehru proposed that instead of a minister becoming a DL let one ordinary member from the Lok Sabha and another from the Rajya Sabha be elected as DLs. Desai had no option left but to agree.

This decision was then approved by the CPP. In fact, after the 1962 elections Nehru even wanted to split the finance ministry into two, presumably to reduce Desai's powers. It was only because of Desai's resistance that the proposal was dropped But on the death of Pant in March 1961, the home ministry was not given to Desai who was eager for it, but to Shastri who "always earned out" Nehru's wishes and "did not do anything which he did not like." The key to his future lay with Nehru and he knew it. "The is considerably more guile in the little man", writes a close observer, "than his manner indicates, and the appearance of mediocrity is often an advantage for a politician." Hangen says:

> "Shastri absorbs praise and abuse from Nehru with equal grace. His equanimity has even won him the Prime Minister's affection, and he is also very close to Indira Gandhi, whom he used to visit when she

was a lonely child in the Nehru family mansion at Allahabad. If she came to power, he would be assured an important place in the government. I have even heard it said that Shastri is planning to use Mrs. Gandhi as his front, but this seems a little far-fetched. It seems more likely to me that Mrs. Gandhi would back Shastri as a compromise Prime Minister, thinking she could use him for her own ends. In any event, the two are not likely to be at odds when the show down comes."

Shastri's opportunity came in 1963 on the occasion of the Kamraj Plan—a device which had quite respectable origins but which was cleverly used by Nehru to get rid of some, if not all inconvenient people, to put Radhakrishnan in his place and to secure his own position at a time when the graph of his popularity was going down because of his China policy debacle. In the spring of 1962. Nehru had his first major illness-a kidney affliction called as pyelonephritis and in spite of his recovery, he had now acquired "a slight loop" so that people around him began to whisper "probably he will never be the same again." He was obliged to rest every afternoon, follow a rigid diet regimen, and reduce his daily work schedule from 17 to 12 hours. His left foot was dragging. The difficulties of the third 5 year plan and food shortages added to his pains.

Foreign exchange reserves were dwindling and communal tensions rising. Early in 1963 the Congress lost three prestige elections to Lok Sabha—Amroha. Farrukhabad and Rajkot— and the victors were Nehru's inveterate foes and bitter critics—Kripalani, Lohia and Masani. On August 16, Kripalani gave notice of his intention to move a motion of No-Confidence—the first formal challenge to Nehru's leadership since 1947. This climate produced a series of moves to cleanse the Congress which, in turn, led to the greatest reshuffle in the union and state governments since independence.

On July 5, 1963 the CWC called a special session of AICC for 9 and 10 August. Behind the scenes "a novel and far-reaching purge was being conceived" by K. Kamraj Nadar, than the chief minister of Madras. In May-June 1963, Nehru went to Kashmir where Biju Patnaik met him and suggested to him that some experienced ministers may be asked to relinquish their posts and take up the organisation work. Soon after the elections of 1962, he suggested to Nehru that he (Patnaik) resign the chief ministership for this purpose. Nehru asked Kamraj to let him think over the matter. After the aforesaid 3 by-elections to the Lok Sabha. Patnaik met Kamraj and agreed to give up the chief ministership of Orissa. It was in this context that Patnaik and Nehru met in Kashmir in June 1963.

It appears that towards the end of July 1963. Nehru discussed the plan with some of his colleagues—Subramaniam, Shastri, Nanda, Indira Gandhi, and of course, Kamraj. Nehru began by offering to resign but as in 1954 and 1958, his indispensability was proclaimed by everyone and Nehru "did not need much persuasion to give up his suggestion." Desai proposed that in the first phase the number of ministers in states and at the centre, be reduced and surplus ministers and those less efficient and having allegations against them be relieved. In the second phase, some three or four efficient ministers be relieved for organisation work. And, after five years, those relieved must return to the ministries and others must be relieved.

But Nehru and others had no interest in the plan proposed by Desai. On 8 August, the CWC adopted the proposal of Kamraj in general terms, and on 10 August the AICC adopted the historic "party before post" resolution embodying the Kamraj plan as approved by Nehru. Patil called Nehru as "leader of leaders" who must "remain there (as PM) till the country gets out of all difficulties". While Kamraj threatened to withdraw his proposal if Nehru insisted on resigning.

Two days before the CWC meeting, Shastri met Desai in the lobby of the Lok Sabha and told him that "he (Shastri) had pressed for his resignation being accepted and that he would give up office but that it is not necessary for me (Desai) to give up office. His resignation should not affect me." Desai adds:

> "When he spoke to me in this manner, I suspected that some game was being played behind the scenes. I told

> him that Jawaharlalji had not talked to me about that matter and that I did not know anything about it He then told me that Jawaharlalji would meet me the next day and tell me about it. This convinced me that he must have had a talk with Jawaharlalji about me also."

> Eventually Nehru told the CWC that Shastri, Desai, Jagjivan Ram, S.K. Patil, Gopala Reddy and K.L. Shrimali from the central Cabinet were to be relieved and the chief ministers of Tamil Nadu (Kamraj), MP (Mandloi), Bihar (B.N. Jha), U.P. (C.B. Gupta), Orissa (Patnaik) had to give up office. Bakshi Ghulam Mohammad of Jammu and Kashmir also decided to resign. Nehru never wanted Shastri to go but accepted the advice of his friends that either Shastri and Desai should go out together or both should stay in the Cabinet; and that if Morarji alone was sent out it would be obvious to the public that it was an unprincipled Chanakya Plan for throwing out Morarji Desai who, in the process, would only acquire sympathy and support".

Lest those who escaped the hatchet should become complacent Nehru added: "It is possible that some suggestions might have to be made by me at a somewhat later stage." In fact, none was made.

Regarding the motives behind the Kamraj plan, we have three points of view: those of Desai, S.K. Patil and Nehru's biographer. Micael Brecher, Desai says:

> "Later, I fully understood the real purpose of the Kamraj Plan. Actually this was the second step taken by Jawaharlalji to prevent me from succeeding him whenever such a contingency arose. Earlier, he had prevented my being elected Deputy Leader to the Congress Parliamentary Party It soon, became clear that he wanted Indiraji to succeed him to show that the Kamraj Plan was not particularly aimed at me. Lal Bahadurji was also included in the plan, but there was an understanding that he would be taken back

in the Cabinet after three of four months This was why he did not give up his official residence, and the government staff, working for him when he was a minister, continued to work for him after his resignation He was taken back into the Cabinet in February 1964."

S.K. Patil's View:

"In 1963 Prime Minister Jawaharlal Nehru and his daughter Mrs. Indira Gandhi worked out a plan to get rid of some unwanted ministers and politicians. This would take place under the name of the "Kamraj Plan." It must be made abundantly dear, beyond any shadow of doubt, that Kamraj had nothing whatsoever to do with it. His name was used as a camouflage. There were various reasons why Jawaharlal wanted to remove some of the Congress leaders from positions of power, one of them was that he felt they did not share his ideology. His own partymen had compelled him to get rid of Krishnan Menon, a friend of his, while K.D. Malviya had to go because of alleged charges of corruption.

"Both Menon and Malviya were considered leftists and friends of the Soviet Union. With their departure, the Soviet Union, on whom Jawaharlal was coming to rely a great deal, may have suggested to him that his Cabinet was weighed down to the right Possibly. Jawaharlal, may have thought that the Kamraj Plan may restore the balance in the Cabinet between right and left. But if only Morarji and I were removed, that would have aroused suspicion and hence some padding became necessary. Under the plan not only were Morarji and I, but ten other ministers, a few from his Cabinet and others from state Cabinets, were asked to resign and work for the organisation On the face of it this was a fraud and smelled of a deep plot. The Soviet Union would have been happy if only Morarji and I were removed but along with Cabinet ministers like Jagjivan Ram and Shrimali, Gopala Reddi was also removed. Lal Bahadur himself suggested that he would go since otherwise people would smell a rat..Shrimali had to go because he had displeased Mrs. Gandhi in the allotment of government accommodation to Dhirendra Brahamachari. The excuse for getting rid of Gopala Reddi was that he had opted for a powerful transmitter used by the Voice of America in the sensitive northeastern region. C.B. Gupta, chief minister of Uttar Pradesh, was asked to resign because Jawaharlal did not like him."

Michael Brecher's version of Nehru's motives behind the Kamraj Plan:

"Kamraj genuinely wished to step down from government office in order to strengthen the Congress machine in the Madras countryside against the growing heat from the separatist Dravida Munnetra Kazhgam (DMK) Patnaik, too wished to throw off the burden of daily state administration— for the larger, All-India stage; at the time he held a position of some importance in the 'Nehru Circle' Gopala Reddy, a poor administrator and an ineffective minister, was the obvious scapegoat for Nehru's error in the Voice of America fiasco earlier that summer. Shrimali's failure to make a mark in the vital sphere of education and his strong espousal of Hindi and Vernacular languages had long been known—but Nehru's style had never been to dismiss colleagues Bakshi's standing in Kashmir, the Achilles Heel of India's international image, was alarmingly low. The choice of Gupta, Jha, and Mandloi reveals the pressure of factionalism; there continued presence as chief ministers of the most faction-torn states in the Union was a barrier to the most formal reconciliation of competing Congress groups and a threat to Congress dominance in the Hindi hinterland.

"Jagjivan Ram was the ideal case for renunciation of power— he had been in the union Cabinet since 1946. As for Shastri, it is known that his resignation was genuine; his willingness to withdraw was reported even before the Kamraj. Plan came before the Working Committee. It may also be, as some surmised at the time, that his inclusion spared Nehru the possible charge of discrimination against Morarji. It seems plausible, however, that Nehru, a consummate politician, suddenly realised the plan's potential, in a flash of genius He could eliminate from the Cabinet two men, Morarji and Patil, whose ideology and personality he found distasteful. He could pave the way for another untouchable representative to replace the otherwise immovable Jagjivan Ram. By adding Shastri to the list, he could avoid the charge of discrimination and, at the same time, nullify Morarji's advantage by virtue of seniority More than that, he could send all potential successors to the wilderness and see which commanded the greatest support in the Congress and the country. and by this complex decision Nehru had fully restored his political power, temporarily jarred by the China debacle in the autumn of 1962.

"As to the effects of the Kamraj Plan, the most notable was to consolidate Nehru's own power in party eclipsed by the China debacle of 1962. Amongst the Right, the Plan made Nehru unpopular. The media understood the game "in pursuance of principles undefined, at least unstated" (The Statesman). The exclusion of Shastri was seen to be "well-calculated". The Tribune called it a "purge preparatory to the feast." In the long term, it robbed Desai, Patil and Jagjivan Ram of a great deal of power and patronage and it eliminated Desai's tactical advantage of being second in the Cabinet. It placed the ineffective Nanda at number to who could be easily outwitted by the power-brokers. On August 29, Nanda got the home ministry. Shastri's own version was that he himself had suggested to Nehru that Desai need not be Kamrajed but that Nehru felt "Morarji's stature would grow out of office." As for Shastri, he was, in a sense "a decoy elephant, leading out those whom Nehru wished to exclude without seeming to be animated by personal reasons." Desai, in particular, Nehru wished to see out of office. At this time there was no strong reason to believe that the succession to Nehru was imminent. This Prime Minister," Nehru told a press conference. "happens to be very much alive at the present moment." But as it happened, the Kamraj Plan helped considerably to bar Desai from the prime ministership a few months later. So, Nehru had perhaps not too consciously, taken a hand in determining the course of Desai's destiny And who, "having seen Desai in the office of Prime Minister many years later, can say that Nehru was wrong?"

"The fact is that nobody took the brighter side of the Kamraj Plan seriously except for Krishna Menon who offered to work and speak for the Congress Everybody else regarded it as no more than a move m the game of jockeying for power. Desai, sore at losing office, retaliated by bringing down the Congress ministry in Gujarat; and Nehru's retort was to appoint the displaced chief minister as High Commissioner in London to Nehru it was all to the good that suppressed feelings had come out on the surface, hidden things had emerged in the open, and the curtain had been

> raised. In the short term, it was an effective act of political spring-cleaning; but, in the long run it weakened the basis of Nehru's way of running the Congress party."

Kamraj Plan

A major consequence of the Kamraj Plan was the public recognition of the fast emerging "Syndicate". A little before the Chinese attack in October 1962, some four or five CMs were regularly discussing issues of national policy and leadership at National Development Council meetings and sessions of the Emotional Integration Committee Some union government officials derisively began to call them as "the Syndicate", although the term was first used by Inder Malhotra in his "Political Commentary" in the Statesman on 16 June, 1964.

It is also ascribed to Romesh Thapar, the then Delhi correspondent for the Economic Weekly (Bombay) and the editor of the Seminar. In October 1963 in Tirupati, Kamraj, Atulya Ghosh, Sanjiva Reddy (chief minister of AP). Nijalingappa (Mysore) and S.K. Patil (on telephone) met and since then the terms "caucus" and "syndicate" were used interchangeably for these power-brokers.

The caucus knew that Nehru wanted Shastri to be the Congress president. Desai was keen for this position even in 1960 but Pant had punctured the proposal, tentatively made by Atulya Ghosh then. At Tirupati they settled for Shastri, and failing him, on Kamraj.

The aim was to exclude Desai from the centre of power and so they decided that there should be no contest. At Tirupati they arrived at a consensus both about the next Congress president and succession to Nehru as PM. It was, however, not made public at that time because they thought it would offend Nehru. Desai deposed on July 7, 1970 in the Congress Election Symbol case before the Chief Election Commissioner in New Delhi that the term 'Syndicate' was first used in 1964 to refer to a group of top leaders in the Congress party and that Lal Bahadur Shastri was the inspirer of it.

Atulya Ghosh set the ball rolling by issuing a press statement proposing Shastri as Congress president Desai believes that the bosses had decided already that Kamraj should be elected as Congress president and that the proposal for Shastri was merely a cover Nehru, he says, had proposed Shastri's name but when he declined, Kamraj was the syndicate's choice. "I understood", Desai says, "That Shri L.B. Shastri was also present in these consultations.

The next day two members of the Syndicate met me. They told me that they had proposed Kamraj in order to prevent Smt. Indira Gandhi from becoming president, and that I should have no misgivings in the matter. I told them that I could not understand their action but did not want to discuss it." Kamraj was thus, unanimously elected on 20 November, 1963 because he was Nehru's real choice.. to see through the party reorganisation flowing from the Kamraj Plan." This was the beginning of the "politics of consensus." Kamraj took charge as Congress president at the Bhubaneshwar session on 8 January, 1964.

That very day, however. Nehru suffered a serous stroke affecting his left side. This witnessed the emergence of a 'duumvirate" of Nanda and TTK in the Union Cabinet. On 11 January, Nanda presided over a meeting of the Emergency Committee of the Cabinet at Delhi, where they confirmed the arrangements made for the duration of Nehru's illness with Nanda attending to Nehru's work as the PM and TTK to look after Nehru's work as the external affairs minister Nehru would be consulted only when it was absolutely necessary.

Both would act jointly on all major issues. The Emergency committee of the Cabinet would include both of them as well as defence minister Chauhan, and food minister Swaran Singh. Nanda was to preside over the meetings of the Cabinet and the NDC.

On 15-16 January, 1964 the media began to speculate about Shastri's return to the Cabinet and Mrs. Gandhi's appointment as external affairs minister. On 17 January Kamraj returned to Delhi from the south and on 18 January Shastri was appointed minister without portfolio and Sanjivayya (Harijan), minister for labour (Jagjivan Ram's replacement). On January 29, a presidential order stated: "Shri Shastri will perform such functions in relation to the business of the ministry of External Affairs the department of Atomic Energy and the Cabinet Secretariat as may be assigned to him by the PM from time to time."

Thus, the clever, silent, little man became "assistant to the PM" even though great care was taken not to rouse any suspicions by continuing his fourth ranking in the Cabinet Nanda inside and Desai outside the Cabinet were obviously very unhappy at this development The "duumvirate" now became "triumvirate" with Kamraj very close, backed up by the caucus. Inder Malhotra wrote in the Statesman on 31 January. 1964 that for the first time since independence, power was shared between the PM and the Congress president and that "the era of a unifocal centre of power is coming to an end."

Mrs. Gandhi, had lent only her passive support to Shastri's return to the Cabinet. In fact, both understood each other very well, both were suspicious of each other, and both were ambitious. Shastri knew that Mrs. Gandhi was the real danger to his chance of becoming the PM. After all even Nehru had fondly though of inducting her into the Cabinet in January 1964. This is confirmed by Desai. When Shastri eventually became Prime Minister, Mrs. Gandhi candidly expressed herself about Shastri to Mrs. Pandit who writes in her memoirs:

> "...immediately after becoming Prime Minster, he (Shastri) had come to me and, in the usual Indian way had asked for my blessings and cooperation as an "elder sister". I told him he had both, including my affection, and hoped he would always trust me. Some time later I repeated this to Indira and she said with quiet sarcasm I hope you will not trust him too much."

But during her father's illness, she could not prevent Shastri's return to the Cabinet even though all concerned felt that Shastri's return would make him Nehru's immediate successor. Shastri, however, shrewdly and modestly lay low and never asserted his newly gained status. But both at home and abroad, everyone was certain that Nehru's crown was now guaranteed to Shastri.

Meanwhile, as weeks rolled by, Shastri's position became stronger and stronger. On 30 March, 1964 Nehru told the Lok Sabha that he had not yet thought about appointing a deputy Prime Minister. Referring to Shastri, he said that he was performing the heavy duties of a Prime Minister very efficiently and that we are working very well together.

This was treated by Prem Bhatia as "PM's final verdict about a deputy". In April, in an interview with Arnold Michaelis, he stated: "If I nominated somebody, that is the surest way of his not becoming Prime Minister. People would be jealous of him, dislike him." He also said that Mrs. Gandhi was unlikely to succeed him and that he was "certainty not grooming her for anything."

Between January and May 1964, the period of his apprenticeship. Shastri visited Kashmir (January 30) to supervise the solution of the holy relic (Prophet's Hair) incident and in February to sort out the differences between factions of the National Conference He also made a major speech on external affairs in Parliament, advising against undue haste in the integration of Kashmir into India, condemning the Chinese policy towards India, warning Sheikh Abdullah against secessionist activities and ruling out an exchange of population with East Pakistan.

But his style remained cramped and his performance lacked vigour or decisiveness Despite an adverse poll forecast made in February 1964, Shastri moved ahead, like a professional practitioner in the art of politics and marched to the summit. In less than a year, casting aside his usual modesty, he boasted that he never had any doubt about the outcome of the contest.

A close account:

> "The story of the 6 day drama of succession has been narrated in the first chapter Shastri's triumph was the triumph of his "low posture", his subtle yet quite decisive approach to politics—the product of three decades in the jungle of U.P. politics characterised by factionalism and casteism. It was there that he had acquired those qualities which made him unique in

> the Congress elite—a man without political enemies, and always successfully hiding the stuff of which he was made. He moved deftly and lightly, always self-effacing and soft-spoken, more feline than canine. The Syndicate knew that none of them—Sanjiva Reddy. Nijalingappa, Atulya Ghosh, Patil and Kamraj— could possibly have become Nehru's successor. If they could not be the "king", they could at least play the "kingmaker" but the one they would make the "king' must be someone who could be made to steer in the direction they desired Desai was exactly the kind of man they did not want, while Shastri looked so. Desai was disliked and feared. Shastri was liked but not feared. While to some of his close associates he was known as extremely tough, even ruthless, positive, manipulator of his own group, and a man as able to press his own interests as any other U.P. politician, the syndicate looked at him as "a sort of lilliputian Pygmalion, material ready for the mould."

The battle of succession was conducted by Kamraj with the thoroughness of an experienced general who used his special weapons of silence and "parkalam" (we'll see) with devastating effect. The game was played so well indeed that Desai withdrew from the contest and offered to propose Shastri's name in the CPP meeting on June 2, 1964.

Right from the start Shastri functioned as a political professional even if he was wholly the product of Nehru who lifted him from complete obscurity into the central Cabinet. Without his unflinching support and goodwill. Shastri, at best, would have ended as an insignificant minister in U.P. On one occasion. Nehru had wanted Shastri to accompany him to London for the Commonwealth Prime Ministers' Conference Aware of his shabbiness, Nehru asked Shastri to acquire an 'achkan' and some 'churidar' pyjamas. Shastri complied with the order, but complained to a friend, *"pyjama to paihen lia, magar uska utarna mushkil hogaya"* (I can wear the pyjamas alright, but how am I supposed to take them off!). That particular trip to London was cancelled, but his fate took him there finally as the Prime Minister to attend the Commonwealth Prime Minister's meeting in June 1964.

Nehru's Demise

The 27th of May 1964 is an unforgettable day in the history of India. On that day the citizens of Delhi woke and attended to their routine work. During the day came shocking news from Teen Moorti Bhavan. The first Prime Minister of free India, Jawaharlal Nehru, lived in Teen Moorti Bhavan; the citizens learnt that he had a heart attack.

After Nehru, Who?

A few months before Nehru had suffered a mild heart attack. But he had recovered from it quickly. He was certain that he would live for some more years. But he passed away on May 27, 1964. Nehru was no more. It was unbelievable but true. One question echoed from Kashmir to Kanyakumari: 'After Nehru, who?'

The leaders of the ruling party, the Congress Party, thought deeply over the question. They counted a few suitable names on their fingers. Which of them was the best choice? Who could be the Prime Minister?

Finally all the leaders came to the decision that Lal Bahadur Shastri was the only person to pilot the nation at such critical times.

A short man. A lean body. Eyes wide as the wheels of a cart. His clothes were simple, his voice soft and almost inaudible. But there was always a smile, which overarched his words. There was not the slightest sign of pride or authority in his bearing. Could he administer a nation of five hundred million people, doubted some.

Lal Bahadur never praised himself. On the contrary he used to say: "I am an ordinary man and not a very bright man." He never aspired to power. He never worked for it.

And yet power and authority came in search of him. Fame set a crown on his head. The short man grew into a colossus. He showed by his work that, though he was tender like a flower, he could be hard as diamond, too. He filled the Four Corners of the world with the fame of India. At a time when the world sang his praises as a hero, an incomparable patriot-hero and as the architect of peace, and just as he touched the peak of his life, Lal Bahadur passed away all too suddenly. He came to power unexpectedly, and he left the world equally suddenly.

Bharat Ratna

Lal Bahadur was a star of great brightness in the history of India, After his death the President of India conferred on him, on behalf of the nation, the award of ' Bharat Ratna'; it was a most fitting.

A small body but mighty man-so runs a Kannada proverb. It applies to several great men. Shivaji was not tall. But like a magnet he attracted people, and organised and built a great empire. Napoleon was short. But he shook the whole world. Lal Bahadur Shastri was not taller than those two; but he was not second to them in greatness. Firmness, love of adventure, patience and skill in administration cannot be acquired in a day or a year. Only when we study his growth from childhood can we understand how he acquired all these qualities.

4

The Prime Minister

Pt. Nehru died suddenly on May 27, 1964. The ruling Congress Party elected Lal Bahadur unanimously as its leader. He did not show any interest in the discussions before the election of the leader. He remained aloof as if it had nothing to do with him. The detachment he showed then was surprising.

Nehru's Successor

Jawaharlal Nehru was succeeded by a mild-mannered and soft-spoken Lal Bahadur Shastri on 9 June, 1964. He was a follower of Nehruvian socialism. Despite the strong influence and desire of becoming the Prime Minister, of some party stalwarts Shastri emerged as the consensus candidate.

Shastri tackled many elementary problems like food shortage, unemployment and poverty. To overcome the acute food shortage, Shastri asked the experts to devise a long-term strategy. This was the beginning of famous "Green Revolution". Apart from the Green Revolution, he was also instrumental in promoting the White Revolution. The National Dairy Development Board was formed in 1965 during Shastri as Prime Minister.

After the Chinese aggression, the major cross-border-problems Shastri faced was caused by Pakistan. It sent her forces across the eastern border into the Rann of Kutch in Gujarat. Shastri showing his mettle, made it very clear that India would not sit and watch. While granting liberty to the Security Forces to retaliate He said:

"Force will be met with force".

The Indo-Pak war ended on 23 September 1965 after the United Nations passed a resolution demanding a ceasefire.

The Russian Prime Minister, Kosygin, offered to mediate and on 10 January 1966, Lal Bahadur Shastri and his Pakistan counterpart Ayub Khan signed the Tashkent Declaration.

In the Steps of Nehru

Jawaharlal Nehru's untimely death on May 27, 1964, was considered to be a big blow in the Indian political scene. China had already betrayed and gave a rude shock to the foreign policy of our country. And in less than two years thereafter, India lost its great Prime Minister in Jawaharlal Nehru.

There was a feeling of some vacuum to search for a leader. But soon the natural successor, the real Indian, a simple and a short sutured yet a seasoned leader (whom Jawaharlal had trained during his last days) Lal Bahadur Shastri was identified and was elected as leader of the Congress Party in Parliament On June 9, 1964.

India's second Prime Minister, Lal Bahadur Shastri took over the reigns of this country. There is no doubt that Lal Bahadur had a spotless and unblemished reputation. Behind his soft and sweet words were hidden his iron will and olid determination.

From May 27, 1964 to June 6, 1964, Gulzari Lal Nanda acted as an interim Prime Minister and Shastri assumed the office of Prime Minister on the forenoon of June 9, 1964.

Dr. S. Radhakrishnan was the President of India and Dr. Zakir Hussain was the Vice-President of India.

Following were the Council of Ministers in the Cabinet of Lal Bahadur Shastri:

Cabinet Ministers	*Portfolios*
Shri Lal Bahadur Shastri (Prime Minister)	Atomic Energy. Also external Affairs (later on External Affairs was given to Sardar Swaran Singh)
Shri Gulzari Lal Nanda	Home Affairs
Shri T.T. Krishnamachari	Finance
Mrs. Indira Gandhi	Information & Broadcasting
Sardar Swaran Singh	Industry & Supply (Foreign Affairs w.e.f. 18-7-1964)
Shri S.K. Patil	Railways
Shri A.K. Sen	Law & Communication
Shri Y. B. Chauhan	Defence
Shri N. Sanjiva Reddy	Steel and Mines
Shri C. Subramaniam	Food and Agriculture
Shri Humayun Kabir	Petroleum and Chemicals
Shri Satya Narayan Sinha	Parliamentary Affairs and Civil Aviation
Shri H.C. Dasappa	Irrigation and Power
Shri M.C. Chagla	Education
Shri D. Sanjivayya	Labour and Employment
Ministers of State	
Shri Mehr Chand Khanna	Works and Housing
Shri M.M. Shah	Commerce
Shri Nityanand Kanungo	Cultural Affairs
Shri Raj Bahadur	Transport
Shri S.K. Dey	Community Development and Cooperation
Dr. Sushila Nayar	Health
Shri Jaisukh Lal Hathi	Home Affairs
Smt. Lakshmi N. Menon	Foreign Affairs
Shri K. Raghuramaiah	Labour and Employment
Shri O.V. Alagesan	Petroleum and Chemicals
Dr. Ram Subhag Singh	Social Security/Railways
Shri R.M. Hajarnavis	Supply/Cultural Affairs
Dr. K.L. Rao	Irrigation and Power

Contd...

Cabinet Ministers	*Portfolios*
Shri B.R. Bhagat	Planning
Shri A.M. Thomas	Food and Agriculture
Shri T.N. Singh	Heavy Engineering and Industry
Deputy Ministers	
Dr. M. M. Das	Rehabilitation
Shri Shah Nawaz Khan	Food and Agriculture
Shri S.V. Ramaswamy	Commerce
Shri Ahmed Mohiuddin	Transport
Shri B.S. Murthy	Community Development and Cooperation
Shri L.N. Mishra	Home Affairs
Dr. Smt. T.S. Sundaram Ramachandran	Education
Shri D.R. Chavan	Food and Agriculture
Shri C.R. Pattabhiraman	Information and Broadcasting
Smt. M. Chandrasekhar	Social Security
Shri Jagannath Rao	Law
Shri Sham Nath	Railways
Dr. D.S. Raju	Defence
Shri Dinesh Singh	External Affairs
Shri Bihudhendra Mishra	Industry
Shri B. Bhagawati	Communications
Shri Shyam Dhar Mishra	Irrigation and Power
Shri P.C. Sethi	Steel and Mines
Shri Ratan Lal Kishori Lal Malaviya	Labour and Employment
Shri Bhakt Darshan	Education
Shri P.S. Naskar	Health
Shri Rameshwar Sahu	Finance

Second Prime Minister of Independent India

Lal Bahadur Shastri was the second Prime Minister of independent India and a significant figure in the struggle for independence. Shashtriji was born in Mughal Sarai, in Uttar Pradesh. To take part in the non-cooperation movement of Mahatma Gandhi in 1921, he began studying at the nationalist, Kashi Vidyapeeth in Kashi, and upon completion, he was given the title Shastri, or Scholar, Doctor at Kashi Vidyapeeth in 1926.

He spent almost nine years in jail in total, mostly after the start of the Satyagraha movement in 1940, he was imprisoned until 1946. Following India's independence, he was Home Minister under Chief Minister Govind Ballabh Pant of Uttar Pradesh. In 1951, he was appointed General Secretary of the Lok Sabha before regaining a ministerial post as Railways Minister. He resigned as Minister following a rail disaster near Ariyalur, Tamil Nadu.

He returned to the Cabinet following the General Elections, first as Minister for Transport, in 1961, he became Home Minister. After Jawaharlal Nehru's death in May 27, 1964, he became the Prime Minister. Shastri worked by his natural characteristics to obtain compromises between opposing viewpoints, but in his short tenure was ineffectual in dealing with the economic crisis and food shortage in the nation.

However, he commanded a great deal of respect in the Indian populace, and he used it to advantage in pushing the Green Revolution in India; which directly led to India becoming a food-surplus nation, although he did not live to see it. His administration began on a rocky turf.

In 1965 Pakistan attacked India on the Kashmiri front and Lal Bahadur Shastri responded in kind by punching towards Lahore. In 1966 a ceasefire was issued as a result of international pressure. Lal Bahadur Shastri went to Tashkent to hold talks with Ayub Khan and an agreement was soon signed.

Lal Bahadur passed away in Tashkent before returning home. All his lifetime, he was known for his honesty and humility. He was the first person to be posthumously awarded the Bharat Ratna and a memorial "Vijay Ghat" was built for him in Delhi. The slogan 'Jai Jawan, Jai Kisan' is attributed to Shastri. 'If one person gives up one meal in a day, some other person gets his only meal of the day.': made during the food crisis to encourage people to evenly distribute food.

Cabinet Making

Shastri's Cabinet-making was interesting although 'Cautious, undramatic and even unimaginative". All the 13 senior ministers of the Nehru team were retained: Mrs. Gandhi, S. K. Patil and Sanjiva Reddy were new faces; Desai and Jagjivan Ram remained out. As for Mrs. Gandhi. Shastri had been shocked by the discourteous letters of her aunts.

Mrs. Pandit and Mrs. Hutheesingh, who had written to him, virtually ordering him not to live in Teen Murti, the official residence of the Prime Minister, since it had been hallowed by the presence of their brother. "Whatever Shastri's respect for Nehru, his feelings for the rest of the family must have been mixed." And, thirdly, Shastri had his own misgivings about Mrs. Gandhi's ambition, which he understood more than the syndicate did.

The syndicate expected Shastri to consult them before the Cabinet was formed, for they wanted to extend the formula of consensus to Cabinet making. But Shastri insisted on his right to choose his Cabinet He sounded Mrs. Gandhi through Dr. Zakir Hussain and discovered that her own choice was the image-building information and broadcasting portfolio.

Krishna Hutheesingh has recorded the story of Shastri's offer to Indira thus:

> "It was settled on the ninth day after my brother's death and while the urns were still standing under the tree in the garden. Mr. Shastri came to ask Indira to become Foreign Minister in he Cabinet. That was the first time in all those days that Indira broke down. Weeping she told Mr. Shastri that she did not want any place in the government: she only wanted to work for the memorial to her father. I would like to have six months of quietness' she said, 'before I take any job in the government.' But day after day, sometimes twice a day. Mr. Shastri came back, not only he, but the Vice-President and the other ministers as well. I think they felt they needed her, not only

> because of her knowledge and ability, but because they wanted the Nehru name to give a sense of continuity that would bolster the new government and win the confidence of the Indian people. They all arrived and tried to persuade her and in the end she gave in and took a smaller job in the Cabinet, which they told her was Minister of information and Broadcasting."

But Shastri himself did not really want to give her the influential external affairs ministry where he put Swaran Singh. Shastri was pro-West and he wanted to shift some emphasis in India's foreign policy. He had felt that India's neighbours like Afghanistan. Ceylon (Sri Lanka). Nepal and Burma had not received the attention they deserved and he was determined to atone for the lapse For this reason, he was happy, when Indira opted for information and broadcasting.

As for Desai, on 8 June, Shastri invited him to join the Cabinet at number three, as Nanda having been the acting PM had to be second. "I told him", Desai writes. "That he was my junior and his being an acting Prime Minister was an accident. I also said that if the Kamraj Plan had not come into effect. I should have continued in the Cabinet and would have become the acting Prime Minister. I, therefore, told him that his stand was not correct He said: Indiraji is also insisting that Gulzarilalji join the Cabinet."

As Prime Minister, Shastri refused to shift to the Teen Murti House where. Mrs. Pandit's and Mrs. Hutheesingh's letters notwithstanding, "he would have felt out of place." He remained austerely in his own house. Mrs. Hutheesingh says:

> "Later he moved next door to number 10, Janpath, a house formerly occupied by the Canadian High Commission. There he lived with his wife, three unmarried sons and his eighty-one year old mother. One of the boys slept in the same room with him. One of the charming sights of Delhi was Shastri happily playing badminton on the lawn with his sons, dressed in a dhoti and kurta. He hardly ever wore the more

> formal sherwani until he became Prime Minister and then only on state occasions."

The Teen Murti House became the Nehru Museum. Shastri dismantled "the elaborate culinary service which the external affairs ministry had created for Nehru." When he was asked by some of his colleagues to take over the entire retinue of J. L. Nehru to assist him, he replied "Panditji was a great man with a great style. I am a simple man and my ways will also be simple.

These fellows will not be able to reconcile themselves to my set-up." The actual reasons were concealed by him under the cover of innocence. These reasons perhaps were that Shastri wanted to keep himself a little aloof from the Nehru line, as Yunus Khan puts it:

> "He later allowed himself to be caught by an anti-Nehru clique. They had their own ideas about how to project this little man so different from Nehru. They thought he should be kept aloof from the public with none of the participatory excitement that marked the Nehru era. The result was unfortunate. It was a total media failure also. These were times when even his own chief ministers could not tee him, while his image on the screen would evoke the most derisive guffaws from the audiences."

As a leading politician, Shastri had about half-a-dozen assets in his political and personal make-up He represented the Hindi heartland, his political reputation was unblemished, he had administrative and a good deal of organisational experience; ideologically, he was a centrist, he combined ability and humility with natural ambition effectively concealed by gentility; and he was seen by the US diplomats as pro-West and had the US confidence.

On November, 16, Galbraith recorded that "the Indians are beginning to see the need for persuading the US of their problems and perils:

> "I think they are going to send a mission, possibly headed by L. B. Shastri to explain their predicament.

> Shastri would be good. He is a nice gentleman, very Indian in appearance. He is also very reasonable where Pakistan is concerned" Without doubt Shastri was respectful of the opposition, was aware of his limitations, knew India very well, had ably managed the elections of 1952, 1957 and 1962. He was the only one who had "an all-India stature and known to Congress workers all over the country." His Prime ministership was of course, in sheer contrast with that of Nehru. There was "a more-relaxed atmosphere" and "greater freedom in discussion" for now charisma was missing There were more spirited exchanges of ideas in the Cabinet which as an institution came to life once again. Decisions reflected a more genuine consensus. Shastri, unlike Nehru, met officials only at the secretary level and invariably sent a copy of the minutes of discussions to the ministers concerned, which Nehru never did. He permitted endless discussions in the Cabinet and listened to his colleagues patiently, even if indecision prevailed. The emergency committee lost its glamour and was confined only to a crisis like the Rann of Kutch of 1965."

Shastri did show some independence of the caucus in the matter of formation of his Cabinet, his denial of the External Affairs ministry to Mrs. Gandhi, and himself took the portfolio which later on was given to Swaran singh, whom he appointed at a time when TTK and Mrs. Gandhi were in London at the Commonwealth PMs' Conference, Nanda was away and Kamraj was not even consulted.

When Kamraj expressed reservation about the appointment, Shastri quietly said that it was the Prime Minister's prerogative. When P. S. Kairon was obliged to resign as the chief minister of Punjab, Kamraj wanted Swaran Singh to be relieved from the Centre and head the government there. Shastri refused. Against the advice of his Cabinet colleagues, Shastri extended the ceasefire in Nagaland.

Changes by Shastri

Shastri did not introduce any material change in the procedure of the Cabinet meetings Any ministry could submit a paper or an item to the Cabinet Secretariat (CS) for circulation to all members. The agenda was prepared by the CS which also recorded all decisions and minutes Members of the Cabinet attended meetings by right as in Nehru's days, while the ministers of state by specific invitation, whenever a matter falling in their domain was to be discussed. The Cabinet secretary with aides remained present throughout. Secretaries of other ministries were present only when the items concerning them were discussed.

Nehru's Cabinet met only once in a week for one to four hours Shastri's Cabinet met oftener and for longer periods. Meetings were called at Shastri's discretion The tea meetings at different homes commenced by Nehru but discontinued later, were restored, as Wednesday afternoon tea meeting and, in these, officials were not present and discussion covered all live and controversial matters These meetings became the nerve centre of decision-making As in Nehru's days, the Prime Minister remained *primus interpares* but Shastri was less 'primus' than Nehru.

The principle of collective responsibility continued to operate in distorted fashion. In January 1965, food minister Subramanium and oil minister, Alagesan resigned on the government's language policy. But they were persuaded by Shastri to return. Home Minister Nanda launched his ill-fated anti-corruption campaign through the unofficial Sadachar Samiti without the Cabinet sanction and when he got into trouble "all he got was a shrug of the shoulders from colleagues."

Structurally also, Shastri introduced no change in the old pattern— the Emergency Committee of the Cabinet (6 members), the Cabinet (16 members), ministers of state (15) and the deputy ministers (20).

Of all the ministers in Shastri's Cabinet. Mrs. Gandhi exercised a special influence, particularly after January 1965, even though she rarely spoke in the Cabinet. Until then, the charisma of her father seemed to have by-passed her. Though some observant pressmen noticed that when she addressed crowds, she carried conviction and they listened to her, more than they did to most ministers In 1965, there arose the language trouble in the south, because Hindi under the Constitution had to be the national language of India by 1965. Violence broke out in Madras, trains were derailed, and northerners killed. Amid this chaos, Mrs. Gandhi flew to Madras. She went around, unafraid, she talked to the people: she talked to the leaders. All she said was what Shastri had already said, but there was a difference.

Similarly, in August 1965 she flew to Srinagar for a rest But in the hours before her arrival, several thousand Pakistani troops, disguised as swaggering, filthy Pathan tribesmen, had crossed the border. When Indira's plane landed, they were within a few miles of the airport.

She was advised to turn back to Delhi, but she would not She insisted on being driven to the military control room which had hastily been set up. She, more or less, took over command and demanded to be driven through the city, though the senior officers warned her it was unsafe.

She was in constant touch with Shastri in Delhi. On this trip, the charisma had manifested itself once more, but also a quality of initiative and authority, a quality of leadership, which nobody, perhaps not even she had ever dreamt she possessed. Conversely, even a man like Desai at one time ranking second in Nehru's Cabinet could not exercise that degree of influence which lower rankers could.

Ideologically, Shastri's Cabinet was "essentially centrist" but with clear rightist and leftist orientations. Patil, Sanjiva Reddy and Subramaniam were broadly rightist; Sanjivayya was a socialist and Chauhan a sophisticated but uncommitted leftist; Mrs. Gandhi a centrist, further to the left; and the Prime minister himself a conservative but pragmatist and a believer in the "middle path" TTK, Patil, Sen, Kabir and Chagla were modernist; Tyagi a reactionary with a touch of the buffoon, Nanda, an obscurantist and Shastri, a traditionalist.

The states represented were Tamil Nadu (2). Andhra (2), Bengal (2). Maharashtra (2). Punjab (1). Gujarat (1), U.P. (3). Bihar

(1), Bombay City (1). There were two Muslims (Chagla and Kabir). One Sikh (Swaran Singh) and one Harijan (Sanjivayya).

Institutional Innovations

Shastri had made two major institutional innovations—the creation of the PM's Secretariat (PMS) and the setting up of the Grand Council of the Republic (GCR) The PMS was set up in July 1964 with the overambitious ICS officer—L.K. Jha with 3 joint secretaries with staff usually related to Shastri's (Kayastha) cast and region (east U.P.). The PMS drafted the Prime Minister's speeches, statements and letters because Shastri was weak at drafting (Nehru had superb drafting ability) and gradually it became a major centre of power. As Dharama Vira has put it in his memoirs:

> "The Cabinet secretariat being the secretariat of the entire council of ministers has always been an impersonal body. With the Prime Minister's secretariat gradually assuming the shape of a miniature government within the Government of India, there is a danger of this impersonal aspect being dimmed and a bottleneck being created through most decisions being centralised in the PM's secretariat. This centralisation is already showing signs of delaying decision-making processes at the centre, a development which is fraught with danger to the smooth and efficient working of the administration."

This only led to inter-secretary jealousies, chagrin among ministers whom LK Jha treated with scant respect and the decline of the office of the Cabinet secretary, now reduced to the position of a postman.

As for the GCR, it had no legal basis and it met irregularly at the Prime Minister's discretion. But it reflected "the new balance of power between the Union and the States and between the government and the party." It was much broader than the NDA which continued to function, and its jurisdiction also was much wider. It included all the real wielders of influence in the party, the Union government and the State governments—19 members of the CWC, 13 chief ministers, two representatives of the CPP, and eight members of Shastri's Cabinet who were not included in the other three groups, and 4-5 special invitees like Menon and Dhebar. Its total membership was about 45. The caucus was there in full force. It was conceived as the Crisis Committee' to which any issue of all-India importance—food, language, communalism, foreign policy and defence could be referred a sort of a "Political Court of last appeal or "the collective substitute for Nehru's charisma."

In Nehru's days, party decisions were taken by him with the advice of men like Azad and Pant and the help of the CWC and CPB. Under Shastri, they were taken by Kamraj and Shastri with the aid and advice of the caucus, the CWC and the CPB. Government decisions under Nehru were taken by him with the advice of a minister-Gopalaswamy Ayangar or Qidwai, or Pant or Menon or TTK or Shastri and routed through the Cabinet, and after 1962, on the advice of the Emergency Committee.

Under Shastri, government decisions were rare but they were taken by him with the aid of the Cabinet or the Emergency Committee. Shastri's tenure as Prime Minister witnessed "the fragmentation of decision-making." this adversely affected efficiency at every level and by June 1965, everyone, except a few close friends of Shastri began to feel disappointed at the sharp fail in standards.

From the early days of independence, Nehru had totally repudiated Kripalani's doctrine that the source of all power of the government lies in the party, and had insisted that the government was responsible to Parliament and not to the Congress or its president. But he had realised the danger involved in diminishing importance of the Congress. In January 1954 he wrote to his colleagues:

> "...many people say that the Congress has become some kind of a camp follower of the government. This is, I think basically not true, the push forward in regard to basic policies has come from the Congress organisation, representing public urges, and the

> Government and the Planning Commission have followed these up and worked them out in detail."

The party was however, safe under Nehru who was no dictator and was tolerant of criticism and open to pressures of the people, the party, groups and even individuals. But without doubt the influence of party *qua* party had declined and until his death in May 1964, it was the leader and not the party that held the key to every lock The China debacle had, of course, shaken Nehru's position to an extent. But the Kamraj Plan, more or less, had restored his position.

The centre-states equation of the Nehru era also underwent a change, with the advent of Shastri. In 1950-51 the unitary stress of the Constitution, the emergence of a highly centralised planning mechanism, the traditional all-India role of the CWC and AICC and Nehru's charisma tilted the scales in favour of the centre.

Nehru was "the Great Unifier", "the Ultimate Source of Unity." And even after his death. Nehruism perpetuated itself and India held together. But Shastri was not even a fraction of Nehru's stature. In his own selection as the PM, the chief ministers had played a crucial role which had given them a great leverage with the centre. Shastri always ran after consensus, which he institutionalised through the GCR that symbolised decentralisation.

Shastri was elected leader of the CPP on 2 June and was at once invited to form the government He and his Cabinet were sworn in on 9 June 1964. He died at Tashkent (USSR) on 11 January, 1966. In his tenure of 18 months and 10 days, can he be said to have achieved anything of a lasting value?

In June 1964, the Indian economy was at its lowest ebb—a stagnant agriculture, foreign exchange crisis, slowing down of industrial growth, massive unemployment, terrible inflation and acute food shortage. It took a modified GCR about 5 months to hammer out an all-India food policy in consultation with a fragmented opposition.

It reflected confused thinking, it lacked drive and direction, and it amounted to a total surrender by the centre to the dictates of the states. From June to November 1964 Shastri called the chief ministers four times for consultations.

The chief ministers refused to agree and on 5 November 1964 Shastri had the Essential Commodities (Amendment) Ordinance promulgated to combat hoarding. But it remained a dead letter and except for three important middle-men merchants of West Bengal, no hoarder could be touched By January 1965.

Shastri admitted total failure The third conference of CMs met at Guntur on 7-8 November, 1964 but it also failed to break the impasse, they opposed rationing. The AICC resolution was "goody goody". On 17-18 November, the fourth conference of CMs met where Shastri eventually capitulated to the state chiefs, Statutory rationing was now to be introduced only in Calcutta (not in 8 cities) and even that was at the insistence of West Bengal's chief minister, PC sen.

Shastri's bid to have an all-India food policy ended in a fiasco, he neither had the guts, nor the will, nor the resources, nor the influence or charisma to deliver the goods. President Radhakrishnan delivered a broadside at Baroda which led the *Times of India* editorially to accuse the states of regionalism and the failure of the centre to arrest the march towards anarchy.

Earlier, the *Hindustan Times* had referred to the "pathetic exercise in evasion" at Shastri's "interminable parleys with the CMs". It was only in April-May 1965, that the question of food receded in the background because of a favourable crop prospect. Shastri's bankruptcy was fully exposed.

The same would have happened at the language front but for the initiative Mrs. Gandhi took by going to Madras in February 1965. Nehru had laid down the governing principles for a stable language policy, stressing the importance of the study of English and yet gradually having Hindi as our national language. He had said:

> "These principles are (1) that decisions can only be largely by consent and cannot be imposed by a majority over a minority. (2) that every language should be given full scope and, in our Services, nothing should be done, which puts a person from a non-Hindi area at a disadvantage. So far as English is

> concerned. I am all in favour of the study of English being continued and even made more widespread. But I confess that I do not understand how we can lay down for the future that English should be our all-India language."

In April 1963, during the debate on the Official Language Act (OLA), he had said:

> "Any real upsurge in India from the people, an awakening of the people cannot take place through the English language.. Then inevitably we have to deal with Hindi for the simple reason that Hindi is the most feasible for this purpose. (And while encouraging Hindi) it becomes necessary and almost inevitable for English to continue to be a ink language. The process is not a sudden thing that you fix a date for."

Section 3 of the OLA provided that English "may" continue to be used after 1965 in addition to Hindi for all the official purposes of the Union and for the transaction of business in Parliament Nehru's personal assurance given on the floor of the House, though not incorporated in the OLA had satisfied the South.

As 1965 approached closer, the South was on fire. On 4 October, 1964 the home ministry asked all the Union ministers to report by 15 October, 1964 as to the steps taken to promote the use of Hindi for official purposes and to say what steps they proposed to take to use Hindi after the stipulated day, 26 January, 1965 (by the Constitution).

It foolishly asked the Delhi secretariat to issue some communications in Hindi to the Hindi speaking states from that day. All letter heads and printed forms were to have headings in both Hindi and English Hindi appearing first. The Statesman expressed the coming danger in their editorial "changeover" on 9 October 1964 each ministry in New Delhi will be engaged in an identical exercise on January 27. 1965—composing an epistle in Hindi. All this would be Gilbertian if it were not so regrettable. If the pace of the change-over to Hindi is forced, the results can only be chaos.

From 10 to 13 February, there was a fury of agitation all over the South. On 11 February, about 400 were kilted It was then that the Rip *Van* Winkle woke up and belatedly announced a 4-point policy in a broadcast to the nation, first, every state would have complete freedom to continue to transact its own business in the language of its choice; secondly, interstate communications would continue to be in English or would be accompanied by an authoritative English translation; thirdly, non-Hindi states would be free to correspond with the centre in English, as in the past, and fourthly. English would continue to be used in the conduct of business at the Centre.

This was a reiteration of Nehru's assurances but it came too late And it miserably failed to say what food minister Subramaniam was asking Shastri to say, that Nehru's assurances would be given a statutory form. Mrs. Gandhi then flew to Madras and her mere appearance did what a hundred speeches by Shastri would have never done.. that wast he power of her charisma.

TTK went at Shastri's request But Subramaniam remained in Delhi. On 11 February night he resigned alongwith Alagesan. This shocked Shastri into sanity and he accepted, in principle, the statutory incorporation of Nehru's assurances. The resignations were withdrawn and the agitation suspended.

The issue, however, reopened on 27 February. 1965 with the President's address to Parliament which *inter alia* stated:

> "We wish to state categorically that the assurances given by the late Shri Jawaharlal Nehru and reaffirmed by our Prime Minister will be carried out without qualification and reservation. While Hindi is the official language of the Union, English will continue as long as the non-Hindi speaking people require (sic) it Parliament was to deal with the legal, administrative and executive aspects and the chief ministers would consider the situation shortly. Kamraj pressed for the amendment of the OLA (1963) to provide for the continued use of English as long as the non-Hindi speaking people wanted it. The Cabinet discussed it

on 20 February but to no result, with Shastri arading the poster of "a national consensus." Meanwhile, the Hindu extremists led by the Jan Sangh and the irrespressible Lohia were beating teachers who spoke in English and defacing all signboards in English with coal-tar."

They, however, produced only a rat — an uneasy compromise in their report, saying that:

> ".. every state will have complete and unfettered freedom to continue to transact its own business in the language of its choice which may be the regional language; communications from one state to another will be either in Hindi accompanied by an authentic English translation or in English. Thirdly, non-Hindi states will be free to correspond with the Central Government in English. Fourthly in the transaction of business at the central level English will continue to be used as an associate official language in the intervening period. No change will be made in these arrangements without the consent of the states."

The vagueness was clear—"the intervening period" was not defined and no way was indicated to ascertain "the consent of the states." The only concession made to the south was beautifully vague—the government (union and states) would examine the steps to be taken including the amendments to the OLA (1963) to give effect to the assurances given by Nehru.

A confused Shastri, as usual, made the confusion worse confounded by telling the Lok Sabha on 24 February that there were undecided issues which are being "examined". On 26 February, 106 MPs led by Bhagwat Jha Azad, K. D. Malviya, and A. P. Jain (all U.P.) demanded in a letter that no amendment be made to the OLA (1963).

The muddle-headed PM only listened, saying nothing, hoping that the agitation would talk itself out. In March, he again talked of the need for "national consensus" to the making of which he had nothing to contribute.

Early in April, a Cabinet committee of Nanda, Patil. Sen, Chagla, Sinha and Tyagi was set up to propose amendments to the OLA.

This committee had two formulas—one put by Sen and the other by Patil the Sen formula would permit the use of English for all-Union purposes, in addition to Hindi, until three-fourths of the states, through resolutions passed by their legislatures, accepted the change-over to Hindi.

This meant a veto to the four southern states but if three of them could be pursued to accept Hindi, they could Impose it on the fourth state also that was the fear of the Madras leaders the Patil formula was more pro-English, for it allowed each state to use English in communication with the centre or states, indefinitely, and it could retain English even after the rest of India had adopted Hindi as the link language Parliament could use English until it decided by two-third majority to switch over to Hindi but even then the President, in his discretion could direct the continued use of English in consultation with the non-Hindi states the Hindi enthusiasts ruled out the Part formula as one designed to perpetuate the use of English.

The central issue was how to avoid the imposition of Hindi on the non-Hindi states and of English on Hindi states For this, Shastri had no solution except to talk of "national consensus." Gradually, he was losing ground and he now ended in surrendering to the South.

The GCR met on 1-2 June, 1965 and it accepted the Patil formula. The specific items on which the use of English could be compulsory in Union affairs would be specified in the Bill itself. The media of examination for all-India Service would be all the fourteen major languages, The proposal of Andhra Pradesh chief minister. Brahmanand Reddy, for state quotas in the all-India services was rejected, and poor Reddy was nicknamed as "Quotanand Reddy."

Superficially, Shastri's "consensus" technique succeeded but it only opened Pandoras box. For all times to come, he destroyed the prospects of achieving Nehru's dream of having Hindi as the national language of India. He only succeeded in encouraging interest-group politics, not national consensus.

Another contribution of "the little sparrow" was the development of the "Civil Services Raj—a product of his "self-conscious reliance on his professional advisers" (unknown in Nehru days). Shastri's own administrative incompetence and lack of imagination and "a vacuum in authority" from which he suffered it was reflected in the changed working of the Cabinet with the Prime Minister's authority gone, in the emergence of the party's autonomy, the growing importance of the Congress president, the Syndicate and the CWC, in the new power of the State's bosses, and in the further fall of India's prestige in world affairs.

LK Jha, his supreme conscience-keeper championed the cause of world capitalism whose influence shot up during Shastri's regime. His policies encouraged the growth of regionalism, linguistic chauvinism, the arrogance of bureaucracy and business lobby.

His weakness in dealing with the communal-obscurantist forces is reflected by an incident narrated by Chagla. When the Aligarh Muslim Bill was being debated in Parliament and Muslim feelings had been roused to a pitch of fanaticism. Shastri asked Chagla that he had received a request from several Muslim members that the debate should not continue on Friday as they wanted to go for their prayers.

Chagla replied that would be unprecedented, the Parliament had never adjuourned on any Friday and that it would form a very bad precedent And he added: "Other members would also ask for suspension of parliamentary business on their own important festival days. I could see that Shastri was not very happy at my reply. He said it was a small thing and I should not unnecessarily irritate the Muslim members of the House. But I was adamant, and much to his displeasure, Parliament continued discussion of the Aligarh Bill on a Friday."

In foreign affairs also, Shastri turned out to be a flop in spite of the legend spread by interested parties about his being a "man of steel, and his rhetoric from the Red Fort on 15 August 1964 that force would be met by force. The US lobby in India hailed him because his economic policies based on what they called "realism" was acceptable to the Johnson administration. But he had little understanding of international affairs and this, combined with his "sense of inadequacy" and the absence of "the Nehru legend" prevented him from projecting an impressive image of India abroad.

Shastri's essay in foreign affairs comprised of his participation in the second non-aligned summit at Cairo in October 1964; his stand vis-a-vis Pakistan on the Rann of Kutch incident (April-June, 1965) and the 3-week war (September, 1965); his participation in the Commonwealth Conference in June 1965, and his relations with India's immediate neighbours, especially the Indo-Ceylonese agreement (October, 1964) on the problems of Indians in Ceylon (Sri Lanka).

At the Cairo non-aligned summit, an attempt was being made by an organised group of countries to diminish the importance and the urgency of peaceful coexistence almost to the point of repudiating the concept. Here, the so-called New Emerging Forces (NEF) led by Indonesia and including Cambodia.

Tanganyika Burundi. Guinea. Mali. Cuba, Congo (Brazzavile) and often Algeria and Ghana were face to face with India leading such states as Sri Lanka, the UAR and Yugoslavia, the last two wavering. Indonesia had taken the line that peaceful coexistence was importable between states of differing political and social systems and that war was preferable to it.

This was the Chinese thesis in its purest for. There was no one here of the stature of Nehru to oppose the propagandist approach of the NEF. Shastri only added fuel to the fire by declaring that nuclear disarmament came "first and foremost" and that "the peaceful settlement of border disputes "came before "anti-colonialism".

In a controversial aside he declared that the non-aligned must strive "to resolve all difference through peaceful methods", by conciliation as distinct from confrontation But while in the Belgrade NA Summit (1961) the Nehru thesis had been accepted that "imperialism is weakening" and colonialism "disappearing" at the Cairo conference they had asserted that these two forces were very much alive Shastri gained nothing except some pious references to the sanctity of frontiers which were as relevant to the substance of the Sino-India conflict and as efficacious as the words on the Lamaist prayer-flags that further in the cold winds of the Himalayan passes through which the Chinese army attacked.

A further initiative launched by Shastri at Cairo was his proposal (in the context of persistent reports that China was about to explode a nuclear device) that the conference send a mission to China to ask her to stop making atomic weapons. But inefficient and timid as he was, the idea was inserted into his speech at the last minute, and other delegates had not been sounded before hand. The UAR thought such a mission "was unnecessary" and others ignored it altogether.

Only Makarios supported it. The conference did nothing about it at all. All that Shastri got was a single, flat, interpolated sentence calling on countries without nuclear arms to refrain from making them. In return Shastri offered, and the conference accepted the proposal that the forty-seven signatories should renounce any idea of making atomic weapons India was in a position to make the atomic bomb, the other 46 could not Thus, jeopardising his country's national security. Shastri bed India's hands in return fora worthless non-aligned moral interdiction on China. A mere sot days after the conference.

China slapped Shastri and other non-aligned nations by detonating its nuclear device. Apart from India only four of the 46 non-aligned states—Ghana. Cyprus. Uganda and Zambia—criticised the Chinese action. Cambodia and Indonesia praised it. Indonesia declared that it would soon have its own atom bomb—a mere bluff though And all this happened because there was no Nehru there; a second Nehru had not emerged. The discerning missed the great man at Cairo.

On his way home, Shastri stopped over for a few hours at Karachi on 12 October 1964 and met President Ayub. In their joint communique they affirmed that it was necessary to settle the outstanding disputes on an equitable basis and agreed to hold discussions "at the earliest possible moment", and to "remain in touch" to determine how these objectives could be best realised. On December 3, Shastri declared that the Kashmir problem occupied "a secondary place" and on December 4. Home Minister Nanda announced government decision to apply to Kashmir. Articles 356 and 357 of India's Constitution With regard to Article 370 which had allowed Kashmir a special status Nand a said: "It is not a well. It is a tunnel. A good deal of traffic has passed already, more will pass now."

On 9 January 1965 the Congress decided to establish its own branch in Kashmir and chief minister Sadiq declared that the National Conference would be dissolved. The Plebiscite Front of Abdullah appealed to Kasmiris to observe 15 January as a day of protest against these decisions The Economist, as the mouthpiece of British imperialism and advocate of Pakistan, wrote on 16 January 1965: "If one thing is absolutely plain about Kashmir, it is that after 17 years with India, the Kashmir Valley—bar its few Hindus—wants to join Pakistan."

Thus, encouraged, the Pakistani troops opened fire on Indian troops in the Indian enclave of Dahagram (East Pakistan) on 17 March, 1965. The Economist declared that "for this, Indian actions tending to integrate Kashmir are directly to blame. On 9 April, the Pakistanis opened fire across the border in the Rann of Kutch.

Our case was that the Kutch-Sindh border is a well-defined, well-known and well-established border clearly marked in the various editions of the Survey of India maps ever since 1871.

The Pakistani case was that the Rann was the bone of contention between the princely state of Kutch and the British Indian province of Sindh. Kutch acceded to India in 1947, and Sindh joined Pakistan. Thus, the issue was inherited by India and Pakistan. They said that the border between India and Pakistan ran through the middle of the Rann, while India claimed that the boundary ran along the northern edge of the Rann.

Each side contended that the boundary claimed by it was the traditional, well-established, and well-recognised boundary. Diplomatic notes were-first exchanged between India and Pakistan in 1948. On 23 December 1955 India had categorically told Pakistan that its claim was baseless Pakistan complained that Indian troops had attacked Pakistani border posts at Chhad Bet on 17, 19 and 25 February and 2 March 1956. In January 1960, they he did discussions at diplomatic level and India made it clear to Pakistan that they had no case From January 1965 taking advantage of a weak leadership in India. Pakistan began to manufacture incidents which culminated into large-scale fighting on 9 April 1965.

All attempts made by India to have ceasefire failed because of the negative approach of the US. On 28 April, Shastri told the Lok Sabha:

> "If Pakistan continues to discard reason and persists in its aggressive activities, our army will defend the country and it will decide its own strategy and the employment of its manpower and equipment in a manner which it deems best."

In May-June. Shastri went to the USSR. Canada and London where he attended the Commonwealth Prime Minister's Conference.

On June 30, a ceasefire agreement was signed under which Pakistan agreed to the withdrawal of her armed forces from the area, and India agreed to vacate the forward positions her troops had occupied Both sides agreed that the position as obtained on 1 January 1965 be restored.

Besides making the ceasefire permanent the agreement laid down a self-executing procedure for the settlement of the dispute. It was stipulated that an effort would first be made to settle the question by bilateral discussion at minister's level. If no agreement was reached within two months of the ceasefire, the two government would have recourse to a tribunal as contemplated by the joint communique of 24 October 1959. It was agreed further that the decision of the tribunal shall be binding' on both governments and that the tribunal 'shall remain in being until its findings have been implemented in full.'

Eventually, the issue was referred to the tribunal which announced its verdict on 19 February 1969 awarding about 350 square miles in the northern part of the disputed Rann of Kutch to Pakistan and the rest to India. India's share was much larger but it was mostly sea-marsh, often under water, while Pakistan's included some crucial elevation points. Though neither side had got all it wanted, there was much more criticism of the tribunal's decision in India than in Pakistan. The curtain on this episode was rung down at Islamabad on 4 July 1969, when Indian and Pakistani plenipotentiaries signed the last documents and maps, in token of finally ending the dispute.

J.P. Narain, a close friend of Shastri had hailed the Kutch agreement "As an object lesson in peace-making" and even made the most irresponsible statement that this method be extended to all "disputes' including that of Kashmir." Significantly, Pakistan, had fully used against India arms supplied by the USA for the purpose of containment of communism.

The Rann incident was followed by the 3-week September 1965 war. Shastri had already allowed passport to Abdullah to get abroad to mobilise support for an independent Kashmir, the ultimate goal of US imperialism and its lackeys such as Pakistan and Britain. In Algiers, he met Chou-En-lai who invited the Sheikh to China It was only then that Shastri woke up to his mistake and had all the endorsements of Abdullah's passport invalidated, save those necessary for going to Mecca, and asked him to return to India. On 8 May, as he landed in India, he was arrested.

On 30 March, the Kashmir legislative assembly had adopted the Constitutional Amendment Bill providing that (i) the Sadr-e-Riyasat be called Governor to be appointed by the President of India instead of being elected by the Kashmir Assembly and (ii) the Prime Minister be styled as chief minister as in other states of the Indian Union. This led to riots in Kashmir. On 9 August, a clandestine radio station, operated by Pakistan, described itself as Sada-e-Kashmir (Voice of Kashmir) and announced that "a Revolutionary Council to conduct an all-out war of liberation against Indian imperialism- had been set up to mark the 12th anniversary of Abdullah's arrest on 9 August, 1953.

Infiltrators from Pakistan began to pour in large numbers and it soon developed into an attack by Pakistan in the Poonch-Rajouri area and thereafter in a full-scale war on all fronts Throughout August, the Pakistan troops fanned out in Kashmir, crossing the ceasefire line. The Indians had to counter these moves so that defence minister Chauhan said: "Wherever it was found necessary to cross the cease-fire line in order to defend the ceasefire line and other areas, we have done so." By the end of August the Indian forces began their drive south of Uri to link up with Indian units near Poonch.

But on 1 September Pakistan troops occupied 2 Indian posts in the Chhamb area of the Jammu Bhimber sector, and opened a new front at Rajouri. General Chaudhary asked for air support immediately. 'What aircraft is available" the General said, "should be put to use". Air action was immediately approved by the secretaries and the very aircraft which we were thinking of scrapping were the only ones immediately available for use.

These planes went into attack and stopped the advance of the Pakistan army." By 6 September, the Indian army launched a three-pronged offensive against Lahore and on 8 September, attack was mounted in the Sialkot sector and a third front was opened in Pakistan.

The civil servants such as Dharma Vira wanted to capture at least Lahore and Sialkot. Shastri after some hesitation concurred but it did not come off. All the senior civil servants had felt that it was the only effective way of diverting Pakistan army from Kashmir. Swaran Singh was opposed to the idea of attacking Pakistan for "fear of adverse reactions abroad." He was however, handled by the civil servants.

As the external affairs minister remained adamant in spite of the arguments advanced in favour of an offensive, the Cabinet secretary, Dharma Vira, whispered to Shastri that the meeting be adjourned so that the officials could discuss the issue privately with Swaran Singh. They then told Swaran Singh that if Kashmir fell to the invaders and the Indian troops trapped in the state were compelled to surrender, the government would be thrown out. This had the required effect. When the committee met next morning, the foreign minister kept silent and a decision was taken without further discussion. Durga Das adds:

> "Shastri told me that Chaudhary, too, did not at first favour attacking Pakistan in reprisal for the infiltration in Kashmir. But when the Pakistani army started

> operations along the international border, the military experts took the view that the situation now justified a massive counter-attack The General Staff did not expect a major Pakistani attack in the Chhamb-Jaurian sector. This was a clear, calculated act of aggression to catch India unawares. Intelligence reports revealed that Pakistani strategy was to go down the Beas, penetrate the Feorzepur area in the Punjab, capture the road leading northward from Delhi and thus choke the lifeline to Kashmir. Having achieved this, the Pakistanis felt sure they would be able to impose a dictated peace."

Now, while Shastri and Chauhan had led the Parliament to believe that Lahore and Sialkot would be taken, Chauhan had instructed the army "to press forward and capture both Lahore and Sialkot, though he would be satisfied if Lahore was merely encircled." In fact, all communication from the Pakistan side with Sialkot had been cut and Pakistan had practically pulled out of the city. Despite all this, Shastri failed to egg on General Chaudhary to fight, and the General replied to him:

> "We must move with the caution and wisdom of an elephant We will take them (Lahore and Sialkot) in God's good time."

The failure to occupy Sialkot was significant against the background of pronouncements at the highest level Indeed. Shastri was not leading; he was being led.

General Chaudhary's excuse was that by occupying the big towns we "would be unnecessarily frittering our forces and resources", and that this would involves severe fighting with much damage which might have left bitter lasting memories behind." And so he devised ways of by-passing towns by surrounding them and moving forward. He was also reported to have said: "I know these politicians. The UN will intervene and they will agree to give up all our gains. Why then should I sacrifice my manpower to this end or that? My policy is to inch forward, not to gallop."

A more determined political leadership such as that of Indira Gandhi (later), and a more dynamic General, such as General Thimayya (earlier) would, of course, have acted differently. After all, he had driven Pakistanis out of Chad Bet in Kutch in 1956 by a bold stroke, even while the Cabinet was debating schemes to accomplish this. Chaudhary's plans for cleaning Kanjarkot in the same area, in March-April 1965 had, on the other hand, remained just paper schemes.

Shastri had made yet another declaration in the CWC and in public that "we would not return to Pakistan the areas of Kashmir which we had recovered." Desai had advised him against such declaration as "it would put him in a very awkward position. When the war ended and negotiations took place for. peace.. both sides would have to return the areas which they have conquered during the operations. This is a general rule. But Lal Bahadurji did not pay any heed to my advice and repeated his declaration."

While the US and Britain kept silent in July-August 1965 when Pakistan was on the offensive, they were unnerved at India's victories, and apprehending Pakistan's destruction they began to ask for cease fire and peace.

The Indian forces had captured the vital Haji Pir pass. The UN Secretary-General. U Thant, flew to Pindi and New Delhi and a ceasefire came into effect on 23 September 1965 Even Kosygin, who at the time was busy striking equidistance with both Pakistan and India "took exception to India's crossing the international border" and asked Shastri to withdraw his forces behind the ceasefire line in Kashmir and the international border elsewhere." And Nasser had told Menon that: "The attack on Lahore was a gross violation of international frontiers" All of them, however, failed to notice that September 1965 war was Pakistan's attempted military solution of the so-called Kashmir dispute and, if the USA had not supplied arms.

Pakistan would not have sought a military solution. This is what Gaibraith had told the Senate Foreign Relations Committee This attempt was entirely and qualitatively different from what Pakistan tried to do in 1947-48, and it had nothing to do with what US defence secretary Robert S. McNamara called "centuries and centuries of conflict between Hindus and Muslims, and that at the time of partition, without any aid from us".

One aspect of the September war was the "ultimatum" of 16 September 1965 China handed over to the Indian Embassy in Peking demanding that India dismantle all "its military works" on the Chinese side of the China-Sikkim boundary, or on the boundary itself, within three days, and return the kidnapped Chinese border inhabitants and seized live stock, or else "bear full responsibility for all the grave consequences arising therefrom". This meant that if the war continued.

China might intervene on behalf of Pakistan, and the USA on India's side, resulting in a major war of unpredictable consequences. And the possibility of Chinese intervention was there even in August 1965. Wisdon, therefore, demanded that Shastri act with utmost urgency and clip the wings of Pakistan in 3-4 days of rapid strike, as (later) Indira did in 1971-72.

But that was not to be for Shastri was not that strong. The Chinese ultimatum roused the USA and caused everyone to sit up and take notice. U Thant said "a real danger to world peace" was imminent The British ambassador to the USA flew to London for consultations and the British foreign secretary Michale Steward called the Chinese move "a serious, indeed dangerous development."

As early as September 4. Kosygin had expressed concern to Ayub and Shastri at the military conflict "in an area directly adjacent to the borders of the Soviet Union" and offered the Soviet good offices for a peaceful settlement. On 8 September, he criticised the Indian action to cross the international frontier and asked for withdrawal of troops.

Moscow was warned about China intervening on Pakistan's behalf, and the USA, in that case, supporting India. On 17 September, he renewed his offer to mediate and invited them to confer at Tashkent offering to "take part in this meeting" if desired by both sides. After the ceasefire the Security Council lost interest in the matter and Moscow continued to press both sides for peaceful settlement of all disputes On 11 November, foreign minister Bhutto accepted the Soviet offer. On November 28, Shastri agreed to meet Ayub at Tashkent if he agrees to discuss the "total relationship between India and Pakistan." Moscow announced on 8 December that Shastri and Ayub would meet at Tashkent on 4 January, 1966. Shastri confirmed it in his statement to Parliament on 10 December, 1966.

The Tashkent conference lasted from 4 to 10 January, 1966. Kosygin argued his case very convincingly. He wanted both India and Pakistan to renounce war and seek a solution of the Kashmir problem and other questions across the conference table. At the same time, he proposed that in accordance with the Security Council's resolution both countries should withdraw to the positions prior to the conflict.

While Ayub was unwilling to renounce the use of force on the Kashmir issue, Shastri was unwilling to give up Haji Pir, having categorically told Parliament that "we shall not withdraw fro it" since the whole of Kashmir lawfully belonged to India. Under the insistence of the Soviet Premier and having regard to the terms of the UN Charter. Ayub after much hesitation agreed to reaffirm the obligation under the Charter and to settle the question only through peaceful means.

As these obstacles developed. India proposed a no-war-pact Pakistan rejected it and asked troop withdrawals only. This sabotage was engineered by Bhutto and aided possibly by L. K. Jha. On the 8th night, the deadlock was complete, and the conference appeared to have broken down. Kosygin then tried the old-timer, Gromyko, his able foreign minister who met Swaran Singh at 11 p.m. on 8 January and told him. "The eyes of the whole world are on us. Some solution must be found." Gromyko worked through the night to prepare a neutral draft and produced it at 10 30 a.m. on 9 January. Kosygin at once gave it to Shastri.

The talks were resurrected and Kosygin went back and forth six times during the day between the villas occupied by Shastri and Ayub and more or less finalised the declaration A few missing details were filled in at the lunch Ayub had with Shastri on 10 January, a few hours before the declaration was signed.

Even after Ayub had, in his own handwriting, agreed to include "non-use of force" in the draft declaration, Bhutto omitted these words from the fair draft sent back by the Pakistanis to the

Russians. The Soviets were indignant and decided not to let Bhutto, who by now they were describing as a "gariachi giava" (hot head) to get away with it They successfully poured cold water on him by going back directly to Ayub and holding him to his earlier commitment. Bhutto, thereafter, cut a sullen figure at Tashkent At the glittering ceremony at which the declaration was signed, those present saw Bhutto quietly rapped by Ayub for blowing smoke rings and conducting himself in a manner which was not in keeping with the dignity demanded by the occasion.

Shastri had convinced himself about the fairness of the Tashkent Declaration which he thought was "a charter of peace between India and Pakistan" and "an honourable basis for their peaceful coexistence". He had got the approval of Chauhan and Swaran Singh and had even sounded the reaction of some of the Indian newsmen. He had turned down Ayub's suggestion conveyed through Kosygin, for a plebiscite in Kashmir by saying 'Mr. Chairman, you will have to talk to some other Prime Minister, not me." But, then, what did India gain out of it?

It was, at best a face-saving compromise, capable of differing interpretations The parties agreed to withdraw, not later than 25 February 1966 "all armed personnel" to the positions held before 5 August 1965. In doing this, neither party gave up its basic contentions. Each held to its own position on the question of who the infiltrators were and why they had crossed the ceasefire line Pakistan failed to obtain a self-executing machinery for the settlement of the Kashmir dispute, India had to vacate all the territories in Pakistan-occupied Kashmir without obtaining any clear guarantee that there would be no repetition of armed infiltration from Pakistan-occupied Kashmir. The issue of the infiltrators to which Shastri had attached great importance "practically faded out of the Tashkent discussions."

Shastri's demand that the declaration should contain a clause to dissuade Pakistan from having relations with third countries that might injure the vital interests of India (meant to circumscribe Pakistan's friendly relations with China) was not accepted. Nor was the ceasefire line frozen as the permanent border. His desire to have no-war pact without a definite arrangement for the settlement of disputes met with rebuff. Shastri interpreted the parties reaffirmation, in the declaration, of "their obligation under the UN Charter not to have recourse to force" to mean that it amounted to a no-war declaration. It was, however, countered by Bhutto who quoted Article 51 of the Charter that. "Nothing in the present Charter shall impair the inherent right of individual of collective self-defence." He argued that under this article, nothing in the Charter precluded "Pakistan's right to assist Kashmiris who are victims of Indian agression".

While Shastri contended that the agreement in the declaration not to interfere in the "internal affairs of each other", barred Pakistan from interference with India's possession of Kashmir, Bhutto argued that a disputed territory cannot be regarded as the internal affair of one of the claimants. "On the contrary, Pakistan succeeded in eroding, to an extent, the Indo-Soviet amity and improve Soviet-Pakistan relations.

Soviet economic assistance to Pakistan progressively increased, and later on, Moscow offered military aid to Pindi on the same terms as to New Delhi. The Soviet support of Afghanistan on the Pakhtun question dropped. While India's relations with China and the USA worsened, and those with the USSR cooled off, Pakistan improved her relations with China, the USSR and the USA on a bilateral basis.

China's response to Tashkent was not hostile to Pakistan; it was hostile to the USSR and the USA. For Beijing saw in it a Soviet attempt to wean Pakistan away from the close relationship which China had so assiduously built up with her. The Ren Min Ribao alleged that the declaration was "a product of joint US-Soviet plotting" and that the Soviet objective had been To weaken the united struggle against imperialism in Asia and Africa."

The entire Muslim world with the exception of Yemen and the UAR expressed sympathy for Pakistan's cause, and even the Yemen and the UAR did not side with India but professed neutrality. It was only Malaysia which stood by India; Yugoslavia and Singapore being the other countries that favoured India.

In fact, if any country had reason to be happy at Tashkent it was the USSR, not India and not even Pakistan. Emphasising the difficult nature of the task facing Kosygin at the conference, the *Times* had observed that the Soviet Union was trying "to open a lock that has no key." Soviet success in getting Pakistan and India to talk on neutral ground, and agree to a statement, was a feat no other country had performed before. It greatly raised the prestige of the Soviet Union in the Afro-Asian arena where she was competing for influence with China. At home, Shastri was criticised by many people for going to Tashkent, even though India had won the war As Desai wrote:

Pakistan was soon convinced that, if the war continued, they would have to suffer terribly and also be put to great shame. They, therefore, accepted the appeal for truce and we than agreed to it The negotiations after the truce should have realty taken place in Delhi but the Prime Minister of Russia. Mr. Kosygin, suggested Tashkent for holding the negotiations and also offered to help in the negotiations. It was not proper, in my view, to go outside the country for negotiations, even though we had won the war I had given expression to my view publicly also. But Lal Bahadurji accepted the suggestion of Mr. Kosygin and went to Tashkent along with defence minister and other.

In retrospect, Shastri appears to have made the fatal mistake of taking for granted that Ayub would honour the agreement. India should have delayed the withdrawal of troops until he had normalised relations and returned the Indian property he had seized having got the Indian troops out and having got the right for Pakistani planes to fly over India he refused to fulfil the other clauses of the agreement unless India discussed Kashmir. The plain fact was that the Pakistani leaders feared that Pakistan would cease to exist if she normalised relations with India.

Shastri succumbed to the strains of six days of hard bargaining, and the emotional reaction to his long distance talk by telephone with his wife and son brought on him a severe heart attack which claimed him in the early hours of 11 January 1966 at Tashkent. Death silences all controversies. But there is not the slightest doubt that if he had returned from Tashkent alive, he would have been subjected to a ruthless criticism for his performance there. But in his case death made him a hero and his uncritical admirers began to cultivate the myth that for all his pliancy, "the mouse well roared" at the hour of crisis. Even Chagla quotes the saying, "Those who came to laugh stayed to pray" and says that "those who used to jest about his unimpressive extensor and his humble ways, suddenly realised that there was the stuff of greatness in him. It is there that people have made a mistake that. Shastri had no trace of "greatness" in him and he was essentially a very weak person He was not "the man of steel", he was perhaps "a man of cheese", who did not even know where our forces were deployed in the western front."

MO Mathai says:

> "Fortunately our Chiefs of Staff then, particularly General J. N. Chaudhary and Air Chief Marshal Arjan Singh, were first class men. During that short war Lal Bahadur and family never slept in their house. Radhakrishnan told me that they slept in a rat hole—a sprawling underground cellar from the basement of Rashtrapati Bhawan, dug deep and far into the far-flung vegetable garden and the small woods beyond in Lord Linlithgow's time, during the second world war. Radhakrishnan refused to go underground. He told me that he preferred to die with his fellow-men breathing fresh air."

It has been said that Shastri signed the Tashkent Declaration "with considerable misgivings, but he signed it because he felt that war between the two countries was an evil thing." Chagla says.

He realised what human suffering it entailed, and he wanted to put an end to it even if it meant some sacrifice on the part of India. He knew that when he went back home he would have to face an angry Parliament and a resentful nation. When he responded to the call of peace he did so without thinking of his own future.

Now, nothing can be farther from the truth Nehru had been able to stave off open war with Pakistan with his inimitable gestures and utterances of peace. But Shastri, possessing much less political skid and stature than Nehru, could ill afford to incur the criticism of the extreme elements in India by saying or doing anything which might have smacked of a concession to Pakistan.

It is true that while initially Shastri's appearance on news reel in the popular cinemas packed with millions every night throughout India had been greeted with ribald comments and jokes, in August-September, 1965 his images were greeted with applause.

One of his admirers says:

> "Two weeks before he left for Tashkent, he spoke at a public meeting in Bombay: a million people turned up to hear him. Even Jawaharlal had not seen such a big audience during the last five years of his reign. Shastri's efficient handling of the war and his new-found popularity gave him new confidence. He appeared far more decisive and all the signs were that on his return from Tashkent he intended to reshuffle the Cabinet and choose his own ministers. Kamraj and the Syndicate were not too pleased by this turn, but in the face of Shastri's determination they were powerless on the political level, the transition of power from Nehru to Shastri had now been completed, the war had finally enabled the new Prime Minister to exercise his predecessor's shadow, and the Congress leaders awaited his return from Taskhent with a mixture of anticipation and fear.

All this is part of the tradition of making a dead person a martyr. The discerning eyes had become aware of Shastri's small stature and his failings. On 24 March, 1965 one of his admirers and a critic of Nehru and Indira, namely Mrs. Pandit made a scathing attack on Shastri's government calling them "prisoners of indecision." The country, she said, was ready to move ahead, but leadership was wanting "What is the government afraid of?" She asked "The whole country is behind it wanting the government and the Prime Minister to mould the destiny of the people." Referring to India's declining position in the world, she went on to say: We had a very fine position in the world yesterday. If we want it tomorrow, we had better look to it today." There was a great deal of truth in it even through India's fine position in the world" had become shattered by the China debacle and Shastri had inherited a tarnished image of India But there was no doubt about Shastri's infinite capacity for indecision and for drift.

That very day, Menon spoke in similar vein ending with the *bon mot* that "Even drift had a direction which the government lacked." When Shastri protested: "It hurts me", Mrs. Pandit apologised, "if my speech hurt any body. But I do not take back a single word." Even the pontific J. P. Narain expressed his disenchantment for Shastri's government which had begun so well but which had, in a few months, declined steadily into "ineptitude, indecision and uncertainty." He decried Congress factionalism, the lack of a sense of purpose, and the absence of thinking about India's future KD Malviya agreed with JP Narain

Nandan Kagal in a write-up said

> "The Shastri government is barely ten months old but it already has a tried and dispirited look." And referring to the people's mood, he said: "Despair is perhaps the wrong word.. (It) is rather one of urbane frustration concealed by cynical boredom."

The caucus, by and large supported and admired Shastri—Atulya Ghosh and Sanjiva Reddy in particular. Frank Moraes acknowledged some commendable achievements such as the Indo-Ceylon (Sri Lanka) Agreement of October 1964, and the Nagaland negotiations. But he did refer to the "discordance in the statements by ministers" and to the disorder amongst the chief ministers. And, then, there was this telling comment: The Prime Minister must show that he can be tough.

His policies should develop teeth." Mulgaokar referred to Shastri's "striking failures" which were more conspicuous than his achievements relating to planning, the Naga problem and relations with Pakistan. The failures included the centre's surrender to the states, the continued faction-fighting in the Congress in U.P. corruption, food crisis, and lack of coordination in government.

Pran Chopra had in June 1964 drawn attention to the two valuable legacies of Nehru—"a reasonably complete and distinctive framework of policy and a climate of moderation" although there were bad legacies also—lack of harmony in the Cabinet, lack of orderly relations with the states, corruption, misrule, and grave, persisting economic crisis. He also referred to Shastri's greatest liability—the lack of charisma.

On 26 January, 1965 he certified to Shastri's good record although there was gloom within the body politic.

> "In the political sphere, his weakness was reflected in the deepening internal squabbles among Congress factions, fomenting a sense of defeatism and failure and generating a climate of irresponsibility and triviality. The Congress in the middle of 1965, reminded one of the Kuomintang and the Wafd. The image of Parliament and state legislatures was being tarnished and the incidents of indiscipline and disturbances in the legislatures of West Bengal, Rajasthan, Maharashtra and U.P. in July-August 1965 set the tone of India's political life, which continues even today. The Lok Sabha became unruly for the first time in 1965 and erring members had to be suspended about a dozen times and were asked to withdraw even more often. While Nehru religiously attended the Parliament, Shastri was frequently absent."

In April 1965, Prem Bhatia wrote in anguish:

> "Parliament today is faced with the crucial problem of survival as the focal point of democracy. It can be saved only by itself and not by an external authority.. A great deal is on trial in India at the moment and the future of parliamentary democracy is one such test.
>
> "Again, Shastri's obsession with "consensus" was based on his desire for personal popularity which he thought would be a substitute for Nehru's charisma.

> But in the process his policy became an open invitation to stagnation in areas demanding "dynamic initiative", sadly weakened the authority of the centre, and led to a dangerous dispension of power in the states. His cover of consensus only sought to hide his own personal weakness, lack of will, vision, direction and determination, and basic disagreements within the Congress at all levels. The quest for consensus landed him in indecision, drift, abdication and surrender at home and abroad."

A Shield for India's Honour

Lal Bahadur Shastri was the Prime Minister of India at a crucial time in India's history. He was physically weak, but he faced the problems confronting the nation like a hero. The first problem that he had to face after he became the Prime Minister was one caused by Pakistan. Pakistan took shape by eroding India's land, and was instigating Indian Muslims. After the Chinese aggression, when India's confidence in her strength had been shaken, Pakistan was creating trouble along the borders.

But Shastriji would not yield to the wickedness of Pakistan. He first tried to earn the goodwill and support of other nations for India. He visited Russia, Egypt, Canada and Britain and explained to the leaders of those nations India's stand. He attended a meeting of the non-aligned nations (nations which were neutral) and explained India's position. He even tried to reason with President Ayub Khan of Pakistan. The wicked do not like advice. They can understand only one language, the language of war.

Rann of Kutch

It had become Pakistan's habit to provoke India somehow and jump to arms.

Pakistan had been waiting to swallow Kashmir somehow. She pushed her forces across the eastern border into the Rann of kutch in Gujarat State in April-May of 1965. Lal Bahadur was not unnerved by this unexpected attack. He faced the problem with great tact at that critical moment. The Indian Army forced the attackers to retreat. Then both countries agreed to stop fighting.

Force will be Met with Force

But friendly words cannot tame a serpent. There is but one way to do it - to remove the serpent's fangs. Even before the ink with which they had signed the Kutch agreement dried up, Pakistan raised its hood to strike again. Pakistani soldiers entered Kashmir in disguise. In September 1965 there was a large-scale invasion of the territory by Pakistani soldiers in the Chhamb area. War broke out all along the Ceasefire Line on the Kashmir border.

The enemies who had managed to enter Kashmir were cunning and mischievous. Pakistan also tried to incite Indian Muslims. The Pakistan army was engaged in forcibly occupying areas, which belonged to India. There was the danger of the fighting spreading to the eastern border also.

In addition to this, there was the threat posed by the Chinese on the northern borders of India. Lal Bahadur Shastri faced all these problems with a will of iron. It was at this time that the country understood the greatness of Lal Bahadur Shastri. He decided that was the time to teach Pakistan a lesson. He gave full freedom to the Commander of the Army. 'Go forward and strike' was Shastriji's command to the generals.

Addressing the nation on 13th August 1965 Shastriji referred to Pakistan's threats and said, "Force will be met with force." Two days later, during the celebration of Independence day, he declared from the ramparts of the Red Fort: "It does not matter if we are destroyed. We will fight to the last to maintain the high honour of the Indian nation and its flag."

China Cannot Frighten Us

Just at this time another danger threatened India. China sent a letter, which said, "The Indian army has set up army equipment in Chinese territory. India should pull down this equipment. Otherwise it will have to face the wrath of China."

At that moment India was fighting against the Pakistani army equipped with the latest weapons supplied in plenty by the United States of America. And, at this very moment how was India to resist China?

China's allegations were a bundle of lies. If India removed the military equipment she would be admitting that China's charges were true. Also, that would mean India was afraid of China.

Even the big nations waited breathlessly to see what Lal Bahadur would say and what India would do.

Lal Bahadur did not take long to give a reply. The letter from China was received on the morning of 17th September 1965. He made a statement in the Parliament the same afternoon. He declared: "China's allegation is untrue. If China attacks India it is our firm resolve to fight for our freedom. The might of China will not deter us from defending our territorial integrity."

China kept quiet.

India's soldiers had no fear of death and fought most splendidly and heroically. The army and the air force functioned like the two arms of a single body. The invaders were beaten. The Pakistani army could not stand against the Indian army. It was then that, for the first time, the world came to realise the supremacy of the Indian army.

War with Pakistan

Seeing the Indian nation at the nadir of its morale in the year 1965 and the disillusionment that followed the military humiliation of 1962. Pakistan thought of striking at India. President Ayub Khan selected the Rann of Kutch, a weak chunk in India's defences. The Indian forces were completely taken by surprise and were found unprepared. Pakistan thought that it would push over under these circumstances. Lal Bahadur warned Pakistan that if it did not de-sist from its aggressive activities on the Kutch border, he would give the army a free hand to settle the question as it saw fit.

To quote Dr. Mankekar: "The Kutch incidents which started towards the end of January, 1965 accelerated into a regular fighting in March, 1965 and towards the end of April burst out into a full scale warfare between the armies of two countries."

On April 28, Lal Bahadur in a memorable speech in the Lok Sabha declared—"If Pakistan continues to discard reason and persists in aggressive activities, our Army will defend the country and it will decide its own strategy and the deployment of its manpower and equipment in the manner in which it deems best."

On August 13, 1965, Lal Bahadur in a broadcast to the nation warned Pakistan that if the latter had any idea of annexing any part of our territory by force, she should think afresh. "I want to state categorically that the force will be met with force and aggression against us will never be allowed to succeed."

On September 1, 1965 President Ayub launched a full scale attack on India in the Chhamb sector on the Jammu front. And the die was cast.

Shastriji was true to his word; force met with force. He plunged the Indian Air Force into the fray and he ordered a three pronged attack across the Punjab border. Thus, opening a new front at points of India's choosing.

Shastriji addressed National Development Council and said "If Pakistan wants to compel us by use of force to discuss the main question of Kashmir, I say it is just out of question, we cannot accept it and we will not accept it, come what may."

On September 6. 1965, Indian Army marched across the Punjab border at three points and within a week of the hostilities. Pakistan found itself desperately fighting in defence of Lahore and Sialkot, the two strategically most important cities of West Pakistan. At one point, the Indian Army was sitting in the suburb of Lahore.

It is a fact that Lal Bahadur wanted to have good relations with China as well as Pakistan. For that very reason, he encouraged the Jayaprakash Mission to Pindi in the hope of breaking the ice and setting in motion efforts to improve relations between the two countries. Though he was soft and gentle, yet if situation demanded he would prove his mettle.

After the war with Pakistan, Lal Bahadur no doubt emerged India's man of destiny. His stocks at home and abroad soared high. He rehabilitated India's image in the world's eyes; provided the Indian Army with an opportunity to prove its mettle and wipe out the smear it suffered in 1962, and restored his people's self confidence and morale, which had reached a pathetic low.

But the Tashkent Agreement at Moscow gave him a severe blow and he could not survive and died in a foreign land. Shastriji felt in his mind that certain concessions, he had made at the Tashkent Agreement might bring some protest at home and cause him unpopularity. To know about the public reaction, Lal Bahadur is reported to have made telephone calls, one at his residence and the other to the Home Minister. He is understood to have been told that there was adverse reaction of the public on his Tashkent Agreement. His death continues to be a mystery; whether it was a natural death or unnatural is anybody's guess.

Tashkent - Treaty

Some big nations feared that, if India won a total victory over Pakistan, it would lower their prestige. The Security Council of the United Nations called on India and Pakistan to stop fighting.

On the invitation of Kosygin, the Premier of Soviet Russia, Lal Bahadur Shastri and Ayub Khan met in Tashkent on January 4, 1966. The leaders agreed that their armies should withdraw to the old Ceasefire Line in Kashmir and that the two countries should live in peace and friendship.

Many people in India felt that we should not return the territory taken from Pakistan- occupied Kashmir. They argued that the entire Kashmir belonged to India. But Shastriji wished to give one more chance to Pakistan to live in peace and friendship with India. So he signed the treaty of friendship.

Tashkent Declaration, January 10, 1966

Text of the Tashkent Declaration signed on January 10, 1966 by the Prime Minister of India and the President of Pakistan.

The initiative for a meeting of the Prime Minister of India and the President of Pakistan at Tashkent was taken by Mr. Kosygin, Chairman of the Council of Ministers of the USSR Mr. Swaran Singh had said that Kosygin not only sponsored the idea of the Conference, but also at all stages, and particularly when difficulties arose, acted as a messenger of peace and helped to resolve all obstacles. He did not pro-pose, much less impose, any particular solutions. Yet without his good offices, the Tashkent Declaration could not have taken shape.

The Prime Minister of India and the President of Pakistan, having met at Tashkent and having discussed the existing relations between India and Pakistan, hereby declare their firm resolve to restore normal and peaceful relations between their countries and to promote understanding and friendly relations between their peoples. They consider the attainment of these objectives of vital importance for the welfare of the 600 million people of India and Pakistan.

I

The Prime Minister of India and the President of Pakistan agree that both sides will exert all efforts to create good neighbourly relations between India and Pakistan in accordance with the United Nations Charter. They reaffirm their obligation under the Charter not to have recourse to force and to settle their disputes through peaceful means. They considered that the interests of peace in their region and particularly in the Indo-Pakistan subcontinent and, indeed, the interests of the people of India and Pakistan were not served by the continuance of tension between the two countries. It was against this background that Jammu and Kashmir were discussed, and each of the sides set forth its respective position.

II

The Prime Minister of India and the President of Pakistan have agreed that all armed personnel of the two countries shall be withdrawn not later than 25 February, 1966 to the positions they held prior to 5 August, 1965, and both sides shall observe the ceasefire terms on the ceasefire line.

III

The Prime Minister of India and the President of Pakistan have agreed that relations between India and Pakistan shall be based on the principle of non-interference in the internal affairs of each other.

IV

The Prime Minister of India and the President of Pakistan have agreed that both sides will discourage any propaganda directed against the other country and will encourage propaganda which promotes the development of friendly relations between the two countries.

V

The Prime Minister of India and the President of Pakistan have agreed that the High Commissioner of India to Pakistan and the High Commissioner of Pakistan to India will return to their posts and that the normal functioning of diplomatic missions of both countries will be restored. Both Governments shall observe the Vienna Convention of 1961 on Diplomatic Intercourse.

VI

The Prime Minister of India and the President of Pakistan have agreed to consider measures towards the restoration of economic and trade relations, communications, as well as cultural exchanges between India and Pakistan, and to take measures to implement the existing agreements between India and Pakistan.

VII

The Prime Minister of India and the President of Pakistan have agreed that they would give instructions to their respective authorities to carry out the repatriation of the prisoners of war.

VIII

The Prime Minister of India and the President of Pakistan have agreed that the two sides will continue the discussion of question relating to the problems of refugees and evictions/illegal immigrations. They also agreed that both sides will create conditions which will prevent the exodus of people. They further agreed to discuss the return of the property and assets taken over by either side in connection with the conflict.

IX

The Prime Minister of India and the President of Pakistan have agreed that both the sides will continue meetings at the highest and at other levels on matters of direct concern to both countries. Both sides have recognised the need to set up joint Indian-Pakistani bodies which wilt report to their governments in order to decide what further steps should be taken.

The Prime Minister of India and the President of Pakistan record their feelings of deep appreciation and gratitude to the leaders of the Soviet Union, the Soviet Government and personally to the Chairman of the Council of Ministers of the USSR for their constructive, friendly and noble part in bringing about the present meeting which has resulted in mutually satisfactory results. They also express to the Government and friendly people of Uzbekistan their sincere thankfulness for their overwhelming reception and generous hospitality.

They invite the Chairman of the Council of Ministers of the USSR to witness this Declaration.

10 January, 1966

Shri Lal Bahadur Shastri	Shri Ayub Khan
Prime Minister	President

The Great Little Man Left the Country in Lurch

Hardly could the nation forget the death of its beloved leader, Jawaharlal Nehru, the Indian people on the fateful morning of 11th January, 1966, heard the death of the country's new hero, Lal Bahadur Shastri.

Lal Bahadur had hardly set firmly on the road to success when the cruel hands of death snatched him from his be-loved people. The transparent sincerity of Shastriji had won the hearts of even the opposition parties. Shastriji's death was a great tragedy and a calamity for the Indian people.

World's Statesmen and leaders once again congregated in Delhi to pay homage to the leader of the nation. Rites and ceremonies were performed; a mourning nation bid a sorrowful and affectionate farewell to a hero whom they had begun to love and admire—"He was our man of destiny—he had piloted the nation's destiny through the most critical time. We are once again orphaned," wailed the people.

Lalita Devi regretted that she should not have allowed herself to be persuaded not to accompany her husband to Tashkent. She was all set to accompany him but Lal Bahadur got round her to agree to stay behind, saying it would be too cold and uncomfortable for her there and that she might catch a chill and get unwell. "I will be busy with talks and meetings all the time and who would be able to take you out anywhere. You will just get bored", he had said. The world seemed to have crashed around Lalita Devi. She fell unconscious and remained in that condition, regaining consciousness now and again for the next twenty four hours.

During her last days she vaguely remembered the sea of humanity that suddenly seemed to have engulfed the house. The body was brought to Delhi and home the next day. "It was a strange face, it had gone blue. It had patches everywhere. It was not the same face that I knew," she insisted.

The Shastri family was plunged into an agonising sorrow. To Lalita Devi, the very object of life had been lost.

Foreign Policy

After having taken over as the second Prime Minister of India, Lal Bahadur streamlined the operation in the sphere of External Affairs Jawaharlal held the External Affairs portfolio with himself, but for the first time, Shastriji had a whole time External Affairs Minister in Sardar Swaran Singh. Basically Shastriji did not deviate from the foreign policy accepted and adopted by his predecessor—Jawaharlal Nehru. Diplomatic moves got in motion to genuinely have closer relations with neighbouring countries like Afghanistan, Nepal, Burma and Ceylon.

Lal Bahadur assured the Indian people from the very beginning of his premiership that he would continue the broad policies laid down by the first Prime Minister. Pandit Jawaharlal Nehru, in the field of international politics. On the policy of non-alignment. Lal Bahadur, in his first broadcast to the nation on June 11, 1964 made it clear that he was committed to non-alignment and would implement the same in letter and spirit.

Addressing the Cairo Conference, Lal Bahadur said that time had now come to formulate a positive programme in the furtherance of peace. The five points outlined by him were:

- Nuclear disarmament;
- Peaceful settlement of the border disputes;
- Freedom from foreign domination, aggression, subversion, and racial discrimination;

- Acceleration of economic development through international cooperation; and
- Full support to the United Nation and its programmes for peace and development.

An Ocean of Humanity

"For a long time to come. Indians, their children and their children's children will speak with gratitude of the great 'Little Man' who so briefly and yet indelibly illumined the pages of modern India's history. In whose light, physical frame, gentle nature, humility and strength of character they saw embodied the Indian ideal of a "Public Servant" so completely dedicated to *'nishkam karma'*, thus ob-served Dr. Mankekar.

Ram Nath: Shastriji's Valet

(An Insider's Account)

"The other day I had an occasion to meet Shri Ram Nath, the man who served as valet to the late Lal Bahadur Shastri. He served him for more than 10 years. The small humble-looking man belongs to the native place of Lalita Shastri, i.e., Mirzapur in U.P. He had many things to tell about his beloved master.

"Ram Nath told me that it was sheer chance that he came into close contact with the family. Once Shastriji was in jail, at that time Lalita Shastri fell seriously ill. Ram Nath went to Allahabad to see Lalita Shastri, as she had been an elder sister to him. He stayed until Shastriji came out of jail. From then onwards, he stayed with the family.

"When asked as to what he had been doing when Shastriji was not in office, Ram Nath replied "continued to be with Shastriji." Ram Nath had all along been treated as a member of the family.

"Overwhelmed with emotions Ram Nath further told me that once his wife was in an advanced stage of pregnancy, he could not manage to get someone from his household to look after his wife during that period. His wife was moved to Shastriji's bungalow. A room was set apart for his wife. She was looked alter with all the care which a member of the family warranted. The wife of Ram Nath gave birth to a son, it was a day before when Shastriji was to vacate the house on his resignation as Union Railway Minister. Shastriji decided to stay in that house for another month to accommodate the family of his valet. Narrating this event, Ram Nath broke down.

"I further asked him if he could recall some moments, when Shastriji was in an angry mood. Ram Nath told me that once on the eve of his departure from Allahabad, he (Ram Nath) did a stupid thing. He was required to keep Shastriji's clothes ready for a change. He forgot to keep his cap along with the other dresses. When Shastriji dressed up to go to Bamrauli airport, he found his cap missing. As usual, the unruffled Shastriji asked him for the cap. Ram Nath felt very nervous as he had sent all the luggage to the airport and it was impossible to produce the cap. Ram Nath sent a car to fetch the bag containing the caps; but it was getting late. Ram Nath could not muster courage to face Shastriji. Shastri knew Ram Nath's discomfiture. Anybody in that situation would have flown into limitless rage but Shastriji went on waiting quietly though he was a bit irritated. When the Governor of U.P. came to know that Shastriji's departure was being delayed due to the non-availability of a cap, he sent a few caps urgently but none would fit on Shastriji's head.

Ultimately the "bag was brought back from the airport and the cap was sent to Shastriji in his room by Ram Nath When Shastriji came out. Ram Nath found it to his great amazement that there were no signs of anger on the face of his revered master. Beyond that. Ram Nath does not recall any situation when he found him annoyed.

"I asked Ram Nath if he had gone with Shastri abroad. He told me that he had gone on many occasions with him on foreign tours. Ram Nath was with Shastriji when he was in Russia to sign the memorable Tashkent Agreement. He remembers that he was with Shastriji half an hour before he passed away suddenly.

"Ram Nath is still staying with Shrimati Lalita Shastri. Of course this gives him some consolation, lie feels himself a part and parcel of his family and will serve them with full devotion to his last breath."— (Published in *Women on the March*, November 1968)

Shastriji is Immortal

Shastriji had suffered heart attacks twice before. And during the period of the Pakistan war and the following days, his body, already battered, had to bear a very heavy strain. He signed the joint Declaration on 10th January 1966. He died the same night.

The news of Lal Bahadur Shastri's death struck India like a bolt from the blue. The entire nation was plunged in grief. Some people suspected foulplay also. Gone was the war hero and the messenger of peace, gone was the great statesman who restored to India her honour and self- respect in the assembly of nations. A tiny, tidy figure. A soul that had lived in perfect purity of thought, word and deed. The very embodiment of selflessness, detachment and simplicity. Such was this man who had lived in our midst. He belongs to the race of the heroes of India.

5

A Great Leader

Shastri's Profile

Shri Lal Bahadur Shastri was born on October 2, 1901 at Mughal Sarai, a small railway town seven miles from Varanasi in Uttar Pradesh. His father was a school teacher who died when Lal Bahadur Shastri was only a year and half old. His mother, still in her twenties, took her three children to her father's house and settled down there.

Lal Bahadur's small town schooling was not remarkable in any way but he had a happy enough childhood despite the poverty that dogged him.

He was sent to live with an uncle in Varanasi so that he could go to high school. Nanhe, or 'little one' as he was called at home, walked many miles to school without shoes, even when the streets burned in the summer's heat.

As he grew up, Lal Bahadur Shastri became more and more interested in the country's struggle for freedom from foreign yoke. He was greatly impressed by Mahatma Gandhi's denunciation of Indian Princes for their support of British rule in India. Lal Bahadur Shastri was only eleven at the time, but the process that was end day to catapult him to the national stage had already begun in his mind.

Lal Bahadur Shastri was sixteen when Gandhiji called upon his countrymen to join the Non-Cooperation Movement. He decided at once to give up his studies in response to the Mahatma's call. The decision shattered his mother's hopes. The family could not dissuade him from what they thought was a disastrous course of action. But Lal Bahadur had made up his mind. All those who were close to him knew that he would never change his mind once it was made up, for behind his soft exterior was the firmness of a rock.

Lal Bahadur Shastri joined the Kashi Vidyapeeth in Varanasi, one of the many national institutions set up in defiance of the British rule. There, he came under the influence of the greatest intellectuals, and nationalists of the country. 'Shastri' was the bachelor's degree awarded to him by the Vidyapeeth but has stuck in the minds of the people as part of his name.

In 1927, he got married. His wife, Lalita Devi, came from Mirzapur, near his home town. The wedding was traditional in all senses but one. A spinning wheel and a few yards of handspun cloth was all the dowry. The bridegroom would accept nothing more.

In 1930, Mahatma Gandhi marched to the sea beach at Dandi and broke the imperial salt law. The symbolic gesture set the whole country ablaze. Lal Bahadur Shastri threw himself into the struggle for freedom with feverish energy. He led many defiant campaigns and spent a total of seven years in British jails. It was in the fire of this struggle that his steel was tempered and he grew into maturity.

When the Congress came to power after Independence, the sterling worth of the apparently meek and unassuming Lal Bahadur Shastri had already been recognised by the leader of the national struggle. When the Congress Government was formed in 1946, this 'little dynamo of a man' was called upon to play a constructive role in the governance of the country.

He was appointed Parliamentary Secretary in his home State of Uttar Pradesh and soon rose to the position of Home Minister. His capacity for hard work and his efficiency became a byword in Uttar Pradesh. He moved to New Delhi in 1951 and held several portfolios in the Union Cabinet - Minister for Railways; Minister for Transport and Communications; Minister for Commerce and Industry; Home Minister; and during Nehru's illness Minister without portfolio. He was growing in stature constantly. He resigned his post as Minister for Railways because he felt responsible for a railway accident in which many lives were lost.

The unprecedented gesture was greatly appreciated by Parliament and the country. The then Prime Minister, Pt. Nehru, speaking in Parliament on the incident, extolled Lal Bahadur Shastri's integrity and high ideals. He said he was accepting the resignation because it would set an example in constitutional propriety and not because Lal Bahadur Shastri was in any way responsible for what had happened.

Replying to the long debate on the Railway accident, Lal Bahadur Shastri said; "Perhaps due to my being small in size and soft of tongue, people are apt to believe that I am not able to be very firm. Though not physically strong, I think I am internally not so weak."

In between his Ministerial assignments, he continued to lavish his organising abilities on the affairs of the Congress Party. The landslide successes of the Party in the General Elections of 1952, 1957 and 1962 were in a very large measure the result of his complete identification with the cause and his organisational genius.

More than thirty years of dedicated service were behind Lal Bahadur Shastri. In the course of this period, he came to be known as a man of great integrity and competence. Humble, tolerant, with great inner strength and resoluteness, he was a man of the people who understood their language.

He was also a man of vision who led the country towards progress. Lal Bahadur Shastri was deeply influenced by the political teachings of Mahatma Gandhi. "Hard work is equal to prayer," he once said, in accents profoundly reminiscent of his Master. In the direct tradition of Mahatma Gandhi, Lal Bahadur Shastri represented the best in Indian culture.

A Selfless Leader

When he was the Railway Minister, he owned moral responsibility for a train accident in south India and resigned, in 1956. He did not have a house of his own, even when he was the Home Minister and people used to tease him the "homeless Home Minister".

That was Lal Bahadur Shastri, who shares his date of birth with Mahatma Gandhi and was a staunch follower of the latter's path of truth and non-violence. In the first general elections of the Indian Republic, the Congress was returned to power with a huge majority.

Shastri, who was the general secretary of the party at that time, had complete control over the selection of party candidates. But he did not contest the elections.

The Prime Minister, Jawaharlal Nehru, however, did not wish to leave such an able and honest man outside the government. He persuaded him to seek election to the Rajya Sabha. He won the election and was appointed the Railway Minister.

At that time there were four classes in the railways: first, second, inter and third. The first class compartments offered extreme luxury while the travails of passengers in the third class was beyond description. Shastri made relentless efforts to remove the wide disparity between the first and third class compartments. The first class, which offered royal comfort, was abolished. The old second class was converted into first class and the inter class was turned into second class. His idea was to have only two classes in course of time.

He provided greater facilities to passengers in third class compartments. It was during his time that fans were provided in third class compartments. He resigned as Railway Minister owning moral responsibility, when an accident occurred in Ariyalur in Tamil Nadu in 1956 in which 144 persons were killed. In fact, he had put in his papers when an accident had occurred in Mahboobnagar three months earlier, killing 112. But Nehru had not accepted it. He refused to continue in the post after the Ariyalur accident.

He became Home Minister after the death of Govind Ballabh Pant in 1961. He had rented a small house in Allahabad. Whenever he went to Allahabad, he used to stay in that house. After some time, the house owner had let it out to another family. When Shastri resigned as minister, he vacated the Government quarter and he did not have a place to live in.

Born at Mughal Sarai in Uttar Pradesh on October 2, 1904, Lal Bahadur Shastri had spent his early childhood at his maternal uncle, Raghunath Prasad's house. His father, Sharda Prasad, died when Shastri was hardly one-and-a-half years old, leaving his mother, Ram Dulari Devi, to take care of their three children. After the death of her husband, Ram Dulari Devi shifted to her father's house in Mirzapur. She played a vital role in shaping Shastri's life by imbibing the right values in him.

After completing his primary education at Mirzapur, Shastri went to Banaras for further studies. He joined the Harish Chandra Vidyalaya, where he was deeply influenced by his mathematics teacher, Nishkameswar Prasad Mishra, who inspired his students by telling them stories of great leaders like Guru Gobind Singh, Rana Pratap and Chhatrapati Shivaji.

He graduated from the nationalist university, Kashi Vidyapeeth, in 1925 and was given the title, 'Shastri', meaning one who is learned in the scriptures. The next year, he joined the 'Servants of the People Society' started by Lala Lajpat Rai and plunged into the freedom movement. Shastri married Lalita Devi, the youngest daughter of Ganesh Prasad, in 1928. He did not believe in the dowry system and refused to take dowry. However, on the insistence of his father-in-law he took five yards of khadi cloth as dowry.

Inspired by his political guru, Purushottamdas Tandon, Shastri joined the Congress Party. He became the City Congress secretary and the president of the Allahabad Congress Committee in 1930. He participated in all national movements between 1921 and 1942 and went to jail seven times. He was elected to the U.P. Legislative Assembly in 1937.

Once when Shastri was in jail, he received the news that his daughter fell ill. He requested the jailor to release him on parole to attend to his daughter. The jailor granted him 15 days parole.

On reaching home, he learnt that his daughter had died. He performed the last rites of his daughter and told his family members that he was going back to the jail. When they reminded him that he was granted 15 days parole, he said, "That was to attend to my sick daughter. But when she is no more, there is no reason for me to take leave."

He became the Prime Minister after the death of Jawaharlal Nehru. He tackled several problems like food shortage, unemployment and poverty. To overcome the acute food shortage, he initially imported food grains and distributed them throughout the country. Later, he drew long-term plans to make the country self-sufficient in food production.

He showed his mettle during the Indo-Pak war, which broke out in 1965. He made it clear to Pakistan and the world that India would not take it lying down, if Pakistan continued to encourage cross-border terrorism. He gave full freedom to the Armed Forces to retaliate and the military bases in Lahore and Sialkot were attacked.

The war had established the supremacy of India and brought Ayub Khan on to his feet. The United Nations passed a resolution demanding a ceasefire. The Russian Prime Minister, Kosygin, offered to mediate and Shastri and Ayub Khan started negotiations at Tashkent. A 'no-war' agreement was signed between the two countries on January 10, 1966, and peace was restored. Shastri suffered a fatal heart attack the same night.

He was awarded the highest civilian award, the Bharat Ratna, posthumously in 1966. A statue of this great little man has been installed in a corner at the park opposite the Municipal Corporation office.

An Exemplary Life

As mentioned earlier, Lal Bahadur was born on 2 October in the year 1904 in Ram Nagar, Ahmedabad Mughal Sarai, United Provinces, British India as Lal Bahadur Shastri. His father Sharda Prasad was a poor school teacher, who later became a clerk in the Revenue Office at Allahabad. When Lal Bahadur was three months old, he slipped out of his mother's arms into a cowherd's basket at the ghats of the Ganges. The cowherd, who had no children, took the child as a gift from God and took him home. Lal Bahadur's parents lodged a complaint with the police, who traced the child, and returned him to his parents.

Lal Bahadur's father died when he was only a year and a half old. His mother Ram Dulari Devi took him and his two sisters to her father's house and settled down there Lal Bahadur stayed at his grandfather Hazari Lal's house till he was ten.

Since there was no high school in their town, he was sent to Varanasi where he stayed with his maternal uncle and joined the Harischandra High School. While in Varanasi, Shastri once went with his friends to see a fair on the other bank of the Ganges. On the way back he had no money for the boat fare. Instead of borrowing from his friends, he jumped into the river and swam to the other bank.

As a boy, Lal Bahadur loved reading books and was fond of Guru Nanak's verses. He revered Bal Gangadhar Tilak, the Indian nationalist, social reformer and freedom fighter. After hearing a speech of Mahatma Gandhi at Varanasi in 1915, he dedicated his life to the service of the country. He also dropped his surname, as it indicated his caste and he was against the caste system.

During the non-cooperation movement of Mahatma Gandhi in 1921, he joined processions in defiance of the prohibitory order. He was arrested but let off as he was a minor. He then enrolled at the nationalist Kashi Vidyapeeth in Varanasi. During his four years there, he was greatly influenced by the lectures of Dr. Bhagawandas on philosophy.

Upon completion of his course at Kashi Vidyapeeth in 1926, he was given the title *Shastri* ("Scholar"). The title was a bachelor's degree awarded by the Vidyapeeth, but it stuck as part of his name. He also enrolled himself as a life member of the Servants of the People Society and began to work for the upliftment of the Harijans at Muzaffarpur. Later he became the President of the Society.

In 1927, Shastri married Lalita Devi of Mirzapur. In spite of the prevailing hefty dowry tradition, Shastri accepted only a *charkha* and a few yards of *khadi* as dowry. In 1930, he threw himself into the freedom struggle during Mahatma Gandhi's Salt Satyagraha. He was imprisoned for two and a half years. Once, while he was in prison, one of his daughters fell seriously ill. He was released for fifteen days, on the condition that he not takes part in the freedom movement.

However, his daughter died before he reached home. After performing the funeral rites, he voluntarily returned to prison, even before the expiry of the period. A year later, he asked for permission to go home for a week, as his son had contracted influenza. The permission was given, but his son's illness was not cured in a week. In spite of his family's pleadings, he kept his promise to the jail officers and returned to the prison.

Later, he worked as the Organising Secretary of the Parliamentary Board of U.P. in 1937. In 1940, he was sent to prison for one year, for offering individual Satyagraha to support the freedom movement. On 8 August, 1942, Mahatma Gandhi issued the Quit India speech at Gowalia Tank in Mumbai, demanding that the British leave India.

Shastri, who had just then come out after a year in prison, travelled to Allahabad. For a week, he sent instructions to the freedom fighters from Jawaharlal Nehru's home, Anand Bhavan. A few days later, he was arrested and imprisoned until 1946. Shastri spent almost nine years in jail in total. During his stay in prison, he spent time reading books and became familiar with the works of western philosophers, revolutionaries and social reformers. He also translated the autobiography of Marie Curie into Hindi language.

Achievements

Played a leading role in Indian freedom struggle; became Parliamentary Secretary of Pandit Govind Vallabh Pant, the then chief minister of Uttar Pradesh; became the Minister of Police and Transport in Pant's Cabinet; appointed as the Railways and Transport Minister in the Central Cabinet; also held the portfolios of Transport and Communications, Commerce and Industry, and

Home Ministry in the Central Cabinet; became Prime Minister of India in 1964; led India to victory over Pakistan in 1965 war.

Lal Bahadur Shastri was the second Prime Minister of independent India. Though diminutive in physical stature he was a man of great courage and will. He successfully led country during the 1965 war with Pakistan. To mobilise the support of country during the war he coined the slogan of *"Jai Jawan Jai Kisan"*. Lal Bahadur Shastri also played a key role in India's freedom struggle. He led his life with great simplicity and honesty and was a great source of inspiration for all the countrymen.

Mystery of Death

After the declaration of ceasefire, Shastri and Pakistani President Muhammad Ayub Khan attended a summit in Tashkent (former USSR, now in modern Uzbekistan), organised by Kosygin. On 10 January 1966, Shastri and Khan signed the Tashkent Declaration. The next day Shastri, who had suffered two heart attacks earlier, died supposedly of a heart attack at 1:32 AM. He was the only Indian Prime Minister, and indeed probably one of the few heads of government, to have died in office overseas.

Although officially it was maintained that Shastri died of heart attack, his widow, Lalita Shastri kept alleging that her husband was poisoned. Many believed that Shastri's body turning blue was an evidence of the poisoning. Indeed a Russian butler attending to him was arrested on suspicion of poisoning Shastri, but was later absolved of charges.

In 2009, when Anuj Dhar, author of CIA's Eye on South Asia, asked the Prime Minister's Office under an RTI plea (Right to Information Act), that Shastri's cause of death be made public, the PMO refused to oblige, citing that this could lead to harming of foreign relations, cause disruption in the country and cause breach of parliamentary privileges.

The PMO did inform however that it had in its possession one document related to Shastri's death, but refused to declassify it. The government also admitted that no postmortem examination had been conducted on him in USSR, but it did have a report of a medical investigation conducted by Shastri's personal physician Dr. R.N. Chugh and some Russian doctors. Furthermore PMO revealed that there was no record of any destruction or loss of documents in the PMO having a bearing on Shastri's death. As of July 2009, the home ministry is yet to respond to queries whether India conducted a postmortem and if the government had investigated allegations of foul play.

Circumstances of Shastri's death do indeed make a case for close enquiry. On the night of January 11, Shastri was awakened by a severe coughing fit. Dr. R.N. Chugh came to his aid. Shastri was unable to speak and pointed to a flask kept nearby. A staffer brought some water which Shastri sipped. Shortly afterwards, Shastri became unconscious and attempts to revive him proved futile.

A cold case forensic enquiry which keeps these facts in consideration, could point to three causes – in order of probability.

- Myocardial Infarction (ordinarily known as Heart Attack)
- Cafe Coronary (impaction of food in windpipe – in this case, drops of water)
- Poisoning by some very quick acting poison, say cyanide although its probability is minimal.

Kashmir Issue

Prime Minister Nehru made the last effort of his life to settle the Kashmir issue in May, 1964. He invited Sheikh Abdullah to come to Delhi as his personal guest. This esture made it clear that he wanted to placate Abdullah and made a new beginning in the spirit of forgive and forget.

Shaikh Abdullah has given a graphic account of his meeting with Pt. Nehru after eleven years of estrangement in his autobiography. He claims to have suggested to Pt. Nehru to invite President Ayub of Pakistan to Delhi for direct talks on Kashmir and other related issues. According to him Pt. Nehru accepted his suggestion and requested him to visit Rawalpindi and invite Ayub on his behalf. According to Abdullah's version Pt. Nehru was Prepared to consider all earlier proposals as also any alternative proposals that may be brought forward during talks to arrive at just, fair and mutually acceptable conclusions.

Sheikh Abdullah received an invitation from President Ayub to visit Pakistan just at that time. It appeared to be prearranged and not just a coincidence. This cleared the way for his visit to Pakistan in the third week of May, 1964.

Before leaving for Rawalpindi Abdullah issued a press statement in which he gave his thinking about the possible solution of the problem. "The solution" he said, "should be such as does not create the feeling of defeat in any party, strengthening the foundations of secularism in India and satisfies the urge for freedom of the people of Kashmir". It pointed to a compromise solution suiting his ambition about freedom for Kashmir through some kind of mutual arrangement between New Delhi and Rawalpindi.

Abdullah and his entourage, which included his son Farooq Abdullah, got red carpet reception at Rawalpindi. He had detailed talks with President Ayub and other leaders of Pakistan. He must have conveyed to them his own plan and thinking of Pt. Nehru. Ayub accepted the invitation of Pt. Nehru and June 15, 1964 was fixed as a tentative date of his visit to New Delhi.

From Rawalpindi, Abdullah went to Muzzaffarabad, the capital of the so-called "Azad Kashmir". This Pak occupied area was of vital importance for Kashmir Valley because the roads which linked it with rail-heads of Rawalpindi and Havelian passed through it. He was therefore keen to woo its non-Kashmiri people to unite it with independent Kashmir of his dreams.

While Abdullah was still in Muzzaffarabad, Pt. Nehru breathed his last at New Delhi on May 27, 1964. This marked an end of an era in free-India. It also aborted the plan of direct talks between him and President of Pakistan for the settlement of Kashmir problem.

Pt. Nehru's death at that juncture was a great blow to Abdullah. He was confident of manipulating Nehru to hammer out a solution, suiting his ambition and the plans. He cut short his visit and rushed back to Delhi.

As discussed earlier, special relationship between Nehru and Abdullah was a major factor in the making of the Kashmir problem. There was much in common between them. Both originally belonged to the Kaul Tribe of Kashmiri Pandits, both were voluptuous and ambitious and both shared weakness good things of life. Pt. Nehru banked on Abdullah to retain Kashmir valley in truncketed India.

Apart from his attachment to Kashmir for perochial reasons, he wanted to disprove the two nations theory on the basis of which he had accepted partition of British India in 1947. Sh. Abdullah wanted to exploit Pt. Nehru to put through his three nation theory according to which Kashmir was to be the third nation in the Indian subcontinent besides India and Pakistan. He might have succeeded in his game but for the twist of history mentioned above. Just as transfer of Hyderabad from Nehru's jurisdiction to Sardar Patel shattered the plan of Nizam Osman Ali about "Sovereign Hyderabad", death of Pt. Nehru destroyed the hope of Abdullah about securing an independent Kashmir with the concurrence of India and Pakistan.

Sh. Abdullah has paid handsome tribute to Pt. Nehru in "*Atish-e-Chinar*" but he has also betrayed his distrust for him in a very subtle way. According to him "Pt. Nehru's love for Kashmir was more like love for a beautiful woman whom he wanted to possess and that he had come to regard him (Abdullah) as a Rakib or rival in love-for the possession of the beautiful valley."

Soon after Nehru's death Sh. Abdullah went abroad ostensibly for pilgrimage to holy places of Islam. He availed this opportunity to establish contacts with heads of many Islamic states and also had a long meeting with Premier *Chou-En-lai* of China at Algiers, capital of Algeria.

The reports of his parleys as published in the foreign and Indian press and intelligence reports received by Government of India from its own sources created grave doubts about him. He was reported to be thinking of an Algeria like liberation movement to secure freedom for Kashmir. He was therefore ordered to return to India. On arrival at New Delhi he was arrested and put under detention. This pointed to more realistic thinking on the part of the new Government led by Lal Bahadur Shastri.

Lal Bahadur Shastri had little in common with Pt. Nehru. He was short in size, rustic in looks and unassuming to a fault. He had a mind of his own. Like Sardar Patel he was a man of the masses who had risen from ranks by dint of hard work. He was a nationalist and realist. He had gained first hand experience of the tricky mind of Kashmiri Muslims during the planned disappearance and reappearance of the reputed hair of prophet Mohammed (Pbuh) kept in Hazrat Bal Shrine at Srinagar, in winter of 1963 and the anti-India frenzy that it had created. He had no misconception about Abdullah.

By his decision to arrest and detain him he made it clear to all concerned that he was not prepared to treat Kashmir as anybody's fief. This step sent right signal to Pakistan also. It made President Ayub realise that he could not expect a soft line on Kashmir from the new government of India. President Ayub had his own assessment of the new leadership at New Delhi and State of military preparedness of India.

According to his assessment Indian military machine had been badly mauled by the Chinese and it would take India sometime to regain its strength and self-confidence. Like many other Muslim leaders, he too had been nursing the fond notion about superiority of Muslim soldiers. He had an exaggerated estimate of the strength of Pak army and capability of Patton tanks that he had acquired from USA. He therefore, wanted to take advantage of what he considered to be Pak military superiority for achieving his objective of grabbing Kashmir by other means.

Pakistan's rulers also banked on cooling off of the relations between India and Soviet Union in the wake of Indo-China war, Anglo-US support and improvement in relations between Pakistan and USSR. He had visited Moscow and developed personal relation with Soviet leaders. At the same time he had continued to enjoy the confidence of USA and was getting massive military aid from her to modernise the Pak army.

But before taking resort to arms he wanted to probe two things. He wanted to know the American reaction if he used

American supplied armament against India. India had been assured by USA that arms supplied to Pakistan will not to be used against her. Secondly, he wanted to have a measure of the mettle of the new Indian leadership. This was the main motivation of Pak incursion into Kutch region of Gujarat in early 1965.

Rann of Kutch was part of the princely state of Kutch which acceded to India in 1947. It is a marshy and sparsely populated region. Some island like uplands called 'Bets" serve as pasture lands. There were unconfirmed reports about reserves of oil and gas in this region. But no exploration had been done until then. India didn't expect any trouble from Pakistan in this sector. Therefore, it was virtually undefended. There were only a few police posts on some of the "Bets".

Pakistan had no valid claim on this area. Maps of the state of Kutch and India as a whole prepared by the government of undivided India had clearly denoted it as a part of Kutch State.

Armed forces of Pakistan backed by Patton tanks made a surprise attack on Kutch, captured some of the Indian posts and laid claims on the whole of Rann of Kutch. Before India could take a defensive action and make a counter attack, UK and USA began to put pressure on India to accept ceasefire which left a big chunk of Indian territory in Pak occupation. Soon after Prime Minister Lal Bahadur Shastri and General Ayub met in London where they had gone for Commonwealth Prime Minister's Conference. There an agreement was signed through the mediation of British Prime Minister. The issue was referred to an International tribunal one of whose members was to be nominated by India and the other by Pakistan.

This was a clear victory for Pakistan. She had succeeded in creating a dispute by unprovoked aggression, tested its newly acquired arms, known the American reaction and internationalised the dispute with the assurance that Pakistan would get something in the bargain. It did get a chunk of about 1000 sq. miles of indisputable Indian territory in Kutch through the award of the Tribunal.

The Kutch adventure and its outcome gave new hope and confidence to Pakistan. It was evident from Ayub's address to

Pakistani students in London in the course of which he bragged that Pakistan's tanks could have a stroll upto Delhi if he had so wished. The way Lal Bahadur Shastri, new as he was to the ways of international politics and diplomacy, acted during this Pak aggression and the negotiations that followed made Ayub think that he could brow beat him and India with impunity. He therefore, decided to go ahead with the main plank of his programme to capture Kashmir.

Pakistan's plan was to launch a sudden attack on Kashmir Valley after sending thousands of armed infiltrations into the state to prepare the ground for proper reception and quick success of the invading army. The infiltration began in May, 1965. The plan was to take the city of Srinagar by surprise on August 9, 1965 when hundreds of thousands of villagers were to come there to celebrate the Martyrs Day call which had been given by pro- Pak leadership of Kashmir Valley. At the same time Pak saboteurs were to become active all along Pathankot- Jammu-Srinagar highway. A major attack was to be made on Chhamb sector to get control of the bridge on the Chenab, at Akhnoor and cut off the north western part of the state from supply bases at Jammu and Pathankot. The bridge on the Chenab at Ram Ban on the highway to Srinagar from Jammu was also to be captured.

The operation in Jammu region began according to plan. But timely information by a Muslim Gujar of Uri about massive infiltration and timely action by the authorities made the part of the operation in the valley a flop.

As a defensive action, the Indian defence forces made an assault on 9000 feet high Haji Peer Pass the only pass leading into the valley from the North West which was under control of Pakistan, and occupied it. An equally daring action led to the recapture of Kargil Heights which command Srinagar-Leh road. These Heights had been captured by Indian forces in April at the time of Kutch war but had been returned to Pakistan in June. These two actions sealed off Kashmir valley and ensured the safety of Laddakh.

Finding its plan of capturing Kashmir through armed infiltrators with the help of local people thus thwarted, Pakistan launched a full scale invasion of the state in Chhamb Jammu sector on September 1, 1965. The object as stated above was to capture Akhnoor bridge and cut off Rajouri and Poonch from the rest of the state and clear the way for capturing the Ram Ban bridge on the Chenab to enable Pakistan to isolate troops in the encircled valley.

Indian troops in Chhamb had no tanks to support them because the one span Akhnoor bridge could not take the load of heavy tanks. Therefore, the capture of the bridge and advance of the Pak forces on Jammu appeared to be a certainty. Indian air force went into action when Pakistani tanks were hardly 10 miles away from Akhnoor. It destroyed a number of them and slowed down their advance.

Even though Pak advance towards Akhnoor and Jammu was slowed down by air action, it was obvious that it could not be halted unless there was counter attack on Lahore and Sialkot sectors by India. Pakistan had planned its strategy on the assumption that as in 1947 India would not extend the theatre of war beyond the boundary of Jammu and Kashmir state and that with the logistic advantage that Pakistan had in Chhamb sector, it would be able to capture Kashmir and that India would acquiesce in the loss of the valley after fretting and fuming for some time.

The experience of first Indo-Pak war when Pt. Nehru did not allow Indian army to make a counter attack on Sialkot, which would have forced Pakistan to come to terms on India's conditions lay at the root of this assumption. Ayub had thought that Prime Minister Shastri would not have the courage to order an all out war with Pakistan. He was also confident that in case of such a war his armoured divisions equipped with Patton tanks would be able to go right up to Delhi.

An Insider's Account Details Thus: I happened to be at Srinagar when Pakistan launched its attack on Chhamb. I had earlier visited Indo-Pak border from Pathankot to Akhnoor and seen with my own eyes the deserted villages, burned vehicles and streams of refugees moving towards Jammu. D. P. Dhar, then Home Minister of State met me on September 2, and apprised me of the imminent threat to Kashmir Valley. He requested me to rush to Delhi to press upon the Prime Minister Shastri to launch counter attack on Sialkot to relieve pressure on Jammu and Kashmir. "You know every inch of Kashmir and can understand the situation better than any other Indian leader. Once Jammu-Srinagar Highway is cut, Kashmir cannot be saved" was his pathetic plea. Fortunately, an Indian Airlines plane was stranded in Srinagar at that time because Jammu airport had been closed. It flew me and some officials and visiting members of Parliament direct to Delhi the same evening. I was happy to learn on reaching Delhi that on the advice of the Defence Chief Shri Shastri had already taken the right decision. He had learned his lesson from the Kutch fiasco and was prepared to call the Pakistani bluff at all costs.

Counter attack on Lahore and Sialkot had the desired result. Pressure on Chhamb sector was relieved. Pak forces fell back to defend Lahore and Sialkot. When ceasefire was ordered on September 21, in response to resolution of U. N. Security Council, Pakistan was nowhere near Kashmir Valley while Lahore and Sialkot were within the range of Indian guns. Lahore had been evacuated and could have fallen into Indian hands if the Indian government had so decided.

Thus the Pak plan to secure by force of arms what it had not been able to get by diplomacy and negotiations failed miserably. Not only Kashmir eluded it once again but it also got a bloody nose. Capture of Haji Pir, Kargil Heights and part of Pak territory up to Sialkot and Lahore retrieved the prestige of Indian armed forces which had suffered badly during the Sino-Indian war of 1962.

But India was once again worsted at the diplomatic table. Attitude of UK and USA during and after the war, as expected, was anything but friendly. Their sympathy for Pakistan was open. But to the great chagrin and dismay of India even USSR maintained a neutral stance. It gave no indication of sympathy and support for India.

After the war Soviet Premier, Kosygin, decided to play the role of a peace maker. He invited both Prime Minister Shastri and President Ayub to meet at Tashkent for peace settlement. Both accepted his invitation. Indian delegation including Foreign

Minister Swaran Singh, Defence Minister Y. B. Chauhan and Indian Ambassador at Moscow, T. N. Kaul. Pakistan delegation included its Foreign Minister, Z. A. Bhutto. The meeting began on January 4th, with an opening address by Kosygin in the course of which he said "India and Pakistan are our southern neighbours. We always came out not only for the strengthening of friendly relations between Soviet Union and India and Pakistan but also for the reign of peace and friendship between these countries themselves." He did not utter a word which could be considered as sympathetic to India which had been subjected to unprovoked aggression. Deliberations continued till January 10, when Tashkent Declaration was adopted and initiated by Lal Bahadur Shastri and Ayub Khan on behalf of India and Pakistan.

Tashkent Declaration was a collection of platitudes. Its only concrete and operative part was clause-II which said "The Prime Minister of India and President of Pakistan have agreed that all armed personnel of the two countries shall be withdrawn not later than 15 February, 1966 to the positions they held prior to August 5th and both sides will observe the ceasefire terms on the ceasefire line."

This was a clear rebuff to India. It not only put the aggressor and the aggressed on par but also committed India to withdraw from Haji Pir and Kargil Heights which belonged to India, had been illegally occupied by Pakistan and had been liberated by Indian armed forces at a heavy cost. It virtually gave legal validity to Pak occupation of the territory it had occupied in 1947-48 without prejudice to its claim on the rest of the state which was still with India.

Lal Bahadur had assured the people and armed forces before his departure for Tashkent that he would not accept any suggestion for the return to Pakistan of Haji Pir pass and Kargil Heights. He stood firm on his word to the nation till the last day. But his aides, Swaran Singh, Y. B. Chauhan and T. N. Kaul, pressured him to accept the Pak demand for withdrawal of troops from there for fear of alienation of USSR. It implied that it was the pressure of the Soviet Union which forced India to accept a patently unjust settlement. Had India not put all her eggs in Soviet basket and had maintained dialogue with USA also before and after going to Tashkent, it might have been saved from the predicament in which Shastri had to sign the Tashkent Declaration against his better judgement.

Prime Minister Shastri was found dead in his room at Tashkent on the morning of January 11, 1966. It was given out that he died of heart failure. But suspicion that he was poisoned to death lingers on. No detailed enquiry into his death was made. Indian physician Dr. Chugh, who had accompanied him to Tashkent was mysteriously liquidated sometime later.

Death of Shri Shastri was the greater loss suffered by India at Tashkent. Had he returned to India alive, he might have given new orientation to India's foreign policy and ended her total dependence on Soviet Union which had proved not only undependable but also dubious.

Soviet leaders were more concerned with global interests and global strategy of Soviet Union than with national interests of India. Independence of character and commitment to national interest above everything else that Lal Bahadur Shastri had displayed during his short tenure was not to the liking of Soviet Union and its supporters in India. They wanted a more pliable person committed to Nehruvian foreign policy to toeing the Soviet line even at the cost of vital national interest of India.

That explained the interest Kosygin, who overstayed in Delhi for 4 days after the funeral of Lal Bahadur Shastri, showed in the election of Mrs. Gandhi as Leader of Congress Parliamentary Party to fill the place of Lal Bahadur Shastri.

Pakistan was not sincere about Tashkent Declaration. This became clear from the statement made by Altaf Gauhar, Press Secretary of President Ayub, soon after the signing of this Declaration. He was reported to have said that nothing but withdrawal of troops to August 5, position which suited Pakistan had been agreed upon and that Pakistan reserved the right to continue its efforts to secure Kashmir by force.

President Ayub confirmed this in his statement made at Hamburg in November, 1966. He said, "It (Tashkent Declaration) settled nothing. All it did was to enable the two countries to disengage their armies from each other."

From the Indian point of view, the futile Pak attempt to grab Kashmir by force had some positive results. In the first place even those parties in India like the Swatantra Party which had been advocating settlement with Pakistan about Kashmir in terms of UN resolutions conceded that Pakistan had forfeited its claim on Kashmir by taking resort to arms.

Mrs. Indira Gandhi, the new Prime Minister, also declared at New York on March 31, 1966, "It is now too late to talk of plebiscite. The second invasion of Kashmir by Pakistan last autumn has destroyed whatever marginal or academic value the old UN resolutions might have had. Kashmir is now also vital to defence of Laddakh against China. Any plebiscite today would by definition amount to questioning the integrity of India. It will rouse the demand for accessation against which is fought a civil war. We cannot and will not tolerate a second partition of India on religious ground. It will destroy the very basis of the Indian states."

Secondly, it had a salutary effect on the minds of those Kashmiris who had been wistfully looking to Pakistan. Had the government of India taken advantage of this situation to fully integrate Kashmir with the rest of India and had it extended Indian Constitution to that State and enabled Indians from other parts of the country to settle there, the Pak design on Kashmir might have been effectively scotched for ever.

But that was not to be Mrs. Gandhi had the same weakness for Sh. Abdullah and his concept of Kashmiri nationalism which had prevented her father to adopt a realistic and nationalistic approach to Kashmir issue. Her policies soon destroyed the wholesome effect of 1965 war on Kashmiri mind.

The net result of Second Indo-Pak war on Kashmir went in favour of Pakistan, as in the case of First War of 1947- 48. Pakistan had gained 30,000 sq. miles of Indian territory by the war of 1947-48. It regained some of this territory which had been taken back by Indian army in the war of 1965. It also established its right on the territory illegally occupied by it since the ceasefire of 1949. It was also able to push out lakhs of Hindus from both wings of Pakistan as refugees into India. Furthermore, it confiscated Indian properties and assets in Pakistan worth hundred of crores of rupees. Thus, in spite of its failure to grab Kashmir by force it was able to strengthen its position against India both internally and externally.

Memorials

All his lifetime, Shastri was known for honesty and humility. He was the first person to be posthumously awarded the Bharat Ratna, and a memorial "Vijay Ghat" was built for him in Delhi. Several educational institutes, Shastri National Academy of Administration (Mussorie) is after his name these were some examples. The Shastri Indo-Canadian Institute was named after Shastri due to his role in promoting scholarly activity between India and Canada.

One of India's Heroes

Lal Bahadur Shastri is one of the great Indian leaders, who emerged from the roots of poverty as a strong, simple and pure figure. He devoted his life for the pride and honour of the country. What are we doing in return?

Lal Bahadur Shastri (also known as *Gudri ka lal*) shares his birthday with the father of the nation. He was born on October 2, 1904, to Ram Dulari Devi and Sharda Prasad in Mughal Sarai. His surname was not Shastri but Shrivastava. Being strongly against the caste system, he dropped his surname. Later he was given the title of Shastri on completion of his graduation degree, in 1925, from Kashi Vidyapeeth in Varanasi and this title became a part of his name.

His father died, when he was only one and half year old, so he, along with his mother and two sisters, stayed at his maternal grandfather's house, thereafter. Early death of father turned Shastri into a bold, strong and patient child. His mother played a very important role in shaping up his strong personality. He was highly courteous and soft spoken. Though physically not very well built but internally he was a very strong, with a determined personality.

In the childhood, he was very fond of reading Guru Nanak's verses and the speeches of leaders like Bal Gangadhar Tilak, Bipin Chandra Pal, Lajpat Rai and Gokhale. He was strongly influenced by the stories, told to him by his maths teacher Mishra, about the way the British took over India's Independence and also the lectures of Bhagwan Das.

Later, while in Varanasi for his higher education, he listened to a speech of Mahatma Gandhi in 1915 and that was the turning point of his life. He decided, then and there, to devote his life to the Indian Independence struggle.

He became an active member of the Independence struggle at a very young age of 17, during the Non-Cooperation Movement of Gandhiji in 1921. He dropped his studies to join the movement and this was strongly opposed by his uncle as well as teacher but his mother believed and supported him for this. Thereafter he never looked back, went to jail several times and joined the Gandhi's Satyagraha.

In between all this, he got married to Lalita Devi in 1927. When his first child, Kusum, was born, he was in the jail. In total, he spent almost nine years in the jail, but he utilised the jail time in reading the social reformers and western philosophers, many autobiographies and even translated the autobiography of Madam Curie into Hindi.

After Independence, he served the nation and the Congress Party in various capacities and finally became the second Prime Minister of India on June 9, 1964, after the death of Pandit Jawaharlal Nehru.

Apart from his incredible contribution in the Indian freedom struggle, Shastri worked remarkably for the uplift of the Harijans. He was a life-member of the Servants of the People's Society. He opposed the dowry system and in his own marriage, he just accepted a charkha and a few yards of khadhi only.

As the minister of police and transport, after independence, he appointed female conductors for the first time and also started the use of water jets rather than lathis for dispersing unruly crowds.

As the minister of railways and transport in the Central Cabinet, he resigned from his post in 1956, taking the moral responsibility of an accident that took place in Tamil Nadu killing 144 people.

He became Union Home Minister in 1961 and people used to call him homeless home minister as he didn't have his own house.

It was highly crucial time in the Indian political history when Shastri became the Indian Prime Minister. As Prime Minister, he introduced various measures to make India self-sufficient in food requirements. He advocated the Green Revolution to increase the productivity of food grains and also played important role in White Revolution. The National Dairy Development Board was also established during his tenure.

Shastriji was highly instrumental in establishing the goodwill of India and getting support from various countries of the world. The other major event of his tenure as Prime Minister, was the 22 days long India-Pakistan war, in which he gave the slogan of *"Jai Jawan, Jai Kisan."* The war ended on September 23, 1965, with the intervention of United Nations. Later, on January 10, 1966, Shastri went to Tashkent to attend the summit and signed the Tashkent declaration with the Pakistani President Muhammad Ayub Khan. After creating this historical moment, he died on the same night due to a heart attack.

Lal Bahadur Shastri was a man who throughout his life believed in simple living and high thinking. He, a tiny tidy figure, represented the honour and self-pride of India in the assembly of nations. He was a pure soul who through his politeness and firmness emerged as a strong Indian leader from the roots of poverty.

He was awarded the Bharat Ratna, posthumously in 1966. A memorial named Vijay Ghat was built for him. Many institutions, roads and monuments have been built on his name. Every year, on his birth and death anniversary, flowers are offered on his statue and a few impressing and heavy words are spoken, by the leaders, in his remembrance.

Is this all that was expected by this great Indian hero from us? He might not need those flowers or words of praise, but what is required out of us, is to follow his steps and principles to achieve his dream India. I doubt if the young generation actually knows who he is? Many youngsters might know him as one of the Indian Prime Ministers but not beyond that.

Today, living in an independent nation, we are unable to realise the sacrifices and the struggle of countless Indians who are behind this independence. Let us not waste their hard and unmatchable efforts, at least.

Dramatic Personality

General J. N. Chaudhary was the Chief of the Army Staff and Chairman of the Chiefs of Staff Committee. Vice Admiral B. S. Soman was the Chief of the Naval Staff. Air Marshal Arjan Singh was the Chief of the Air Staff. Rear Admiral B.A. Samson was the Flag Officer Commanding Indian Fleet (FOCIF).

Mr. Lal Bahadur Shastri was the Prime Minister. Mr. Y. B.Chauhan was the Defence Minister. Mr. Swaran Singh was the Foreign Minister.

In the Ministry of Defence, Mr. P. V. R. Rao was the Defence Secretary, Mr. H.C. Sarin was the Secretary Defence Production Mr. G.L. Sheth was the Additional Secretary and Mr. D.D. Sathe was a Joint Secretary. Mr. L.K. Jha was the Principal Secretary to the Prime Minister. Mr. C.P. Shrivastava, the Private Secretary to the Prime Minister, published his memoirs "Lal Bahadur Shastri" in 1996. Mr. R.D. Pradhan, the Private Secretary to the Defence Minister, published his memoirs "Debacle to Revival" in 1998.

The Little Earthen Lamp

It is a strange fact that so little is known about the nature and character of Shri Lal Bahadur Shastri, the second Prime Minister of India. And this despite the fact that he answered in so magnificent a manner the question which had tormented the whole country for well nigh a decade—namely, "After Nehru, who?" As might be recalled, anyone who wrote about India in the late fifties or early sixties—whether they were foreigners like Michael Brecher or Welles Hangen or Indian writers—they all posed this question as crucial for the future of Indian democracy, and attempted their own answers. In a lighter vein an answer was suggested by one of my distinguished predecessors, the first Director of the National Academy of Administration, Mussoorie, the late Shri Aditya Nath Jha, later Lt. Governor of Delhi. When asked why he had given up the prestigious post of Director of the National Academy in Mussoorie to take up the post of Additional Secretary in the Planning Commission in Delhi, he replied with his characteristic humour. "You see, after some time all the District Magistrates, all the Superintendents of Police, all the Heads of Departments, all the Secretaries to Government, all the Heads of Embassies abroad would have been those who had been trained by me, and the politicians began to fear that the country would have found the answer to 'After Nehru, who?'"

Partly this lack of knowledge about Lal Bahadurji is due to his own shy and retiring nature, which shunned personal publicity. That is why quite a number even today regard him as a rather dull and prosaic sort of person, who rose to the highest post in Government only because of his non-controversial nature, and because of a fortuitous set of circumstances.

This impression is heightened by the contrast with the many-splendoured personality of Jawaharlal Nehru, who bestrode the Indian firmament like a Colossus. Shastriji had no such pretensions, nor did he ever attempt or aspire to the dominant position of his giant predecessor. But in his own quiet, reserved, steady manner he sought to discharge the heavy responsibility cast on him, to the best of his ability and with complete integrity.

One likes to think of the succession of the charismatic Pt. Jawaharlal Nehru by the quiet and self-effacing Lal Bahadur Shastri in terms of the beautiful and moving poem of Gurudev Rabindranath Tagore: The sun is setting and everyone is worried as to what will happen when darkness will fall. Then the little earthen lamp speaks up: "Light me and as long as I last. I will do the best I can". This poem is particularly moving in this context, because this is precisely what Shastriji did in the short span of life vouchsafed to him as Prime Minister of India.

In writing about Lal Bahadurji, I am in no way attempting a biography, or even trying to chronicle a list of his achievements.

I am confining myself to giving some personal glimpses of his character and personality viewed at close quarters over a period of 7 years. These were the last and most momentous years of his life, when he rose higher and higher up to the very summit, and then suddenly and dramatically vanished from the scene.

Even from this brief and somewhat fragmentary account, it will be seen how wrong are those who regard him as a prosaic and colourless sort of person. One may see emerging a very warm human figure, full of wit and humour and the joy of living. And one may get glimpses of the qualities that took him from humble beginnings to the most important and prestigious post this country has to offer.

I had made it a point, as Director of the Lal Bahadur Shastri National Academy of Administration, Mussoorie, for nearly 4 years, to speak to successive batches of trainees about the qualities of the man whose name the institution was privileged to bear. I had kept urging that if only they would remember and put into practice some of his qualities, they would themselves go far in their careers, and would also help to make the country a better place to live in. And most of all, I used to emphasise that if he who rose from humble beginnings to the topmost position, could preserve his humility and humanity to the very end, there was no reason why any of us should lose ours on becoming Class-I officers of the Central Government.

In my own humble way, I think I can claim to be in a unique position to speak and write about him, because I worked with him for seven long years. I joined him as Private Secretary to the Minister of Commerce and Industry on the 11th January 1959, and by a strange and sad coincidence, he departed from this life on 11th January, 1966. It was 7 years of a rich and rewarding experience, but also 7 years of a tortured existence.

The role of a Special Assistant or Private Secretary to a Minister is a combination of the sublime and the ridiculous. He is often the Minister's closest confidant in all official matters and is in touch with issues that even the Secretary to Government in the Ministry knows little about. At the same time, as the nominal head of the Personal Office, he has to keep his eyes and ears close to the ground and keep himself posted with what is happening not only amongst the personal staff—all of them with close and direct links to the Minister—but also in the household. Also, most of the time he has to keep walking on an extremely tight rope, balancing his absolute loyalty to the Minister who trusts him, without displeasing the very highly placed officers of his Service who man the senior posts in the Ministry, and would sometimes like him to get some of their pet proposals approved by the Minister.

Occasionally, the situation would become quite difficult, but the guiding principle was never to do anything which would let down the Minister. All in all, the experience was such that one can get in no other post. Apart from being associated with and seeing Shastriji in a period of his continual rise to ever greater heights of power and responsibility, I had also the privilege of seeing from close quarters the top direction of two wars in which India was engaged—The War with China in 1962 and the War with Pakistan in 1965.

But Shastriji's methods of working, and his habit of sitting till very late at night in office, night after weary night, made this rich experience also a tormented existence, which I would not care to repeat even for the reward of the seven heavens.

Combination of Ancient and Modern

Shastri's qualities of head and heart were moulded by combining ancient tradition with modem temper. He was fortunate in securing an unassuming and pious lady Lalitha Devi as his life partner.

After he took the degree of 'Shastri' in philosophy and humanities, he came to be known popularly as 'Shastri', though it was neither his proper name nor his caste name. As a distinguished Kayastha a community of pioneers in every walk of life, he combined in himself Hindu Dharma and Islamic culture and was scrupulously loyal to the heritage of India marked by a rare integrity of purpose. In public life, he was unassuming and modest to the point of self-effacement. He courted imprisonment during the successive Satyagraha campaigns: and on one occasion, he went up the clock tower in a burqua and unfurled the national flag to the consternation of police in Allahabad. He was a great reconciler and proved to be a bridge between Babu Purushottam Das Tandon, the orthodox puritan, and Pandit Jawaharlal Nehru, the heterodox cosmopolitan. He joined the Servants of the People's Society founded by the late Lala Lajpat Rai, popularly known as the Lion of Punjab, to train lifelong national workers on the model of the Servants of India Society founded by Gopal Krishna Gokhale to carry on constructive work unostentatiously.

It is said that politics is art, statesmanship is science and party organisation is craft. Shastri successfully combined these roles to a remarkable degree. He gained considerable experience in local self-government as the city father of Allahabad. Whenever and wherever there was a critical situation, whether it be Communist Menace in Kerala, linguistic fanaticism in Assam or regional, religious, class and caste cleavage, he was summoned to devise a satisfactory formula.

Whenever he stepped into any critical situation, bones of contention were broken and mists of misunderstanding melted away. He always came out successfully with flying colours. He resigned his position as Railway Minister, assuming personal responsibility for a serious accident at Ariyalur, and his reputation shot up. As Home Minister, he visibly grew in stature, displaying gentleness, patience and understanding.

Though he gave up office in obedience to Kamaraj Plan, he was called back to office within one year as he was the only conceivable deputy for Jawaharlal. Over the issue of trouble in Kashmir, following theft of a holy relic from the Hazratbal shrine in Srinagar, he displayed wisdom and circumspection in dealing with inflammatory assignment. He did well in probation to wear the mantle of leadership.

Thus, he stuck to moral values in public life. He was calm, collected and confident and never fell excited or elated. He presented a picture of quiet strength and competence. When he became the Prime Minister of India, many thought that he would look small in the place vacated by a stalwart like Jawaharlal. But he proved to be a veritable 'Vamana' rising to dizzy heights like Trivikrama as occasions demanded of him. He came out triumphant in war as well as in peace with his path undeflected, ideals unscralched and vision undemmed.

Though a frail little figure, he was unique and seemed to shy away from limelight. Yet, limelight pursued him. He was most undramatic of men, who was destined to pass into history by a quirk of fate. Never a great parliamentarian, he was an upright person exuding humility and integrity, which was Just there but never put on as Hiren Mukherjee opined. At the same time, he was no political innocent.

If so, how could he be chief organiser for Congress elections all over India? It may be recalled that he was Police Minister in Uttar Pradesh a Job that could not be held by a goody-goody person. He made his mark by an unobtrusive, yet firm and principled, formulation of his views. Though he felt deeply about Hindi as the country's official language, he spoke in Parliament often In English instead of Hindi to respect the susceptibilities of members from non-Hindi regions. In a quiet way without frills, he rose to parliamentary heights.

His success was mainly due to his possessing common sense in an uncommon degree. He took to the crowd and the crowd took to him. He mixed with the crowd as sugar In milk. Though he was always in it, he was never of it. He took a detached and dispassionate view of men and matters.

His individually was not offensive but charming. Everyone felt at home in his company. He had no personal or political enemies. He was the most clear-headed and clear-eyed public man looking ahead with crystal clarity and anticipating coming events with an almost alarming accuracy.

He was a man of quick decision and quicker action. He saw no difficulty in accepting the resignation of the Finance Minister. T. T. Krishnamachari and to appoint Sachin Chaudhary as his successor within the twinkling of an eye.

To the strength of a giant and courage of a lion, he added the gentleness of a dove. He was completely free from ego, anger and jealousy and withstood every test with his head erect. As it was said of Brutus by Shakespeare, the life of Shastri was gentle and the elements were so mixed in him that nature might stand up and say that this was a mart when Pakistan violated our frontiers, he rose to the occasion and successfully faced the challenge with the slogan *Jai Kisan and Jai Jawan*. He even envisaged a plan holiday during emergency (external). He met the opposition periodically on issues requiring national approach. He was good and true as one could expect In political pawn.

Life on earth is transitory. While many live and work for themselves, few like Shastri live and work for others. We are helpless against the decree of Providence. His sudden and unexpected passing away in the early hours of January 11, 1966, at Tashkent soon after the conclusion of a pact for peace with Pakistan was a calamity of colossal dimensions.

General J. N. Chaudhary, who arranged funerals of Gandhi. Nehru and Shastri, described the reaction of the crowd in his autobiography thus:- In the case of Gandhi, there was deep and genuine sorrow, "in the case of Nehru, it appeared that they were saying good-bye to a relative. When Shastri died, it was muchless an emotional affair." Government of India awarded him the highest title of Bharata Ratna posthumously.

In those days of uncertainty, crumbling faith and moral nihilism, he proved to be a spiritual rallying centre, a synoptic vision as Plato loved to call it and a 'Samanvaya' as Hindu thinkers put it. His death created a void which cannot be easily and fully filled up. His reputation was self-established, his abilities were self-evidencing and his personality was self-luminous.

He never shone In the reflected glory of others. He conducted the affairs of the country with great dignity and utter simplicity. One wonders whether he was a moderate in the guise of an extremist or an extremist in the guise of a moderate. But all were agreed that he was an ardent patriot.

His conservation was not quietism but consolidation of what was good in our cultural tradition and national genius. A balanced and rhythmic life in harmony with 'Dharma' was his greatest and lasting contribution to our public life. It can be truly said to him that:

His life's race was well run
His life's work was well done
And his life's crown was well worn.

The *lia Upanishad,* which is most commented upon after the *Bhagavad Gita,* in its penultimate mantra (hymn) tells us that after the body is consumed by fire and the components are consigned to the various elements, what remains unconsumed are the deeds of a person. It is no exaggeration to say that the memory of his life and work constitutes a model and a marvel and continues to guide and Inspire the generations yet unborn.

The greatest tribute that can be paid to him is to emulate his example of sacrifice and service:

Lives of great men all remind us
We can make our lives sublime
And, departing leave behind us
Footprints on the sands of lime.

—*H. W. Longfellow*

Short but Shrewd Statesman

Some are born great. On some others, greatness is thrust. A few achieve greatness against heavy odds by sheer merit, ability, integrity and character. Lal Bahadur Shastri can be placed under the third category. He was born poor and he led the life of a common man even after reaching great positions when everything was at his beck and call. He was the embodiment of plain living and high thinking. What is the secret of his tremendous success in a very short time?

He was born on October 2, 1904 at Mughal Sarai near Varanasi, significantly on the same date of the month in which Mahatma Gandhi was born. He lost his father as a baby of 18 months and was brought up at Varanasi by his maternal grandfather. What is more, he was educated at Kashi Vidyapeeth established by the great philanthropist, the late Sri Shiva Prasad Gupta, in the wake of the Non-cooperation Movement launched by Mahatma Gandhi. It was presided over by the late Bharata Ratna Dr. Bhagawan Das, a scholar of Homeric and cosmic proportions. The professorate consisted of stalwarts like Acharya Narendra Dev, Dr. Sampurnanand and Sri Prakasa, who later occupied positions of responsibility and trust and also of opportunity and honour in independent India.

Personal Details — An Emotional Touch

(An Account by a close watcher).

Lal Bahadur Shastri and my father were good friends. My father Late Shri Lala Shrinath Agrawal was a man of strong character and nature. In his entire life he happened to praise only one person and that person was none other than Shastriji. My father was not known to be generous, when it came to praising anybody even Shastriji, in spite of the fact that Shastriji was his very good friend. In fact my father proved to be a good critic. This book intends to bring out the many qualities of Shastriji. I believe that the people should learn about the qualities of this great personality.

During the Indian National Movement Gandhiji called upon the people for their support. Leaving his education midway Shastriji too joined the movement and remained a disciple of Gandhiji throughout his life. After independence Shastriji's life revolved around Anand Bhawan and Pandit Jawaharlal Nehru. My father told me that Shastriji was an honest person in the truest sense of the term. He possessed a very strong character. The honesty aspect is being mentioned even after his death. Shastriji has truly essayed many different roles as a politician, a patriot, a friend, a co-worker and a family man without compromising on his honesty ever.

Before going to sleep at night I use to massage my father's head and feet. It was during such moments that my father narrated to me various anecdotes about Shastriji.

Gandhiji went to South Africa after his studies where he became famous for his fight for the rights of the blacks. Gandhiji's victories were based on truth and non-violence. His concept of non-violence is deeply and indelibly engrained in the annals of history. Adopting these very ideals of truth, Shastriji worked as a common soldier for the Indian independence throughout his life. Shastriji went on to become the Prime Minister of India. The popularity and adulation that Pandit Jawaharlal Nehru enjoyed took two decades to build. However, Shastriji achieved this in a very short span of time.

There are thousands of books on Gandhiji, but very few on Shastriji. My intention is that every politician should know and learn from the character and values of Shastriji. Every student needs such a motivational force, every citizen needs such ideals to follow and for every co-worker it may provide basic values necessary for work ethics. If such is the magnitude of Shastriji's personality then it surely needs to be proliferated. The children of our country and every citizen ought to know that in the absence of morality and honesty the family or the nation cannot progress.

The word honesty has many connotations. This one word can be used to connote the entire character of a person. If a person is honest then he will be tolerant, balanced, judicious and religious. He would essentially be a follower of non-violence and thereby possess all the good qualities of life. An honest person will be moved by the tribulations of others. He would regard their pains as his own and thus would always be besides them whenever the need be. Modern history bears testimony to the fact that, in Shastriji.

India witnessed the life and times of such a stalwart. Shastriji was indeed a dedicated, sacrificing, concerned and hard working personality. Loyalty and a keen sense of patriotism only added to his other exemplary qualities such as dedication, hard-work and concern for his fellowmen.

Shastriji was a dedicated follower of Gandhiji's ideals. From a humble soldier to a commanding officer, he possessed all the qualities to match their skills. It was not an easy job to secure the confidence of Pandit Jawaharlal Nehru, India's first Prime Minister. Only a person with uncommon stature could secure that. Shastriji was capable of securing Nehru's confidence and thus could become the Prime Minister after Nehru. Shastriji truly represented the common person and thus gave the slogan of Jai Jawan, Jai Kisan. It is due to such acts that Shastriji could go on to secure a respected place in the annals of Indian history. I am sure you will enjoy this anecdote.

"Let's go Lalaji," Shastriji had some *supari* (beetle-nuts) from my father's hand and put them in his mouth and stepped down from the *chabutara* (platform of the house), asking my father to accompany him for the election campaign.

"Relax" replied my father. Shastriji thus sat there for a few more moments. Outside there was a huge crowd waiting for them to go for the election campaign. Slogans were being chanted. "Shastriji *Zindabad!"; "Pandit Nehru Zindabad!"; "Bharat Mata Ki Jai!".*

I was a young boy then, probably around twelve years of age. But I realise that from my childhood I was engaged in activities which normally older people perform. I now realise that I was quite mature even then. My conscience was well in place too. Around that age I had formed a Rashtriya Bal Club. Children that age normally prefer to fly kites, play marbles, *gulli-danda,* I-spy, etc. However, I loved to infuse a feeling of patriotism in such young children. My favourite pastime was to educate such young friends on the functioning of the Parliament. Since I was an active member of the Indian Scouts and Guides and was aware of its active environment, I used to tell them the importance of character building. And, in order to remain physically fit and healthy, I would organise several sports activities. Soon some questions arose—Who will be the President of the Club? Who shall be its Secretary? Who shall be the Treasurer? Who shall be the other office bearers? How shall it operate? I had started organising the activities of the Club similar to that of any big organisation. Two of my revered elder brothers' (Shri Raja Ramji's and Sri Motilalji's) very dear associates Dr. Suresh Vaidya, Shri Vyasji, Shri Padamji Mehrotra, Shri Suresh Shrivastava and a Professor at Allahabad University Dr. Shrivastava encouraged me time and again in all my efforts. The members of our Club had also joined my father and Shastriji in their election campaign.

Coming back to the anecdote. Lal Bahadur Shastriji and my father got down from the *chabutra* and joined the election campaign group, which was waiting for them.

At that age we had no idea what the Congress party was? What was Jan Sangh? Or what was Communist party? But we had come to realise that the independence movement was fought by the Congress and it was under the leadership of Mahatma Gandhi that our country got its freedom from the British. Not only this, we learnt that the person who shot Mahatma Gandhiji belonged to some opposition party.

Thus, for children like us the Congress party began to occupy a respectable position in the framework of patriotism. Such feelings were not only present in children like us, even adults began to feel strongly about this issue. In other words all of us equated the Congress party to Mahatma Gandhi.

Lal Bahadur Shastri and my father were very good friends. But in the span of life Shastriji joined politics and served the country, while my father remained occupied in his business. My father was instrumental as a financial supporter whereas Shastriji was involved directly with the national movement and had to go to the jail on many occasions.

My father came to understand that his son (that is me) was inclined towards social service. Children of my age preferred to adorn the walls of their rooms with photographs of cine stars, whereas I preferred to hang pictures of Mahatma Gandhi, Swami Vivekananda and Pandit Nehru, etc. Apart from such interests, my abilities and style of oratory where praised even by elderly persons. They got impressed by my elocution and oratory.

Often my father use to relate to me incidents about Shastriji. More often than not these discussions took place whenever I used to massage his feet at night. Though it was not clear to me then, I am able to understand the significance of these discussions to day. In the event that I enter public life as a leader, my father somehow wanted to ensure that I follow the ideals, footsteps and character of Shastriji. These discussions were his way of creating ever lasting impressions of Shastriji's principles in my mind.

My father had a *Munshi* (an assistant) whose face I can vividly recall even today. He had a long white beard and a stout body. He invariably wore a *kurta-paijama,* a jacket and there used to be a towel on his shoulders. He was a Muslim by religion. But, he was a staunch follower of Gandhiji in the truest sense and, he admired Shastriji too. We used to address him as *Maulanaji.*

Once I requested my father's permission to receive *Chacha* Nehru at the *Bamrauli* aerodrome. Granting my request, my father directed *Maulanaji* to take me to the *Bamrauli* aerodrome which he did.

I was not aware of the protocol of *receiving* or *seeing off* someone at the airport at that time. But, I had come to know that whenever someone arrives from outstation, then the local people went to receive him at the aerodrome or railway station. The pleasure which is associated with the receiving aspect can only be experienced by the person who receives someone. The emotional bond which is created at the time of receiving someone can only be treasured by the person who goes to receive and the person who is being received.

I had never been introduced before to *Chacha* Nehru, but I had come to know that he was known as *Chacha* (uncle) of the nation. In this way he happened to be my *chacha* as well. Not only this, we children had a special affection for him. On one of his visits, my father had introduced me to Shastriji thus - *"he is my son Munnu, he also intends to be a politician."* Hearing so. Shastriji had patted my cheeks. The touch of his hands was warm and full of personal affection.

I was joined by other two children members of our club. One was named Chhammo and the other was Mammo. Both were brothers and lived close to my home. Their house was as big as a castle. So we made this house the office of our Rashtriya Bal Club. This is where we held our weekly meetings. Its huge terrace was used by us as a playground.

Coming back to the Airport scenario there were a number of Congressmen at the Aerodrome. Some others, twenty to twenty-five of them, were of our age as well. People like me who had gathered there to receive the dignitaries, were asked to stand separately in a row behind a thick rope which was specially organised for us. Everyone was eagerly looking at the skies. It was around half past nine in the morning. Suddenly there was some commotion and we saw a small aircraft approaching the runaway. As it came nearer the plane became much bigger. The aircraft landed and a ladder was placed at the entrance of the aircraft. All of a sudden the entire place started to smell of fresh roses, the roses which party workers, citizens and other people had brought along with them to greet Nehruji. Slogans of *"Chacha Nehru Zindabad"* filled the air.

Nehruji was the first to emerge from the aeroplane. He descended from the plane and it was quite a vision to see him do so adjusting his cap. He wore a white *churidar paijama,* a black *sherwani* with a red rose in one of the button holes. This was his favourite attire. On some occasions he wore a Nehru Jacket as well. As he swiftly descended the stairs, we saw Shastriji follow suit. He was wearing a *dhoti-kurta and* a jacket of *khadi.* This was the same dress in which I had seen him at my residence for the first time. It appeared to me as though he had not changed his dress ever since.

Shastriji followed Panditji. After exchanging pleasantries from everyone present there Panditji came towards us. I wanted to welcome him by garlanding his neck. Someone had lifted me for this job.

Panditji bowed down to accept my garland and reciprocated in kind. You can imagine how delighted I was at this gesture! People wanted to garland Shastriji too. But Shastriji very humbly refused, instead insisted that they present those garlands also to Panditji. As Shastriji came near me I too came forward to garland him, which he gracefully accepted.

While accepting it he carefully looked at me and said, *"You are Lalaji's son, aren't you?"* I nodded, at which he once again patted on my cheeks and moved ahead in those fifteen minutes at the Aerodrome I witnessed that Shastriji was like a disciplined, dedicated soldier trying to manage and control the entire situation there. Indira Gandhi was very young in those days. I did not notice when she alighted the plane.

But when she was about to board the car then I saw her struggling to fold back her umbrella. It was probably a folding umbrella. She was finding it difficult to fold it. Shastriji was standing nearby. When he saw this he gently took the umbrella from her and helped her to sit in the waiting car. Indiraji closed the door of the car and it sped off.

I am recounting this incident of Shastriji because today I feel that this small gesture carried with it a whole gamut of emotions. This small act had unusual dimensions to it. It depicted his simple and honest character. At the same time, today I can infer that one can occupy his master's position by serving him loyally as was evident from this incident.

At that small age I had started wearing *Khadi. I* also wore cloth made at the local centres, but the sense of nationality and love for the nation drew me towards *khadi.* Today I marvel at my preference for *khadi.* I had probably come to realise that Gandhiji was promoting his *Charkha* Movement and *Khadi* Movement because our country is poor and an agriculture based country. On many occasions, due to draught or excess rainfall, crops get severely affected. In such times the farmers and the poor could at least rely on the charkha and earn for their livelihood.

6

Memorable Events

Interesting Happenings of the Childhood

A particular incident when Lal Bahadur was an infant is worth mentioning here. One day, when he was just a month old, his mother, went to a Mela – a fair on the banks of the river Ganga, she was carrying the child in her arms when she was suddenly pushed by the surging crowd, and Lal Bahadur fell out of her hands, disappearing in the confusion and bustle. She tried her best to find the child but did not succeed. The loss was reported to the Police and, as if miracle, Lal Bahadur was shortly recovered form the hut of a cowherd in a neighbouring village and restored to his distraught parents. Lal Bahadur had fallen into the basket of the cowherd who had believed that the Almighty and the sacred river, mother Ganga, had granted his fervent prayers for a son. When police explained the facts, the cowherd and his wife readily, though sadly, agreed to part with the child.

At the age of six, while returning from school, Lal Bahadur and his friends went to an orchard that was on the way to home. Lal Bahadur was standing below while his friends climbed the trees to pluck mangoes. Meanwhile, the gardener came and caught hold of Lal Bahadur. He scolded Lal Bahadur and started beating him. Lal Bahadur pleaded to gardener to leave him as he was orphan. Taking pity on Lal Bahadur, the gardener said, "Because you are an orphan, it is all the more important that you must learn better behaviour." These words left a deep imprint on Lal Bahadur Shastri and he swore to behave better in the future.

One day, Lal Bahadur along with his maternal uncle was out for a stroll in Mirzapur. They met an old man carrying a basket full of mangoes. The old man offered to sell hundred mangoes for just one anna. They pooled their resources, two paisas each and Lal Bahadur gave the money to the old man, who began to set apart and count the mangoes. When he reached fifty, Lal Bahadur intervened and told the man not to take out more.

The puzzled man said, "My boy, you have given me an anna and I have to give you another fifty mangoes to make up the hundred." Lal Bahadur replied, "The money is yours. Actually we don't need more than fifty mangoes. Thank you very much." Later on, Lal Bahadur's maternal uncle asked that why he took only fifty mangoes when we paid for hundred mangoes.

Lal Bahadur explained "You remember the old man saying he was prepared to sell a hundred mangoes for just one anna? It was a distress sale. Why take advantage of such a situation? In any case, we don't need more than fifty mangoes for the family." This incident showed that Lal Bahadur had a highly developed conscience nurtured in invisible ways by a moral family environment.

When he was studying in class VI, he noticed that his name was registered as Lal Bahadur Varma in the school records. He was at the age of twelve at that time. He told his mother and family that he did not wish to keep the caste surname 'Varma': he did not like caste differences. With his family consensus, he made an application to the Headmaster for the deletion of surname 'Varma' in Lal Bahadur's school records.

A delicate situation arose because the Headmaster was himself a 'Varma' – Basant Lal Varma. Sensibly, he did not take umbrage and approved the proposal. Lal Bahadur Varma thus became just Lal Bahadur. Shastri was added to his name in 1925 after he acquired the degree 'Shastri' (one who knows the Shatras). This revealed his strong commitment as a social reformer and he was against the caste system.

Premiership of Lal Bahadur Shastri

The premiership of Lal Bahadur Shastri extended from 9 June 1964 to 11 January 1966. Formerly the Minister of Home Affairs, Shastri became the Indian Prime Minister after the death of Jawaharlal Nehru, India's first Prime Minister, on 27 May 1964. Shastri's tenure as Prime Minister lasted only nineteen months due to his sudden death in Tashkent (then in Soviet Union).

Taking Office

After the death of Nehru, several leaders of the ruling Indian National Congress nominated Shastri due to his socialist background, to stand against the conservative, pro-business Morarji Desai. With the backing of Congress President Kumaraswami Kamaraj, Shastri became the party's choice for Prime Ministership. Shastri was officially sworn in on 9 June 1964 taking over from the Acting Prime Minister Gulzarilal Nanda. Commanding a strong majority in the Indian Parliament that it had won in the Indian general election in 1962, Shastri and the Congress party did not call fresh elections. In his first broadcast as Prime Minister, Shastri said:

> "There comes a time in the life of every nation when it stands at the crossroads of history and must choose which way to go. But for us there need be no difficulty or hesitation, no looking to right or left. Our way is straight and clear – the building up of a socialist democracy at home with freedom and prosperity for all, and the maintenance of world peace and friendship with all nations."

Council of Ministers

Shastri retained many members of Nehru's Council of Ministers. T. T. Krishnamachari was retained as the Finance Minister of India, as was Defence Minister Yashwantrao Chavan. He appointed Swaran Singh to succeed him as External Affairs Minister. He also appointed Indira Gandhi, daughter of Jawaharlal

Nehru and former Congress President, as the Minister of Information and Broadcasting. Gulzarilal Nanda continued as the Minister of Home Affairs.

Domestic Affairs

Shastri continued Nehru's socialist economic policies with central planning. He promoted the White Revolution - a national campaign to increase the production and supply of milk - by supporting the Amul milk cooperative of Anand, Gujarat and creating the National Dairy Development Board. While speaking on the chronic food shortages across the country, Shastri urged people to voluntarily give up one meal so that the saved food could be distributed to the affected populace.

Security and Foreign Affairs

Shastri also continued Nehru's policy of non-alignment but also built closer relations with the Soviet Union. In the aftermath of the disastrousSino-Indian War of 1962 and the formation of military ties between the Chinese People's Republic and Pakistan, Shastri's government considerably expanded the defence budget and strengthened India's armed forces.

Madras anti-Hindi agitation of 1965

The Madras anti-Hindi agitation of 1965 are a series of agitations that happened in the Indian state of Tamil Nadu (formerly Madras State) in 1965. The agitations involved several mass protests, riots, student and political movements in Tamil Nadu, and concerned the official status of Hindi in the state and in the Indian Republic.

Adoption of an official language for the Indian Republic was a hotly debated issue during the framing of the Indian Constitution after India's independence from Britain. After an exhaustive and divisive debate, Hindi was adopted as the official language of India with English continuing as an associate official language for a period of fifteen years, after which Hindi would become the sole official language. The new Constitution came into effect on 26 January 1950. Efforts by the Indian Government to make Hindi the sole official language after 1965 were not acceptable to many non-Hindi Indian states, who wanted the continued use of English. The Dravida Munnetra Kazhagam (DMK) led the opposition to Hindi. To allay the fears of the opposition, Indian Prime Minister Jawaharlal Nehru enacted the Official Languages Act in 1963 to ensure the continuing use of English beyond 1965. The text of the Act did not satisfy the DMK and increased their skepticism that his assurances might not be honoured by future administrations.

As the day (26 January 1965) of switching over to Hindi as sole official language approached, the anti-Hindi movement gained momentum in Madras State with increased support from college students. On 25 January, a full-scale riot broke out in the southern city of Madurai, sparked off by a minor altercation between agitating students and Congress party members. The riots spread all over Madras State, continued unabated for the next two months, and were marked by acts of violence, arson, looting, police firing and lathi charges. The Congress Government of the Madras State, called in paramilitary forces to quell the agitation; their involvement resulted in the deaths of about seventy persons (by official estimates) including two police men. To calm the situation, Indian Prime Minister Lal Bahadur Shastri gave assurances that English would continue to be used as the official language as long the non-Hindi speaking states wanted. The riots subsided after Shastri's assurance, as did the student agitation.

The agitations of 1965 led to major political changes in the state. The DMK won the 1967 assembly election and the Congress Party never managed to recapture power in the state since then. The Official Languages Act was eventually amended in 1967 by the Congress Government headed by Indira Gandhi to guarantee the indefinite use of Hindi and English as official languages. This effectively ensured the current "virtual indefinite policy of bilingualism" of the Indian Republic.

The Backdrop

The Republic of India has hundreds of languages. According to the Census of 2001, there are 1,635 rationalized mother tongues and 122 languages with more than 10,000 speakers.[1] During the British Raj, English was the official language. When the Indian Independence Movement gained momentum in the early part of the 20th Century, efforts were undertaken to make Hindustani as a common language to unite various linguistic groups against the British Government. As early as 1918, Mahatma Gandhi established the *Dakshin Bharat Hindi Prachar Sabha* (Institution for the Propagation of Hindi in South India). In 1925, the Indian National Congress switched to Hindustani from English for conducting its proceedings. Both Gandhi and Jawaharlal Nehru were supporters of Hindustani and Congress wanted to propagate the learning of Hindustani in non-Hindi speaking Provinces of India. The idea of making Hindustani or Hindi the common language, was not acceptable to Periyar, who viewed it as an attempt to make Tamils subordinate to North Indians.

Agitation of 1937-40

The Indian Constituent Assembly was established on 9 December 1946, for drafting a Constitution when India became independent. The Constituent Assembly witnessed fierce debates on the language issue. The adoption of a "National Language", the language in which the constitution was to be written in and the language in which the proceedings of the assembly were to be conducted were the main linguistic questions debated by the framers of the Constitution.

On one side were the members from the Hindi speaking provinces like Algu Rai Sastri, R.V. Dhulekar, Balkrishna Sharma, Purushottam Das Tandon, (all from United Provinces), Babunath Gupta (Bihar), Hari Vinayak Pataskar (Bombay) and Seth Govind Das (Central Provinces and Berar). They moved a large number of pro-Hindi amendments and argued for adopting Hindi as the sole National Language. On 10 December 1946, Dhulekar declared "People who do not know Hindustani have no right to stay in India.

People who are present in the House to fashion a constitution for India and do not know Hindustani are not worthy to be members of this assembly. They had better leave."

The pro-Hindi block was further divided into two camps: 1) the Hindi faction comprising Tandon, Govind Das, Sampurnanand,

Ravishankar Shukla and K. M. Munshi and 2) the Hindustani faction represented by Jawaharlal Nehru and Abul Kalam Azad. The adoption of Hindi as the national language was opposed by members from South India like T.T. Krishnamachari, G. Durgabai, T. A. Ramalingam Chettiar, N. G. Ranga, N. Gopalaswamy Ayyangar (all belonging to Madras) and S. V. Krishnamurthy Rao (Mysore). This anti-Hindi block favoured retaining English as official language. Their views were reflected in the following pronouncement of Krishnamachari:

> "We disliked the English language in the past. I disliked it because I was forced to learn Shakespeare and Milton, for which I had no taste at all. If we are going to be compelled to learn Hindi, I would perhaps not be able to learn it because of my age, and perhaps I would not be willing to do it because of the amount of constraint you put on me. This kind of intolerance makes us fear that the strong Centre which we need, a strong Centre which is necessary will also mean the enslavement of people who do not speak the language at the centre. I would, Sir, convey a warning on behalf of people of the South for the reason that there are already elements in South India who want separation..., and my honourable friends in U.P. do not help us in any way by flogging their idea of "Hindi Imperialism" to the maximum extent possible. So, it is up to my friends in Uttar Pradesh to have a whole India; it is up to them to have a Hindi-India. The choice is theirs."

After three years of debate, the assembly arrived at a compromise at the end of 1949. It was called the Munshi-Ayyangar formula (after K.M. Munshi and Gopalaswamy Ayyangar) and it struck a balance between the demands of all groups. Part XVII of the Indian Constitution was drafted according to this compromise. It did not have any mention of a "National Language". Instead, it defined only the "Official Languages" of the Union:

Hindi in Devanagari script would be the official language of the Indian Union. For fifteen years, English would also be used

DMK's anti-Hindi Policies

The Dravida Munnetra Kazhagam (DMK) which split from the Dravidar Kazhagam in 1949, inherited the anti-Hindi policies of its parent -Dravidar Kazhagam. DMK's founder Annadurai had earlier participated in the anti-Hindi agitations during 1938-40 and in the 1940s.

In July, 1953, the DMK launched an agitation for changing the name of a town—Dalmiapuram—to Kallakudi. They claimed that the town's name (after Ramkrishna Dalmia) symbolised the exploitation of South India by the North. On 15 July, 1953, M. Karunanidhi (later Chief Minister of Tamil Nadu) and other DMK members erased the Hindi name in Dalmiapuram railway station's name board and lay down on the tracks. In the altercation with the Police that followed the protests, two DMK members lost their lives and several others including Karunanidhi were arrested.

In the 1950s DMK continued its anti-Hindi policies along with the secessionist demand for Dravidistan. On 28 January, 1956, Annadurai along with Periyar and Rajaji signed a resolution passed by the Academy of Tamil Culture endorsing the continuation of English as the official language.

On 21 September, 1957 the DMK convened an anti-Hindi Conference to protest against the imposition of Hindi. It observed 13 October, 1957 as "anti-Hindi Day".

On 31 July, 1960, another open air anti-Hindi conference was held at Kodambakkam, Madras. In November, 1963, DMK dropped its secessionist demand in the wake of the Sino-Indian War and the passage of the anti-secessionist 16th Amendment to the Indian Constitution. But the anti-Hindi stance remained and hardened with the passage of Official Languages Act of 1963.

The DMK's view on Hindi's qualifications for official language status were reflected in Annadurai's response to the "numerical superiority of Hindi" argument: "If we had to accept the principle of numerical superiority while selecting our national bird, the choice would have fallen not on the peacock but on the common crow."

Official Languages Act of 1963

As the deadline stipulated in Part XVII of the Constitution for switching to Hindi as primary official language approached, the central government stepped up its efforts to spread Hindi's official usage. In 1960, compulsory training for Hindi typing and stenography was started. The same year, India's president Rajendra Prasad acted on the Pant Committee's recommendations and issued orders for preparation of Hindi glossaries, translating procedural literature and legal codes to Hindi, imparting Hindi education to government employees and other efforts for propagating Hindi.

To give legal status to Nehru's assurance of 1959, the Official Languages Act was passed in 1963. In Nehru's own words:

> "This is a Bill, in continuation of what has happened in the past, to remove a restriction which had been placed by the Constitution on the use of English after a certain date i.e. 1965. It is just to remove that restriction that this is placed."

The Bill was introduced in Parliament on 21 January 1963. Opposition to the Bill came from DMK members who objected to the usage of the word "may" instead of "shall" in section 3 of the Bill. That section read: "the English language may...continue to be used in addition to Hindi".

The DMK argued was that the term "may" could be interpreted as "may not" by future administrations. They feared that minority opinion will not be considered and non Hindi speakers' views would be ignored. On 22 April, Nehru assured the parliamentarians that, for that particular case "may" had the same meaning as "shall". The DMK then demanded, if that was the case why "shall" was not used instead of "may".

Leading the opposition to the Bill was Annadurai (then a Member of the Rajya Sabha). He pleaded for an indefinite continuation of the *status quo* and argued that continued use of English as official language would "distribute advantages or disadvantages evenly" among Hindi and non-Hindi speakers. The Bill was passed on 27 April without any change in the wording.

students from Madras city's colleges marched from Napier park to the Government secretariat at Fort St. George to present a petition to Bhaktavatsalam. But he refused to meet with the students saying "Why should i see the students?". The students viewed his refusal as an insult and were further enraged.

Madurai Incident

In the morning of 25 January, students in Madurai took out a procession towards the Thilagar *thidal* (lit. Grounds) at the centre of the city. Their intention was to stage a public burning of Part XVII of the constitution. They burned a huge effigy of "Hindi Demoness" and shouted slogans against Hindi like "Down with Hindi" and "Hindi Never, English Ever". As the procession approached the Congress Party district office at North Masi Street, some Congress "volunteers" who had arrived in a Jeep shouted insults and obscenities at the students. A volley of sandals from the students returned the insult.

The provoked Congress volunteers, who ran back into the Party's office, returned with knives and attacked students, wounding seven. As the riot broke out, students set fire to the pandal in the Congress office, constructed for the Republic day celebrations. When news of the attack spread riots broke out in Madurai and other parts of the State. In retaliation for the attack, students cut down flag poles of the Congress party all over Madurai.

Two Months of Riots

As the riots spread, police responded with lathi charges and firing on student processions. This further inflamed the situation. Acts of arson, looting and damage to public property became common. Railway cars and Hindi name boards at railway stations were burned down; telegraph poles were cut and railway tracks displaced.

The Bhaktavatsalam Government considered the situation as a law and order problem and brought in para military forces to quell the agitation. Incensed by police action, violent mobs killed two police men. Five agitators (Sivalingam, Aranganathan, Veerappan, Muthu, and Sarangapani) committed suicide by pouring gasoline and setting themselves on fire and three more

(Dandapani, Muthu, and Shanmugam) died by consuming poison. (a sixth suicide by self immolatation - by Sarangapani of Mayavaram occurred two weeks later). In two weeks of riots, around 70 people were killed (by official estimates). Some unofficial reports put the death toll as high as 500. A large number of students were arrested. The damage to property was assessed as one crore Rupees.

On 28 January, classes in Madras University, Annamalai University and other colleges and schools in the state were suspended indefinitely. Within the Congress, opinion was divided - On 31 January, a group of Congress leaders including Mysore Chief minister S.Nijalingappa, Bengal Congress leader Atulya Ghosh, Union Minister Sanjeeva Reddy and Congress president K. Kamaraj met in Bangalore and issued an appeal not to force Hindi on non-Hindi speaking areas as they believed it might endanger the unity of the country.

Morarji Desai refused their demands regretting that Hindi was not made official before the anti-Hindi protests crystallized. He said Congress leaders in Madras should convince people there and no regional sentiments should come in the move to forge the integration of the country. Union Home Minister Gulzari Lal Nanda agreed with Bhaktavatsalam's handling of the agitation and commended him for standing "hard as a rock".

Rioting continued through out the first week of February. On February 6, student representatives met Bhatavatsalam to find a compromise. But the talks failed and violence continued unabated. Processions, fasts, general strikes, burning of Hindi books, destruction of Hindi name boards, agitations in front of Post offices became commonplace. By the second week of February the students had lost control of protests.

Annadurai (who had been released on 1 February) condemned the violence and asked the students to suspend the movement. But violence continued unabated. Efforts were made by both sides to find a compromise - Indira Gandhi visited Madras to try and reconcile the situation, while Bhaktavatsalam toned down his stance and started advocating "permanent bilingualism". In a Union cabinet meeting on 11 February, C. Subramaniam, the

Jai Jawan Jai Kisan

Jai Jawan Jai Kisan was a slogan given to India by the Prime Minister of India Lal Bahadur Shastri in 1965. It means hail the soldier and hail the farmer. Soon after Shastri took over the prime ministership of India after Nehru's death India was attacked by Pakistan . At the same time there was scarcity of foodgrains in country. Shastri gave the slogan *Jai Jawan Jai Kisan* to enthuase the soldiers to defend India and simultaneously cheering farmers to do their best to increase the production of foodgrains to reduce dependence on import. It became a very popular slogan.

Tashkent Declaration

The Tashkent Declaration of 10 January 1966 was a peace agreement between India and Pakistan. In September 1965 before the two had engaged in the short run Indo-Pakistani War of 1965. Peace had been achieved on 23 September by the intervention of the great powers who pushed the two nations to a cease fire for fears the conflict could escalate and draw in other powers.

A meeting was held in Tashkent in the Uzbek SSR, USSR (now in Uzbekistan) beginning on 4 January 1966 to try to create a more permanent settlement. The Soviets, represented by Premier Alexei Kosygin moderated between Indian Prime Minister Lal Bahadur Shastriand Pakistani President Muhammad Ayub Khan.

The conference was viewed as a great success and the declaration that was released was hoped to be a framework for lasting peace. The declaration stated that:

- Indian and Pakistani forces would pull back to their pre-conflict positions, pre-August lines, no later than February 25, 1966.
- The nations would not interfere in each other's internal affairs.
- Economic and diplomatic relations would be restored.
- The two leaders would work towards building good relations between the two countries.

The day after the declaration Indian Prime Minister Shastri died of a sudden heart attack. The agreement was criticized in India because it did not contain a no-war pact or any renunciation of guerrilla warfare in Kashmir.

Death and Succession

Prime Minister Shastri died in Tashkent due to a heart attack the day after signing the Tashkent Declaration. He was eulogized as a national hero and the Vijay Ghat memorial established in his memory. Upon his death, Gulzarilal Nanda once again assumed the role of Acting Prime Minister until the Congress Parliamentary Party elected Indira Gandhi over Morarji Desai to officially succeed Shastri.

The Prime Minister was in Washington D.C. recently and he specially asked the American companies to come and invest in the area of post-harvest. So as soon as the harvest is done for fruits, vegetables and general crops, we need to focus on the post-harvest to ensure that they reach the table of our citizens?

To my mind business can play a fantastic role in this particular field. I think, we need more help from the government in terms of resetting some of the archaic laws. It is happening from the central government. Some states have come around to dismantle the APMC Act. Much more needs to be done.

The upcoming GST, which would unify tax rates for goods and services, will assist this process further. But we must build this very important pillar and this is the Jai Kisan pillar. We need to ensure that farmers are remunerated well and the post-harvest piece is taken care off.

One of the important thing the government will have to look at in this area is the Foreign Direct Investment in retail. Retail will automatically ensure that supply chains will come into place faster.

Let's look at some of the other areas of economic activity.

IT is one of the important industries in the country. Millions of jobs, as you know, have been created and many of you are working in the IT and IT services. This is one area for which late Shri Pramod Mahajan used to say had flourished because the government did not intervene in this area. India's IT story as all you know is a world story. The world is either working with an Indian IT company or the large IT companies of the world like IBM, Accenture are putting up big shops here in India. Thousands of young minds are engaged in this area.

So therefore the question whether business is doing vital work in the area of national building is already put to rest.

And now, how do we move from a business which only looks at profit for the shareholders? I'd like to recall a recent speech given just a few days back by Nobel laureate Mohammed Yunus, from Bangladesh when he was addressing the joint session of the Parliament. He spoke about social business. I was very touched

with that particular model. He said that Philanthropy is a one time event. A rupee which is given in philanthropy is a one time event, but a rupee given to a 'social business' is sustainable. It keeps generating more jobs, more momentum. He gave a wonderful example of Grameen Bank, which started by lending very small amounts of money to the poorest of the poor and become an iconic success on the basis of which he was awarded the Noble Prize.

I think a lot of businessmen, a lot of youngsters in business must look at social business as well. Can business be purely found on profits and gains for the shareholders? Certainly they are required but social businesses can also be adopted which are not loss making but which are businesses in which the delivery is of satisfaction. I think that this business model has to be developed in this country. And I therefore really urge all of you who are students of management here to listen to the speech of Mohammed Yunus and read through it and you will find that it is very very valuable for your young minds?

The much touched talked about area is corporate social responsibility. Now that is something which is almost a given now for any good company. A tobacco company will have to do green stuff, they will have to go and provide support to climate change issue, green technology, go into businesses that in some sense compensate for the business they do. You also need to have great corporate governance. That is CSR.

If you are using electricity, consume less power, consume less energy, ensure that all that we do is sustainable in the market place and civil society accepts it. Today civil society gives special attention to those companies who are engaged with CSR activities. But that is really to promote your business and making your business more sustainable and more acceptable in a civil society.

Let us look at Corporate Philanthropy through which you do pieces of Nation building.

There are fantastic examples around the world of Corporate Philanthropy. Bill Gates foundation is one fine example, with which they have dedicated over US$30 Billion of their wealth to programmes which have made huge impact on society. They have even gone outside their home country. They have fantastic programmes. They are also working on mobile money transfer to ensure that poor people are served. But their main thrust area is Health Care and in India HIV AIDS. It is the same in Africa and many other countries.

Warren Buffet has decided to use someone else foundation, in this case Bill and Melinda Gates Foundation to channelise his resources to ensure that more and more work is done in this particular area.

We have set up Bharti Foundation which was mentioned earlier this morning. 237 village schools are already operating and more are being put out. Of the 30,000 children 70 per cent belong to the SC/ST and OBC categories. This is the single largest corporate intervention in the history of India where one company has gone out and taken upon itself to reach out to over 100,000 children, especially the girl children and more importantly from the segments of the society which do not get good education. These 100,000 children who will be admitted in the system, batch after batch, to my mind will contribute to nation building. Some of them will be engineers, some of them scientist or doctors and therefore it is becoming very important that this country in itself and the businesses focus attention on the area of education.

There are 320 million young minds at the age of 6-16 today, i.e. 32 crores. About 75-85 per cent of them will never go to high school. And some of them who will go to school will drop out in one or two years. If out of this 32 crores, 20-25 crores will never complete their education, then what will happen in a 10 years' time? In 10 years' time these kids will be in the age group of 16-26. They will either be a productive global workforce or be a burden on the civil society. You have already seen the first sight of problems coming up in the areas where we have seen the Maoist movements coming up.

These are all indications of what is coming up in 10 years. If we do not handle this particular area, this nation will be in difficulty. And this is where businesses need to walk shoulder to shoulder with the government. We have Kapil Sibbal, a fantastic minister, a young minister with a very sharp mind who is trying to set the agenda in educational reform. I hope India will see it in the next two years - a major reform for universities and investment in education. Because the window is of 10 years. In these 10 years we will fix this and the good news is that we don't have to give higher education for all. We can focus on skills growth.

The world needs certified doctors, certified nurses, certified electricians, certified chefs. We will see millions of people going outside for work and send back money to the country adding to our foreign reserves.

Birlas, Infosys, Wipros, Bharti, all of them are moving into this area to make an impact. Are these businesses doing enough in this area? The answer is mixed.

Its still early days. Many people ask why we don't see stories like Bill Gates or Waren Buffet in India. I have an answer and in fact a very frank answer with all the Indians sitting in the room. Firstly, there is a cultural barrier and a difference between Western and our Cultures as to how we look at philanthropy. If you see after the Independence, there were lot families who saw poverty all around them, and engaged actively in giving.

The Tata, the Birlas, the Dalmias, set up colleges, hospitals, clinics. But this stopped suddenly. In the socialistic world, as we developed in the late 60's, 70's and early 80's taxes were high, profit was a bad word, and it was difficult for businesses to do their own business.

Today, we are seeing the first signs of change because there is confidence. India is on a permanent economic development path. In the worst case scenario, in the bad year we are seeing 7 per cent growth rate. In good year India will grow at 9-10 per cent which means this will be a country of nearly 35-40 trillion dollar economy by 2040.

So in 10 years' time we will see India rise up to be the third largest economy in the world after China, which will probably be number one by the time. But that's going to make serious difference to the lives of the Indian people. Each pocket will be growing by 40 times. India's economy is of trillion dollars today. That's a massive rise. So now it's giving the confidence to Indian businesses that they can share some of the profits they have earned. They are becoming more sure, more confident that this growth is going to continue. The government needs to ensure that the economic climate is such that people are confident and secure. Corporates will come forward to set up more libraries, more clinics, more hospitals.

Coming back to the cultural issue, Indians like to do everything for their children. The parents will scrounge, save and live a very difficult life so that their children can get a better life, get better education than what they have got in their lives. That's why the entire direction is towards saving for the children. Whereas in the western world, children leave home at 15, 16, 17 and parents have very little emotional connect with them later in their lives. The parents start directing their money to causes which they believe in, such as charity. The good part of the Indian family system is that parents take care of their children, and the children take care of their parents. But philanthropy has definitely taken a back seat. That's a cultural piece, it will definitely take a long time to change.

But as far as businesses are concerned I see a very strong connect in the area of giving because as Churchill said 'living is about getting, but life is all about giving'.

And in my concluding statement I would like to say what Gandhiji said "I shall pass through this world but once. Any good, therefore, that I can do or any kindness that I can show to any human being, let me do it now. Let me not defer or neglect it for I shall not pass this way again."

So with these words I would like to say that businesses are an integral part of a nation's progress. The three pillars - the government and the political leadership without which nothing will move because they are the enablers of the ecosystem, the civil society - consisting of all of us, and of course the businesses themselves will move any nation forward. So I do hope the respect and credibility that the businesses are getting now will continue in the future as well. And more and more people engaged in businesses will be conferred with awards like the one I have received today which is a very important symbol of honour for any individual.

I wish every one of you my very best and urge everyone to participate in your own way in this very important nation building process.

Address to Students

(19 December, 1964)

[The following speech (abridged) was given by Lal Bahadur Shastri at the convocation of the Aligarh Muslim University.]

Whatever your station in future life, each one of you should first of all think of yourselves as citizens of the country. This confers on you certain rights, which are guaranteed by the Constitution, but it also subjects you to certain responsibilities, which also have to be clearly understood. Ours is a democracy, which enjoins freedom to the individual, but this freedom has to be subjected to a number of voluntary restraints in the interests of organized society. And these voluntary restraints have to be exercised and demonstrated in everyday life. A good citizen is one who obeys the law, whether there is a policeman around or not, and who takes delight in performing his civic duties. In the olden days sense of self-restraint and discipline was inculcated by the combined effort of the family and the teacher.

The economic stresses of present-day life unfortunately do not leave enough time to the parents to look after the children. In the educational institutions the numbers have grown so large as to take away the benefits, which used to accrue formerly by personal contact between the teacher and the taught. Inevitably, our young students are often left much to their own resources. Often this creates problems, which we all know about. This is an important aspect, which needs thorough examination.

The responsibility of our young citizens is great. In my view every station in life is important in itself. Work has its own dignity and there is great satisfaction in doing one's own job to the best of one's ability. Whatever the duties, we should apply ourselves with sincerity and devotion. Such an approach, apart from being good in itself, also has the added advantage of opening avenues for further advancement. We have to see whether we have done our own job well before thinking of criticizing anybody else. All too often, we succumb to the temptation of decrying others without bothering to look to ourselves. Never forget that loyalty to the country comes ahead of all other loyalties. And this is an absolute loyalty, since one cannot weigh it in terms of what one receives.

It is essential to remember that the entire country is one and that any one who fosters or promotes separatism or fissiparous tendencies is not our true friend. What I have said stems from a desire to see that the youth of our country prepares itself in a disciplined and determined manner for the responsibilities of tomorrow. A democratic country is sustained not by the greatness of a few but by the cooperative effort of the many. The future of the country is in your hands and as the older generations complete their task the new ones come along to take their place. If they are well equipped as individuals and as citizens, the country's future will be bright indeed. At a time when you are at the threshold of a new period in your life I would urge you to play your role with confidence and dignity. Our position with regard to secularism is known so well that it hardly needs any reiteration.

It is embodied in our Constitution, which ensures equal respect for all religions and equal opportunities for all citizens, irrespective of their caste and creed and the faith which they profess. In spite of a seeming diversity, there is a fundamental unity in India, which we all cherish and it has to be our constant endeavour to maintain and strengthen this unity.

The country can progress only if it does away completely with fissiparous tendencies and emerges as an integrated whole. And it is in the field of education that the seed of secularism has to be sown at the earliest stages, so that the plant can be carefully nurtured as it grows. The world is at the moment passing through very difficult times. In fact, it would not be wrong to say that never before in the recent past had mankind to grapple with problems of as complex a nature as are confronting it today. It is imperative that satisfactory and, as far as possible, lasting solutions should be found to these problems without undue delay, otherwise there is a danger of the situation getting out of hand. Mutual suspicions, hatred and ill-will between nations and groups of persons have to be removed at all costs and sincere and determined efforts have to be made to ensure that differences and outstanding problems are resolved by mutual discussion in a spirit of understanding, and not by the use of force.

Wars and conflicts, as we know to our cost, always create more problems than they succeed in solving. The great advances made by science and technology, particularly in the field of nuclear and thermonuclear energy, have placed an almost unlimited power at the disposal of mankind. This power can be used either for constructive or for destructive purposes and it is up to us to try to derive the fullest possible benefit from it. We, in India, have our own special problems. No one can deny that some of them are of a serious nature and must be tackled with vigour and determination. Our national objective has been defined clearly and unambiguously.

We aim that every citizen should be provided with the basic necessities of life and should have complete freedom to lead the life of his or her own choice. We aim at a democratic society, strong and free, in which every citizen, irrespective of his religious belief, will occupy an equal and honoured place, and will be given full and equal opportunities for growth and service. We aim at the removal of untouchability and the doing away of the prevailing serious inequalities in status and wealth. We are opposed to the concentration of wealth in a few hands. Our rich cultural heritage extending over countless centuries is not the culture of this community or that but the synthesis of the cultures of the great peoples who lived here at various times in the past.

The objectives I have mentioned are by no means easy of achievement in their entirety. I know that we have met with only a limited degree of success so far, but we have to persevere until the goal is achieved. It must be remembered that the vast majority of Indians are extremely poor and it is only a small minority that live in relative comfort and have the benefit of university education and other worthwhile things. It is when we look at the Indian scene in such a perspective that Hindus, Muslims, Christians, Parsees and others, instead of feeling that they are different, will together begin to put forth a tremendous effort to fight poverty, to eradicate disease and banish illiteracy.

8

Select Letters

To Rajeshwar Prasad

My dear Rajeshwar Prasadji

Namaskar,

I had received your letter of the 2nd September, and yesterday I also received your letter of the 28th September. I am sorry I could not write to you earlier. I have been extremely busy during the last one month. There was the election of the new Chief Ministers and the formation of their Cabinets etc. and these took a great deal of time. We have not yet been able to resolve the disputes in Uttar Pradesh. The situation there is causing concern. Our colleagues in U.P. do not seem to realize how much harm they arc causing to the State. They are so pro-occupied with their individual rivalries.

Panditji wanted very much that I should continue on my post. He mentioned this several times, but I myself wished to leave office. 1 had always been feeling uncomfortable in my mind about giving advice to others and not acting upon it myself. The speed with which we in the Congress are going down is sometimes frightening. Government administration in the districts is rapidly reaching a low level. No strong opposition party has been able to emerge. In these circumstances if some of us in Government come out and do something, then this relinquishing of office should be welcomed.

So far the signs are not very favourable. But it is hardly surprising that such a big step should give rise to some doubts and hesitations in the beginning. For those of us who are regarded as experienced and elders, this is a testing time. I feel that the fault is ours and not that of our Congress workers in the states or the districts. The next few months will show just how much utility we will have outside. I am not without hope.

Difficulties and hardships in the household will have to be put up with. A person learns to adjust himself. I have not yet shifted from my house but I shall be going to a smaller house. We have reduced one vegetable dish, as well as milk, and have started washing some of our clothes ourselves. I am using Ramji's car and shall put in the petrol myself. We shall have to be careful in raped of other things also. I have left office twice before also and this is the third time.

This time there are a few more facilities than on the previous occasions. Hari is also now employed. There is also the Parliament allowance. It is. however, a fact that the burden of expenditure has greatly increased. The truth is that the help and cooperation of my wife is most sincere and without parallel, and I get great strength and support from her. So we shall manage somehow. It is natural for you to be concerned. It is perhaps better not to think too much about what may come. I believe that whatever HE does, we should accept accept cheerfully.

Hariye na himmat, bisariye na Ram ko Jahi vidhi rakhen Ram, Tahi vidhi rahiye

> Do not lose heurt and forsake Ram.
> In whatever manner HE chooses to keep you
> in that manner should you learn to live.

On the 2nd of October, all of us went to Rajghat. It was the same familiar scene except the new constructions which had come up around the Samadhi. The memory of Gandhiji brings one close to tears. All of us are consumed by the desire for comfort and office. The feeling of service and dedication is so much less evident in office. Gandhiji's renunication was utter and complete. The story of his life is summed up in the beautiful verse of Kabir:

Das Kabir jatan se odhi, Jyon ki tyon dhar deeni Chadariya[3]

Thy servant Kabir used this coverlet with care and left it just as he found it

At Rajghat Panditji recollected that it was my birth-day also. The conversation which took place has been reported in *Navbharat as* follows:

Gandhi's birthday is everyone's birthday

> New Delhi, 2nd October This morning at Rajghat, Shri Nehru asked Shastriji "I hear that today is your birthday?" Shastriji, who does not ordinarily make any mention of this fact, replied, "Today is the birthday of Gandhiji, and hence it is not only mine but everyone's birthday."

I am glad to know that you and your wife are keeping good health and are happy. You will come back with new experience and new knowledge. You will be of even greater utility to Government and to the country. I am sure that you would have put every moment to the best possible use. I would like to convey, even at this stage, the congratulations and felicitations of all of us.

Ajay, Alok. Ravi and Anshu are all well. They came here and had their meals with us on two occasions. We also met them when we went to Maheshwar Prasadji's house for dinner. They are all living happily, although they must be missing you both and looking eagerly forward to your return. You and perhaps more than you, your wife, must also be longing to see them again. She must be wondering why the date for return does not come sooner.

I met your elder brother also. Maheshwar Prasadji is still in the Home Ministry.

All else is well.

Yours

(Sd.) Lal Bahadur

Shri Rajeshwar Prasad,
IAS 7, Prince Albert Road
London, NW-I

To Minister for Transport and Railways

Minister for Transport and Railways,
India

New Delhi 1st May 1955

My dear Sir,

I mentioned to you last evening about Shastri's Tilak ceremony to be performed at my residence this evening at 7.30. We shall all feel honoured if you would kindly be present at this function and also join us in the dinner which will follow at 8.30 p.m.

Thanking you,

Yours sincerely,
Lal Bahadur Shastri

9

Golden Words of Shastriji

- There comes a time in the life of every nation when it stands on the crossroads of history and must choose which way to go. But for us there need be no difficulty or hesitation, no looking to right or left. Our way is straight and clear the building up of a social democracy at home with freedom and prosperity for all and the maintenance of world peace and friendship with all other nations. To that straight road and to these shining ideals we rededicate ourselves today.
- *"Jai Jawan, Jai Kisan"* ("Hail the soldier, Hail the farmer")
- If one person gives up one meal in a day, some other person gets his only meal of the day, spoken during the food crisis to encourage people to evenly distribute food.
- Perhaps due to my being small in size and soft of tongue, people are apt to believe that I am not able to be very firm. Though not physically strong, I think I am internally not so weak.

10

Great Life at a Glance

1904: Lal Bahadur Shastri was born on October 2, to Ramdulari Devi and Sharada Prasad Shrivastava, in Mughal Sarai, (Uttar Pradesh). He shared his birthday with Mahatma Gandhi, the father of the nation. Lal Bahadur was against the prevailing caste system and therefore decided to drop his surname.

1947: Lal Bahadur became the Minister of Police and Transport in U.P's Pant's Ministry. He took many steps to bring discipline into the administration. As Transport Minister he subjected government buses to discipline. He was the first to appoint women conductors. Usually the minister in charge of the Police Department would not remain popular for long. But Lal Bahadur Shastri never allowed the police to resort to lathi charge and firing.

1955: Gandhi Medical College, Bhopal was inaugurated on 13th of August, by Lal Bahadur Shashtri. The college started its functioning in the building of the Polytechnic with a first batch of fifty students and two departments. The College later had twenty three departments with a multi faceted faculty. The Medico-legal Institute, Regional Eye Institute and Cardiac Sciences Centre were well established.

— ***Oct. 16:*** India's Transport and Railways Minister, Lal Bahadur Shastri, said the development operation would increase the efficiency of existing port facilities, 'modernise docks at Calcutta and Bombay, improve shipping channels through increased dredging and provide additional berthing.

1962, Feb. 4: The then Home Minister of India, Lal Bahadur Shastri, declared: "If the Chinese will not vacate the areas occupied by them, India would have to repeat what she did in Goa. She would certainly drive out the Chinese forces."

— ***Jun. 6:*** During a debate on the Demands for the Ministry of Home Affairs, when some Members of Parliament referred to the growing menace of corruption in Administration, Shri Lal Bahadur Shastri, the then Home Minister, proposed to request some Members of Parliament and, if possible, other public men, to sit with his officers in order to review the problem of corruption and make suggestions.

— ***Oct. 8:*** Shri Lal Bahadur Shastri Rashtriya Sanskrit Vidyapeeth was established in Delhi. The University campus is beautiful and large. The Vidyapeeth progressed ahead under the able guidance of a dynamic leadership. This University offered Under Graduate, Post Graduate and Ph.D. courses in many fields. This University also provided courses; Shastri and Shastri Sammanita in Sociology.

— ***Oct. 21:*** China launched a major offensive.

1964, May 22: Union Minister Lal Bahadur Shastri laid the foundation stone for the project, Alamatti Dam, later named as Lal Bahadur Shastri Sagar.

— ***May 27:*** Nehru died and Lal Bahadur Shastri became Prime Minister of India. Shastri and his senior Cabinet members Morarji Desai and Gulzari Lal Nanda were strong supporters of Hindi being the sole official language.

— ***Jun. 11:*** Lal Bahadur Shastri made his first broadcast as Prime Minister.

— ***July:*** In the second week Lal Bahadur Shastri left Delhi for a meeting of Commonwealth Prime Ministers in London. *En route,* the plane stopped for refuelling in Karachi, where the President of Pakistan, Field Marshal Ayub Khan, was at hand to welcome the Indian Premier.

— ***Aug. 15:*** People gathered to listen the first Independence Day speech of the newly appointed Prime minister of the nation, Lal Bahadur Shastri, at the historical Red Fort, in New Delhi.

— ***Sep. 10:*** Prime Minister Lal Bahadur Shastri's three-month-old government, faced a mounting barrage of problems, as Prime Minister witnessed the opposition lodge a no-confidence motion against his government.

— ***Oct. 24:*** On October 24, 1964, on the invitation of Shastri, a high-powered Ceylonese delegation led by P.M Srimavo Bandaranaike arrived in New Delhi. The Ceylon premier was given a red carpet welcome and received at the airport by Lal Bahadur Shastri and the Members of his Cabinet, along with other distinguished personalities.

— ***Nov. 6:*** Lal Bahadur Shastri inaugurated the Tuticorin Port Works.

1965, Jan. 24: Prime Minister Lal Bahadur Shastri dedicated the Sharavati hydroelectric project at Jog in Mysore state — the largest power plant in India to be built with US aid and one of the largest power-generating complexes in the world.

— ***Feb. 11:*** After the resignation of two Union ministers from Madras, Lal Bahadur Shastri announced on All India Radio that he would fully honour Nehru's assurances that English would be used as long as people wanted.

— ***May 8:*** Prime Minister, Lal Bahadur Shastri put Sheikh Abdullah under house arrest in Ooty. After a year or so he was released, when Smt. Indira Gandhi succeeded Lal Bahadur Shastri after his untimely death.

— ***Jun.:*** When Lal Bahadur Shastri took over as Prime Minister, a formal invitation was sent to him to visit the United States. The visit was planned for June 1965, and an invitation was also sent to Field Marshal Ayub Khan. Because of President Johnson's preoccupations with Vietnam, the visit was postponed.

— ***Aug. 13:*** Time Magazine featured Lal Bahadur Shastri on its cover.

— ***Sept.:*** Pakistan President Ayub Khan launched an offensive. He saw India as a weak, nation. He got new tanks from the US and was itching to go at India. The so called Mujahideen sent in by Pak army crept into the Kashmir valley and the locals caught them and handed over to the Indian security. Then Pakistani Sabre jets attacked the Indian territory.

1966, Jan.: Indian Prime Minister Lal Bahadur Shastri signed the joint communique at the end of his talks on the Kashmir issue with Pakistan President General Ayub Khan, at Tashkent in Soviet Union.

— ***Jan. 11:*** Lal Bahadur Shastri died in Tashkent, Uzbekistan (then in USSR). When Shastri's body was flown to New Delhi, where a large crowd gathered on the streets to pay last respects to the late Prime Minister. Later, he was cremated at Vijayghat, near the banks of Yamuna river.

— ***Jan.:*** Following the sudden death of Lal Bahadur Shastri in January 1966, Indira Gandhi became the Prime Minister. When Lal Bahadur Shastri was elected, the Prime Minister of India, Indira Gandhi served as the Minister for Information and Broadcasting.

Appendix

(Procedure of Governance)

Prime Minister and the Functioning of Parliament

In modern times it is the Cabinet which actually controls the Parliament. There is no denying the fact that it is the government which really chalks out the parliamentary time-table. None of the existing devices—the questions, the adjournment motions, the censure motions are adequate to control the Cabinet It is in the light of this statement that the relationship between the Prime Minister and the Parliament is to be examined.

Ordinarily the Prime Minister is the leader of the House in his capacity as the leader of the Lok Sabha, if he is its member But if the Prime Minister belongs to Rajya Sabha, then the Prime Minister can appoint one of the Ministers as the leader For example, when Mrs. Gandhi was appointed as the Prime Minister in 1966, she was a member of the Rajya Sabha and she appointed Satyanarain Sinha, Minister for Parliamentary Affairs, as the leader of the Lok Sabha. It should, however, be noted in this connection that if there is an officially designated Deputy Prime Minister from the Lok Sabha, then he will be the leader of the House.

The leader of the House also appoints the Chief Whip and other whips of the Parliamentary Party. The Chief Whip, according to H. M. Jain, is usually included in the Council of Ministers and is designated as Minister for Parliamentary Affairs. He is authorised to perform the day-to-day parliamentary work on behalf of the leader of the House, and the special tasks assigned to him by the leader from time to time. He remains in close contact with the Prime Minister and keeps him informed of the day-to-day happenings in Parliament He works as the eyes and ears of the Prime Minister so far as Parliamentary affairs are concerned.

He always consults the Prime Minister with regard to the dates for summoning and adjourning the session and election of the Speaker, the fixation of the business of the House, timings of debates, arrangement of speakers, possible strategy of the Parliamentary party and on other important and pressing problems faced by the Government in the house. The timetable of the session is also decided with his approval. He also decides the timings of the no-confidence motion to be taken up in the Lok Sabha. He is always treated as the Master of the House because of his position, as the leader of the house and the Parliamentary party in power. He leads the ceremonial debates and is expected to wind up no confidence motion.

Several times he helps the uneasy Ministers at the question hour to maintain dignity and decorum in the House is his special obligation. He also contacts the opposition on behalf of the Government. For finalising the business of the House, he remains in touch with the leaders of the various opposition groups or the leader of the Opposition, as the case may be For this purpose, in the Indian Parliament, there is a Business Advisory Committee which is chaired by the Speaker of the Lok Sabha and which is represented by the members of the opposition and Treasury benches. The Chief Whip is previously briefed by the Prime Minister.

The Prime Minister plays an important role in the functioning of Parliament. It is on his recommendation that the Parliament is summoned and prorogued and also it is on his recommendation that the Lok Sabha is dissolved.

Summoning of Parliament

According to article 85 (1) of the Constitution, each House of the Parliament is to be summoned by the President to meet at such time and place as he thinks fit but "six months shall not intervene between its last sitting in one session and the date appointed for its first sitting in the next session." Ordinarily the session of the Parliament is summoned on the advice of the Prime Minister and it is expected that the Prime Minister before giving such an advice to the President would consult the Cabinet (a Committee of Council of Ministers). If the Prime Minister without consulting the Council of Ministers, advises the President in this respect, he may refuse to accept that advice.

For example, in 1970 in U.P., when the Congress Party which was a major Partner in Charan Singh's Ministry withdrew its support and the Ministers belonging to Congress (R) did not resign, at that time, such a situation developed. The Assembly was to meet on October 6, 1970, but Kamalapati Tripathy, the leader of the Congress (R), demanded the dismissal of Charan Singh on the ground that he has been reduced to a minority in the Assembly On the same day.

Charan Singh asked 13 Congress Ministers to resign and when they refused to do so, he recommended their dismissal The Governor instead of dismissing the Ministers, asked Charan Singh to resign. But Charan Singh refused to do so and informed the Governor that he still had a majority in the Assembly because the other parties have extended their support to him.

He also informed the Governor that he may be permitted to face the Assembly on 30th of September or on 1st of October, 1970. But the Governor did not accept the recommendation and informed the Chief Minister that the date of the session which has been fixed on the advice of the Council of Ministers can not be changed on the advice of the Chief Minister alone

As already mentioned, the advice of the Prime Minister is ordinarily accepted by the President in this respect but what should the President do if there are large-scale defections from the party in power as was the case in West Bengal, Bihar, Haryana, Punjab, Madhya Pradesh, U.P., Gujarat in 1975 and again in 1977 or when a coalition Ministry breaks because of internal differences, as it happened in Punjab in 1970, in Orissa in 1971 and again in 1972 or when a major partner withdraws support as it happened in U.P. in 1970 in Charan Singh's case and m Jammu and Kashmir in 1977? What should the President do if such a situation emerges at the centre and the opposition requests the President to summon the session of Parliament so that It may pass a vote of no-confidence against him?

If in such a situation, the Prime Minister summons the session on his own then that is the most honourable course of action. If he summons the session on the advice of the President even then there will be no difficulty. At the state level, this course of action was followed in Punjab in 1970 and in Gujarat in 1977.

The problem, however, would arise if the Prime Minister refuses to advise the President to summon the session in spite of Presidential advice. At the state level, such a situation developed in West Bengal in 1967, when Dharma Vira, the then Governor advised Ajoy Mukherjee, the then Chief Minister to summon the session within the time-limit stipulated by the Governor, but the Chief Minister refused. What should the President do if such a situation develops at the centre?

In that case the question would arise: Can he summon the session without the advice of the Prime Minister or not? Eminent jurists and Parliamentarians, the Home Ministry and the Law Ministry have expressed conflicting views in this respect. The Law Ministry is of the view that the Head of the State has no such powers. Even some of the Governors agreed with this view.

For example B. Gopala Reddy, the former Governor of U. P. while rejecting the demand of the opposition to summon the session when C. B. Gupta lost majority in 1969 said that persons belonging to various political parties were criticising him for not summoning the Assembly. He pointed out that he was only acting in accordance with the Constitution. A Governor, he emphasised, could not summon the session without the advice of the Chief Minister Agreeing with this view N. Sanjiva Reddy, the then Speaker of the Lok Sabha said: 'The Constitution gave right to a Chief Minister to recommend to the Governor the date on which the House should be summoned.

The other school of thought, however, does not agree with the view that the Parliament can be summoned only on the advice of the Prime Minister. This school of thought is of the opinion that it the debates of the Constituent Assembly are read carefully, then it will be found that the summoning of Parliament is a duty of the President instead of the right of the Prime Minister. Some of the members of the Constituent Assembly expressed the fear that if in spite of the advice of the Prime Minister, the President does not summon the session of the Parliament, then there is no remedy.

Therefore, Professor K. T. Shah wanted to empower the Presiding Officers of both Houses of Parliament "Provided that if at any time the President does not summon as provided for in this Constitution, for more than three months". Opposing this amendment. Dr. Ambedkar said that if the President did not perform this obligation, then he would be impeached. This shows that even Dr. Ambedkar thought that the summoning of Parliament is a duty of the President and not a right of the Prime Minister K. Santhanam. L. M. Singhvi, Administrative Reforms Commission, C. K. Daphtary and M. C. Chagla agreed with this, while expressing their views in the context of the development which took place in West Bengal in 1967.

Hence, it can be said that if the Prime Minister does not advise the President to summon the session of Parliament, then the President on his own can also summon it in extraordinary circumstances though ordinarily it should be done on the advice of the Prime Minister.

Prorogation of the Session

The President ordinarily prorogues the session of the Parliament on the recommendation of the Prime Minister. It may, however, be asked in this connection as to how far is it obligatory on the part of the President to accept the advice of the Prime Minister? Conflicting opinions have been expressed by persons eminent in the field of Constitutional Law on this point. The occasion for expressing these views arose when some of the Governors prorogued the session in order to prevent the Assembly from passing a vote of no-confidence against the Ministry.

The first school of thought is of the view that in this respect the Head of the State is bound to accept the advice of the Prime Minister/Chief Minister The second school of thought does not agree with this view K. C. Reddy, and B. Gopala Reddy, the former Governors of Madhya Pradesh and U.P. respectively. Y. B. Chauhan, P. Govinda Menon and Ashok Sen agree with the first view.

But N.G. Ranga, N.C Chatterjee, Nathpai Acharya Kripalani and C. K. Daphtary agree with the second view According to C. K. Daphtary, the former Attorney General of India, the power to prorogue the House and to summon the House is an absolute power given under the Constitution to the Head of the state.

Since conflicting views have been expressed on this point the question as to how far the President is bound by the advice of the Prime Minister in proroguing the house should be examined carefully? No doubt, so long as the Prime Minister has a majority in the Lok Sabha, the President has to accept his advice. But what will be the position, if the Prime Minister who after having lost majority in the House of the people, because of defections, advises the President to prorogue the session so that a vote of no confidence may not be passed against him? Will that advice be binding? At the state level, such a situation developed in Madhya Pradesh in 1968, and in Jammu and Kashmir in 1970.

If such a situation ever develops at the centre, then the question would arise as to how far the President will be bound by the advice of the Prime Minister to prorogue the session. Though in the above-mentioned two cases Y. B. Chauhan, the then Home Minister strongly defended the action taken by the Governor, yet if the issue is considered in depth, then it will be found that, the Head of the State as guardian of the Constitution, should not have accepted the advice because acceptance of the advice to prorogue the session on such crucial occasions means that the Head of the State takes sides.

It will be more appropriate on the part of Head of the State not to prorogue the session when the motion of no-confidence against the Ministry is pending or when the fall of the Ministry is imminent because of defections In such a situation, It would be appropriate on the part of the Head of the State to ask the Prime Minister to face the House. This contention has been supported by the Mysore are Punjab and Haryana High Courts. The Supreme Court white agreeing with the view says: "Article 174 (2) (3) which enables the Governor to prorogue the Legislature does not indicate any restriction on this power."

Dissolution of the Lok Sabha

Ordinarily, the President dissolves the Lok Sabha on the advice of the Prime Minister but whether the advice of the Prime Minister is binding on the President in this respect or not on this point there is a difference of opinion. So long as the Prime Minister has an absolute majority in the Lok Sabha, the advice of the Prime Minister to dissolve the House is binding but not otherwise.

Though at the Centre we have no example where the Head of the State refused dissolution to the Prime Minister, yet at the state level, there are many examples of this type. For example, Rao Birendra Singh in Haryana in 1967. Naresh Chandra Singh in Madhya Pradesh in 1969 and Hitendra Desai in Gujarat in 1971 were refused dissolution The President may also do the same in certain circumstances.

Even in England, it is said that King George V temporarily refused dissolution to Asquith in 1910. Asquith himself said on December 18, 1923 that it would be subversive of constitutional theory to contend that the King was bound to grant a dissolution when advised to do so the Prime Minister. Sir Ivor Jennings and Anson, the two constitutional experts are of the view that the Crown may not only refuse dissolution but also can dissolve on his own.

It will not be out of place to mention here that when in 1913 the Asquith Government wanted to pass the Home Rule Bill for Ireland, King George V expressed the view that before its passage there should be fresh election but the Prime Minister opposed it. Then the King wrote to the Prime Minister "Should the sovereign never exercise the right not even, to quote Sir Erskine May, in the interests of the state and on the grounds which could be justified to Parliament?

Bagehot wrote, the sovereign too possesses a power according to theory for extreme use on critical occasion, but which in law he can use on any occasion He can dissolve."

In India, since we have the President as the head of the State and has position is different from the hereditary Crown, therefore, instead of blindly following the advice of the Prime Minister in the matter of dissolution, he, like the Governor-General, the Head of a Commonwealth country, may exercise his powers more independently. This is what has been done in some of the Commonwealth countries.

For example. Lord Byng, the Governor-General of Canada, refused to accept the recommendation of Mackenzie King, the then Prime Minister, to dissolve the Parliament in 1925. After refusing dissolution, the Governor-General invited Meighan the then leader of the opposition, and appointed him as the Prime Minister, but his government was defeated in the House of Commons and the Governor-General then dissolved the House on the recommendation of the Prime Minister Similarly, the Governor-General of South Africa in 1939 refused dissolution to the government of the day.

The government therefore, had no option but to resign In this case also, an alternative government was available, and it kept a majority until after the war had been won. In Australia dissolution was refused to the defeated Prime Minister Watson in 1904, Reid in 1905 and Fisher in 1909, on the assumption that an alternative government with majority in the House was possible.

Since in India at the state level we have followed the practice of Commonwealth countries, whereby the Head of the State can refuse dissolution, the possibility of adopting this practice at the Centre cannot be completely ruled out in future Hence, it can be said that in this respect the advice of the Prime Minister is not binding. Agreeing with this view Dr. Eugene A. Forsey a noted Canadian authority on matters constitutional, examined the subject closely in his comprehensive work *The Royal Power of Dissolution of Parliament in the British Commonwealth*. He wrote, "the enormous increase in the power of the Cabinet and especially of the Prime Minister, raises the question whether the reserve power of the

Crown to force or refuse dissolution may not be one of the few safeguards against dictatorship by the leader of the junta wielding for the moment the power of office.' If, for example, a Cabinet with a majority in both Houses tried to use that majority to prolong the life of Parliament indefinitely, a forced dissolution would be the only constitutional means of preserving the rights of the people." Even the 42nd Amendment act has not changed this position because after the passage of the 42nd Amendment Act, if it is accepted that the President is bound to accept the advice in this respect, then it would mean that the Prime Minister would have the right of recommending repeated dissolution.

Constitutionally speaking this position cannot be accepted. It may be mentioned in this connection that in England, "until the First World War no one doubted that the decision to advise the Crown to dissolve Parliament was a collective decision of the Cabinet. For reasons which are not wholly clear, the practice since 1918 has been for the decision to rest with the Prime Minister alone taking such advice (or none) as he sees fit."

Prime Minister and the Standing Committees

If Parliament is to exercise an effective control over the executive, then the existence of standing committees attached to various Ministries is absolutely essential, because without them an effective and continuous control on the administration of the various Ministries is very difficult.

In fact between 1921-1930, there was a joint standing committee consisting of eleven members from each of the two Houses of British Parliament on Indian Affairs. Even between 1947-52, there were some standing committees which were attached to some of the Ministries but they were abolished in 1951 because Nehru, the then Prime Minister, thought that they might prove inconvenient to administration.

It was therefore argued by the Prime Minister that so long as there was no clear opposition in the House. Standing Committees could manage to remain in existence after the first General Elections, the situation changed The Lok Sabha now contained opposition groups, and the Government decided firmly that the committees should be abolished. The opposition and independents criticised this move as a retrograde and undemocratic step but the Prime Minister was not prepared to change his decision in this respect. He explained that these Committees had been formed in quite different conditions and that they would have no meaning in the changed circumstances.

They, according to Nehru, belonged to a different system of institutions from those in existence in India. The abolition of the standing Advisory Committees has been a relief to the Prime Minister and other Ministers and a disappointment to the opposition Immediately after the election of 1967, the demand for these standing Committees was again made by the opposition.

The Prime Minister, Mrs. Gandhi while rejecting the demand said that informal consultative committees suit the Indian conditions better than the standing committees attached to the various ministries. In her letter to N. G. Ranga on April 6, 1968, the Prime Minister said that American or British practice were not of much help She also said that 'so long as our particular system continues we do sincerely feel that setting up of Standing Committees would be a retrograde step." She supported this contention by recalling that both the former Speaker Mavalankar and the Chairman of Rajya Sabha.

Radhakrishnan, had not favoured the institution of the standing committees. She therefore preferred the informal consultative committees instead of standing committees of the Ministries. The opposition while rejecting this plea said that "it is a matter of regret that you advance the untenable plea that setting up of Standing Committees would net be in the best interest of our system of Government We fad to appreciate your remark that the practice in the United Kingdom is not of much help.

Since the plea of the opposition was not accepted, therefore, the leaders of the Swatantra, Jan Sangh, PSP, CPI and CPI (M) decided to continue the boycott of the informal consultative Committees. The boycott was started in 1967 when the 4th Lok Sabha came into existence. However, after the Congress split in 1969, the parties which supported Mrs. Gandhi joined the informal consultative committees.

Parliament and Vote of no Confidence

Since the Prime Minister remains in office so long as he enjoys the confidence of the Lok Sabha, therefore, whenever, a vote of no confidence is passed against him, he should resign. According to B. R. Ambedkar, holding office during the pleasure of the President means that "the pleasure shall not continue notwithstanding the fact that the Ministry has lost the confidence of the majority The moment the Ministry has lost the confidence of the majority, it is presumed that the President will exercise his 'pleasure' in dismissing the Ministry" The Prime Minister will loose the confidence of the House if:.

- Formal Vote of no confidence is passed against him/her or a formal vote of confidence is rejected.
- Money Bill or a Bill dealing with major policy is rejected.

So far as the formal vote of no confidence against the Prime Minister in India is concerned, it has been a mere formality before 1969 and after 1971. Before 1962 a formal vote of no confidence was moved twice against Nehru and also twice against Shastri. Against Nehru, it was only in 1962 that for the first time such a vote of no confidence was moved but the motion fell through because it secured only seven votes. The no-confidence motion was again moved against Nehru by Kripalani on August 13, 1963 after few months of Chinese attack on India. This time though it was admitted yet after discussion it was rejected by 61 votes in favour and 346 against it.

Two motions of censure against Shastri government probed serious weaknesses in government but they too were rejected after discussion. Between 1967 and 1970 as many as five no confidence motions were moved and admitted against the government which were rejected after discussion. Only two motions of no confidence were admitted for censuring the government by the opposition parties during the tenure of the Fifth Lok Sabha One was rejected on November 22, 1973 and the other was rejected on July 25, 1974. The Congress had a steam-rolling two thirds majority in the House Therefore, these motions failed to make any impact on the fate of the government.

The Prime Minister also will have to resign if his government is defeated on a major policy issue But it is for the government to decide what is a major policy issue. If the government is defeated in a snap vote then the Prime Minister may not resign. 'For example, the Government of India was defeated in a snap vote in 1967 on a Bill to provide for the establishment of the institution of Lok Pal for investigating administrative irregularities and public grievances.

Ordinarily when the government is defeated on a Money Bill in a snap vote or otherwise, it should resign For example. Bhola Paswan Ministry in Bihar at the state level resigned when it was defeated on grants for animal husbandry. Similarly Gurnam Singh in Punjab had to resign when the House refused him permission to introduce the budget.

It should, however, be remembered in this respect that if a Constitution amendment Bill is rejected it will not be considered a defeat of the Government on a major policy. For example in 1970, the Constitution amendment Bill was rejected After the rejection of this Bill, the Prime Minister wrote letters to the Congress MPs who were absent expressing her displeasure. She expressed the hope that, in future, it would not reoccur. The Bill was reintroduced in the same session by waiving the rules and was got passed. Subsequently, for the second time, the Constitution amendment Bill abolishing the privy purses was also rejected by the Rajya Sabha in September 1970.

Another issue on which the question of the confidence of the Lok Sabha may arise is the election of the Speaker. The Prime Minister knows that the office of the Speaker is very important, and therefore, it is he who decides as to who should be the candidate for the office of the Speaker Since in Parliament up to Feb. 1977 the Congress Party has always been having a majority, the candidate put up by the Prime Minister has always won the election. But what will happen if the candidate proposed by the Prime Minister for the office of the Speaker is defeated in the election? This may happen when some of the MPs of his party refuse to vote for the Prime Minister's candidate or when the Prime Minister belongs to a party which does not have a majority.

In that case, the Prime Minister is not bound to resign. For example, at state level in Haryana when Bhagwat Dayal's candidate for the office of the Speakership was defeated, he did not resign immediately. This happened in Bihar also. For instance, immediately after midterm poll in 1969, the nominee of the Chief Minister for the office of the Speaker was defeated by 172 to 155 votes but Harihar Singh, the then Chief Minister, did not resign.

Prime Minister and the Speaker

The Prime Minister knows that the constitutional framework within which the Lok Sabha operates owes much to the Speaker's influence and advice. The maintenance of order and decorum in the House and the smooth conduct of business the decisions on the admissibility of questions and motions; the establishment of the scope and timings of different kinds of debate and their regulation depends upon the way, the Speaker conducts himself.

His Chairmanship of the Business Advisory Committee is central to the planning of the work and timetable schedule of the House and to the fostering of reasonably harmonious relations between the government and the opposition groups. The emerging policy of the House on matters relating to privilege is largely of the Speaker's making. In such matters, the Speaker needs the cooperation of the Prime Minister as Leader of the House.

The position of the Speaker in relation to party-politics is significant. President Vithalbhai Patel held office from 1925 to 1930 and did more than any of his successors before 1946 to assert and consolidate the independence of the chair Successive Presidents during 1930's and 1940's maintained the gains which Patel had made, but the period of consolidation gave way to new period of development with the election of Mr. Mavalankar who won by 66 to 63 votes against the wishes of government after 1947, every Speaker without exception was a Congress politician of some prominence. The position in this respect has, however, changed after the elections in March 1977.

Though it is conceded that the Speaker in India should stand apart from party strife, it is maintained that he should not keep himself entirely aloof from politics as the British Speaker does

Jawaharlal Nehru as the First Prime Minister was eager to allow the Lok Sabha to "develop any form of independence from the Executive." He always showed respect to the Chair in the observance of Parliamentary formalities.

This was mentioned by the speaker on August 27, 1956, when he said that often the members, excepting the Prime Minister did not show due respect to the Chair Nehru advised the members to bow to the chair when they came to occupy their seats. In sharp contrast Prime Minister Mrs. Indira Gandhi left the house when a privilege motion against her was being discussed in the Lok Sabha on March 31, 1966 and the Speaker was still on his feet.

The speaker, on protest from the opposition, said that the Prime Minister should not have left the House Mrs. Gandhi apologised. On November 17, 1969 when Piloo Mody asked a supplementary question and Mrs. Gandhi advises the Minister not to answer, as the question was frivolous several members protested that it was a dangerous precedent if a Minister refused to answer a question after it had been admitted by the Speaker On the Speaker's intervention, the Minister gave the answer.

The impartiality of the Speaker has not caused any conflict with the Prime Minster. In his capacity as leader of the house, the Prime Minister usually keeps the Lok Sabha informed about the government's intention Reference to a Committee of Privileges is generally made with the concurrence of the Prime Minister by the Speaker In 1971, when a question of privilege was raised by an opposition member for alleged indignities practised on him by police officials, indignation was so strong in the house that it wanted to refer the matter to the Committee of Privileges.

But the Speaker wanted first to ascertain certain factual aspects of the matter through the Minister for Home Affairs—an office held by the Prime Minister herself at the time. The Prime Minister was not in attendance, and the entire opposition waked out of the House. But the Speaker refused to be intimidated by this act of opposition, though he very much regretted the absence of the Prime Minister in the House.

Whereas Nehru made all policy statements in Parliament, Mrs. Gandhi has developed the Practice of doing so outside the

House, even when it is in session. Such a tendency to by-pass Parliament has been resented by the members and sometime, the Speaker has also seconded it When Mrs. Gandhi reshuffled her Cabinet in August 1970 and the members asked her to give reasons for it, she refused to oblige. It is well-known that Mrs. Gandhi does not spend even half the time that Jawaharlal spent in the Parliament when it was in session. She "prefers to find time for large number of interview-seekers rather than for Parliament". The Chair has felt constrained to convey the feelings of the House to the Prime Minister Nehru always looked eagerly to satisfy the Parliamentary aspirations of the opposition, who felt a sense of delight and vigour in attacking the governments and of those Congress members, who desired the Prime Minister to hear their best speeches in defence of the government.

Prime Minister and Nomination of Members to Rajya Sabha

As many as 12 members of the Rajya Sabha are to be nominated by the President. It may, however, be asked whether the advice of the Prime Minister in such a matter is binding on the President or not At the state level, a similar power has been given to the Governor, and when certain nominations were made in West Bengal in the name of the Governor by the then Chief Minister, it was contended that they were illegal because they were not made by the Governor.

The Governor himself accepted that he did not know that he has the power of nominating certain persons to the Legislative Council. The Kolkata High Court held that the Governor is to act on the advice of the Chief Minister in this respect. By implication, it means that at the Centre the. President has to accept the advice of the Prime Minister in so far as the nominations to Rajya Sabha are concerned.

Termination of Membership

Prime Minister, in his capacity as the leader of the majority party, has another important power so far as the compositive proceeding for the expulsion of an MP whose conduct is derogatory to the membership of Parliament. For example on September 24, 1951, the Prime Minister moved a resolution to expel H. G. Mudgil from the House and on his recommendation his membership was terminated. On November 16, 1976, Subramaniam Swami, a Jan Sangh member of Rajya Sabha was also expelled because his conduct was also thought to be derogatory of its membership..

It is important to note in this connection that at the state level, the House has no such power to expel its member according to the decision of Punjab and Haryana High Court. If we critically examine this case then, it is difficult to understand why Parliament has the power to expel its member but not the State Assembly.

Prime Minister and the Opposition

For a smooth functioning of a Parliamentary democracy, it is essential that the Prime Minister should not ignore the opposition to the extent that it feels frustrated If that happens, then it may result in confrontation between the opposition and the party in power, since Jawaharlal Nehru was very well aware of this, he had a regard for its views.

For example, when he came to know that the opposition was not happy about the proposed introduction of a Bill to amend the Constitution in regard to the seizure of the property of the persons detained under Defence of India rules, he dropped it Similarly, the Eighteenth Constitutional Amendment Bill was also dropped on similar grounds. "The Bill for the amendment of the Civil Procedure Code was also similarly withdrawn. Preventive Detention Bill, 1952 was sent to a Selected Committee by Nehru against the previous declaration of his Home Minister. On August 28, 1959, the opposition brought a pressure on the government to issue a white-paper detailing the development on India's Northern borders with China and the Prime Minister accepted the suggestion.

This shows that so far as Nehru was concerned he tried to accommodate the opposition as far as possible. He knew that the people who were on his side did not represent the entire public opinion. Shastri also followed this policy. Even Mrs. Gandhi, till 1974, adopted this policy. "An acrimonious debate on an adjournment motion regarding the brutal assault on SSP member of Parliament was hold on 6 April. 1970, though the rules did not permit a discussion on the motion on the same day, the Prime Minister sensing the mood of the House, made a handsome gesture by intervening to agree to a discussion on the motion. Though the motion was defeated by 152 to 113 votes, the Prime Minister announced the appointment of a judicial enquiry by a High Court Judge. Between 1969-70, Mrs. Gandhi, was in minority in the Lok Sabha because of the Congress split and she had no alternative but to accommodate the opposition parties which supported her.

During this period the Preventive Detention Act was allowed to lapse. Even after the 1971 election, the Prime Minister tried to accommodate the opposition. For example, in the Licence Scandal case in 1974, she went to the extent of throwing even the confidential files to the opposition, but this was not done gracefully. All this, however, did not mean that the Prime Minister has accepted each and every suggestion made by the opposition in Parliament For example, whenever the opposition demanded the appointment of an enquiry commission against some of the Central Ministers and State Chief Ministers, the demand was rejected in all cases except that of Karon.

This was the policy of Nehru and it was followed by Mrs. Gandhi. When demands were made to appoint commissions of enquiry against L.N. Mishra, Maruti of Sanjay Gandhi and Bansi Lal, the demands were rejected.

When the opposition demanded her resignation, she instead of accepting the demand of the opposition declared internal Emergency on June 25, 1975 and put all the important leaders of the opposition behind bars. When these leaders were in jail the 38th, 39th and 42nd Amendment Acts which changed the basic structure of the Constitution were passed. All the major opposition parties namely, Congress (O), Jan Sangh, BLD, Socialist and CPI (M) boycotted the special session of the Parliament in which the Constitution was defaced and defiled.

So far as the government of Morarji Desai was concerned, it changed its policy towards the opposition Appreciating the need for showing due consideration and giving it a sense of participation in the national affairs, he told a group of foreign journalists. "I have always respected the Opposition even when I was in the

Treasury benches. But after sitting in the Opposition. I am now more convinced than ever that not only should the Government respect the opposition but should behave in a manner that the Opposition must be have.

The example has to be set by the Government Otherwise the Opposition is bound to become irresponsible. It is for the ruling party to make the opposition responsible." "When Mr. Bhupesh Gupta asked me whether the Government would consult the Opposition. I said I would do that. Am I not doing it now? Now there is no time for formality calling the opposition. But from the next session we propose to have regular meetings with the opposition".

The Janata Government gave the status of a Minister to Y. B. Chauhan who was the Leader of the Opposition in the sixth Lok Sabha When the Prime Minister addressed the nation over All India Radio, the same facility was extended to the Leader of the Opposition, and he also addressed the nation from All India Radio the next day. There has been enough bitterness and controversy in this nation over the last few years. Let us now move towards a broad national reconciliation so that this country which we so dearly cherish can prosper in all spheres of life."

Prime Minister as Mediator between Lok Sabha and Rajya Sabha

When the members of the Lok Sabha came to know about it, there was a heated debate about the remarks of Mr. Biswas. At that time. Nehru, the then Prime Minister, intervened and appealed to the members not to be exercised over the issue. On his appeal the matter ended. Similarly, there were differences between the Lok Sabha and Rajya Sabha about the composition of the Estimates and Public Accounts Committee.

The Rajya Sabha expressed the opinion that its members should be associated with these committees but the Lok Sabha was not prepared to accept this proposal The Prime Minister again intervened and moved a resolution that the Rajya Sabha may be requested "to nominate seven members to associate with the Public Accounts Committee." When the Prime Minister moved this resolution, the Lok Sabha accepted it.

Whenever similar difficulties were experienced by Rajya Sabha, the Prime Minister came to its rescue. In December 1953, when the proposal for a joint Committee came from the Rajya Sabha, the Lok Sabha again became indignant But the Prime Minister intervened, and once more appealed to the members to be reasonable Somewhat suddenly, the Lok Sabha agreed to the proposal of the Prime Minister for the Bill to be considered in the Rajya Sabha where it had originated.

It was again in December 1954 on the intervention of the Prime Minister that the two Houses agreed that the two Privilege Committees, sitting together, would work out an acceptable procedure for cases where a member of one House commits a breach of the Privileges of the other The support was given by the Prime Minister to the Rajya Sabha which strengthened its position in dealing with the Lok Sabha which in its anxiety to maintain the *status quo,* always remained anxious to have the Prime Minister on its side in matters involving the two Houses.

Parliamentary Proceedings and the Prime Minister

Parliament shows his interest in Parliamentary proceedings. It is by attending these sittings, particularly the question hours that the Prime Minister can judge the performance of his colleagues in meeting the challenge of the opposition.

So far as Nehru was concerned, he was mostly present during the question hour and he used to ask his colleagues not to give evasive replies to the questions asked by the opposition. If his colleagues could not satisfy the House, then, he himself used to intervene. It is said that so far as Nehru was concerned "he loved Parliament and its zero hour He had a sense of involvement in running institutions of which he was one of the builders and in the involvement was attached a sense of dedication to the cause of making democracy work".

After Nehru's death, the position changed because Lal Bahadur Shastri neither had the same control over the Congress Parliamentary Party which Nehru had, nor his stature Therefore, the Prime Minister was mostly absent when important debates took place. The position did not improve when Mr. Gandhi became the Prime Minister in 1966. The Cabinet did not function as a team and the Prime Minister was mostly absent from the House and therefore, whenever, a Minister was in a tight comer, there was none to help him. Senior Ministers mostly kept quiet if they were not directly concerned. Even after the election of 1967, the position of the Prime Minister did not improve In 1968, the opposition did not allow the Prime Minister even to reply to the no-confidence motion After the Congress split in 1969, the Prime Minister's position in Parliament further weakened On one occasion in 1969 when Piloo Mody asked a supplementary question, she advised the Minister not to answer it.

In this connection, according to Wilson in England "no Prime Minister looks forward to Parliamentary questions with anything but apprehension; every Prime Minister works long into the night on his answers, and on all the notes available to help him anticipate the instant and unpredictable supplementary questions that follow his prepared answer. It has been said that Harold Macmillan, a highly successful performer at question time, used on occasion to be physically sick, or very near to it before questions on Tuesdays.

The position of the Prime Minister in India in this respect is not much different from that of the Prime Minister in England. Though in the elections of 1971. Mrs. Indira Gandhi obtained more than 2/3rd majority in the Lok Sabha yet it was not very smooth sailling for her because when various scandals involving Bansi Lal, Maruti, Nagarwala and Licence case were raised in Parliament the Prime Minister was in a very tight comer.

Instead of giving a satisfactory reply to the various charges levelled, she used her brute majority in the Lok Sabha to silence the opposition. In fact, by 1977, her position in the Congress party was more or less the same as that of Hitler in the Nazi Party. When the Rajya Sabha met in March 1977 to approve the Presidential Proclamation extending the President's rule in Tamil Nadu, at that time something very unusual happened. After attending the sitting when Mrs. Indira Gandhi rose to leave the House, several Congress members stood up.

Though in theory, it can be said that it is Parliament that controls the Prime Minister, yet in practice, it has been the other way round except between 1969-70. Between 1952-1969 and again between 1971-77, the Prime Minister dominated Parliament because of the clear majority of the Congress Party.

Selection of Ministers

According to article 75(1) of the Constitution, the Ministers are appointed by the President on the advice of Prime Minister. In this respect. I may, however, be asked as to how far the Prime Minister has a free hand in the selection of his colleagues This will, to a great extent, depend upon:

- The position of the political parties in the House of people, and
- The standing of the Prime Minister in his party.

If after the elections, none of the parties has a clear majority in the Lok Sabha and there is to be a coalition Ministry in office, the choice of the Prime Minister would be severely limited, because in that case, it will not be the Prime Minister, but the respective coalition parties, who win select their nominees to be appointed as Ministers. At the state level, there are many examples of this type when the coalition partners were allotted seats in the Council of Ministers and then those parties selected their nominees.

At the centre, more or less such a situation existed in 1946 when the Interim Government was appointed. In that government, the Congress and the Muslim League were the coalition partners and each of these parties selected its own nominees to be appointed as ministers But after 1947, we never had such a situation at the centre. Even the Janata Party which consisted of BLD.

Congress (O). Jan Sangh and Socialist Party did not function as a coalition government so far as the selection of Ministers was concerned because it was the Prime Minister and not the leaders of these parties who selected the ministers.

On the other hand, when elections of the Lok Sabha are held and if after the elections, one of the political parties has a clear majority in the House of the People, the situation would be different.

In that case, whether the Prime Minister would have complete independence in the selection of his colleagues or not, would depend upon his standing vis-a-vis the standing of other group leaders in the party. If the party has another leader who has the potentiality of challenging his leadership, to that extent, his choice would be limited and he would have to include in the Cabinet not only the potential challenger but also some other persons whom he recommends.

For example, between 1947-50 Sardar Patel had this potential capacity and therefore. Nehru not only had to appoint him as the Deputy Prime Minister but also many other Ministers were appointed on his recommendation Even Maulana Azad and Rajendra Prasad were there in the Cabinet not because of the mercy of the Prime Minister but on their own strength. The Prime Minister did not have that control over the Congress Parliamentary Party to ignore their claim.

However, after the death of Sardar Patel in December 1950, the position changed and the balance was tilted in favour of the Prime Minister. In fact in 1952, 1957 and 1962, the Prime Minister Nehru had almost completely a free hand in the selection of his colleagues.

So much so that V. K. Krishna Menon was appointed Minister much against the wishes of a sizeable section of the Congress Parliamentary Party. Though while selecting his colleagues. Nehru might have consulted some of his colleagues like Maulana Azad, Govind Ballabh Pant. V.K. Krishna Menon and Lal Bahadur Shastri, on his own, there was no political compulsion for him to do so.

After the death of Nehru in 1964, when Lal Bahadur Shastri became the Prime Minister, he certainly did not have that freedom which Nehru had between 1952-1962. This was so because after Nehru's death, there was a tussle for power between Morarji Desai (who resigned in 1963 under the Kamaraj Plan) and the Syndicate.

The contest was avoided by evolving the principle of consensus in which not only the important members of Parliament but also the organisational leaders and the Chief Ministers played an important part in order to keep Morarji Desai out Hence. Shastri, who was obliged to some of the important leaders, could not have as much of a free hand as Nehru had after 1952. Though Shastri claimed that while selecting his colleagues, he did not consult anyone and Michael Brecher agrees with this, yet there are others who do not subscribe to this view because this statement is not supported by the Press reports of those days. According to these Press reports, he consulted Kamaraj, Atulya Ghosh, Sanjiva Reddy, Chauhan, S.K. Patil, Swaran Singh, Chagla and other important leaders of the Congress Party.

The very fact that Shastri retained "all thirteen senior Ministers and fifteen Ministers of state and all but two of the Deputy Ministers" Shows that he had a limited free choice in this matter at that time. He added only three new faces; that is, S.K. Patil, Sanjiva Reddy and Mrs. Indira Gandhi. This appears to be so because at that time it was difficult for Shastri to ignore the above-mentioned leaders completely, and Shastri could not have excluded some of these leaders from the Council of Ministers.

But in the interim period. Nanda had succeeded to that rank and had even served as Prime Minister and it would have been embarrassing to downgrade him. Shastri offered him the No. 3 rank. But the proud Morarji declared that it was not consistent with his self-respect and dignity. After sometime, without consulting Kamaraj and some other senior ministers like Nanda and T.T. Krishnamachari, he chose Swaran Singh as his foreign Minister.

On Shastri's death when Mrs. Indira Gandhi became the Prime Minister, her position in this respect was not much different from that of Shastri in 1964. This was so because this time there was a straight contest between Morarji Desai and Mrs. Indira Gandhi in which she defeated Morarji Desai by 355 to 169 votes, but in the process, she was helped by many other senior persons of the party because this time "the struggle for the Succession assumed the character of Morarji Versus Pack."

Hence, while selecting her team, she too did not have a completely free hand and she prepared the list of Ministers after ceaseless rounds of consultation. It is said that Sachindra Chaudhary and Fakhruddin Ali Ahmed were taken in the Council of Ministers in place of Ashok Sen and Humayun Kabir on the recommendation of Atulya Ghosh, and Nanda and Jagjivan Ram were appointed Ministers on the recommendation of Kamaraj. The advice of some of these leaders could not be ignored because without their support, she did not have a majority in the Party.

After the elections of 1967, the position of the Prime Minister in the party became still weaker because the Congress Party had a very narrow majority in the Lok Sabha and Morarji Desai again challenged her leadership. In order to maintain unity in the party, it was considered desirable to avoid a contest and hence the party managers offered Deputy Prime Ministership to Morarji Desai, which he accepted.

When Chauhan and Jagjivan Ram came to know about it they rushed to Mrs. Gandhi's house at Safdarjung Road and asked her that it should be made clear to Desai and Kamaraj that the future Deputy Prime Minister would have no edge over other Cabinet Ministers except that he would have second ranking. He would not and could not be Sardar Patel. They also asked her about the duties of the Deputy Prime Minister Some of the MPs went to Kamaraj's house to emphasise that Morarji should be Deputy Prime Minister by rank but not in terms of power.

Desai did not like all this. He also went to Mrs. Gandhi at that time when Chauhan and Jagjivan Ram were there. Mrs. Gandhi, while making her position clear, said that the Deputy Prime Ministership was an office which was given to Desai because he insisted on having this title. Otherwise all ministers are equal.

After the death of Patel in 1950, the office of the Deputy Prime Minister was abolished by Nehru and he did not agree to appoint a Deputy Prime Minister even when he had fallen ill. It was only in 1967 that the office of the Deputy Prime Minister was revived Hence, the appointment of Morarji Desai as Deputy Prime Minister was not at the pleasure of the Prime Minister.

In 1966, Mrs. Gandhi did not even invite him to join her Cabinet. It should also be noted in this connection that "there is in the British Constitution no such animal as a Deputy Prime Minister. Even where a Prime Minister has formally designated a colleague as deputy Prime Minister, this has not created any presumption that a person nominated should be sent for on the deceases or resignation of the Prime Minister Had Winston Churchill ceased to be the Prime Minister in wartime, his successor would undoubtedly have been chosen from the ranks of the Conservatives, who were by far the largest party in Parliament, Clement Attlee was deputy Prime Minister, as leader of the second most substantial partner in the Coalition.

In the recent past, it appeared again when: "Herbert Morrison was officially designated by Clement Attlee, as deputy Prime Minister. But when Winston Churchill sought to have Anthony Eden recognised as deputy Prime Minister. George VI refused to agree, as he feared it might create a presumption about the succession (Winston Churchill was nearly 77). In 1962, Harold Macmillan refused to designate an official deputy, as he considered that there was no such recognised office under the Constitution, though later in the year, he announced that R A. Butter would act as deputy Prime Minister. This announcement was not followed by any recognition in the officially promulgated list of Ministers."

This position of the Prime Minister, however, changed after the elections of 1971. In these elections, the entire old guard of the Congress Party was against her in the form of Congress (O) but still, the Congress (R) under the leadership of Indira Gandhi got more than 2/3rd majority in the Lok Sabha, which on the one hand enhanced her prestige and power, and on the other hand seriously affected the position of Chauhan and Jagjivan Ram in the party. Since then, she had been the master of the show and then there came an occasion when there was none in the party who could dare challenge her leadership. Her position in the party since 1971 had almost been the same as was that of Nehru between 1952-1962.

This is the position of the Prime Minister when one of the political parties has a clear majority in the Lok Sabha. If none of the parties has a clear majority in the Lok Sabha and if a coalition ministry is to be formed, then in that case, there may be no role of the Prime Minister in the selection of his colleagues In a coalition government, usually the seats in the Council of Ministers are divided in advance among the coalition partners by agreement and the nominees of the parties are to be selected by the concerned parties themselves and the Prime Minister may have no hand in their selection. It is significant to note that after the elections of the Lok Sabha in March 1977, when the Janata Party came into power. Morarji Desai was unanimously elected its leader and was appointed as the Prime Minister. But he did not have a free hand in the selection of his team.

In fact the representatives of various constituent units selected their candidates to be taken into the Cabinet For example. Jagjivan Ram and Bahauguna were the representatives of CFD, Badal represented Akali Dal. When the question of expanding the council of Ministers was considered, it was decided that "Four names were to be submitted by every constituent members of the Janata-Congress (O). Jan Sangh Bhartiya Lok Dal. Socialists and Congress for Democracy.

There are many examples of such coalition Ministries at the state level, which came into existence between 1967-1971. In these Ministries the supremacy of the Chief Minister was challenged. In West Bengal, Jyoti Basu wrote to Ajoy Mukherjee, the then Chief Minister, that "while the Constitution does say that the ministers will be appointed by the Governor on the advice of the Chief Minister, it does not lead to the conclusion that in any and every political situation the Chief Minister has a position of supremacy in the affairs of the Government.

The literal construction of constitutional provisions will not yield their true meaning. Constitutional provisions must always be understood in relation to the particular political scene where they are applied." Though Ajoy Mukherjee was not prepared to accept this position, yet it seems that in practice, the stand taken by Basu was somewhere nearer the truth.

This shows that the role of the Prime Minister in the selection of his colleagues had depended and would always depend upon the prevailing political situation at a particular time, especially with regard to his grip over his party machine in a single party Government, or his hold and his power of appeal among the masses and classes in a Coalition Ministry For example, in 1966, when Mr. Indira Gandhi was elected party leader by defeating

Morarji Desai, she did not ask him to join her Council of Ministers. But in 1967, he was offered a Deputy Prime Ministership. However, the same Morarji Desai was deprived of his portfolio of finance in 1969 when there were differences between him and the Prime Minister on the Presidential candidate.

Allocation of Portfolios by Prime Minister

Besides selecting his team, the Prime Minister allocates portfolio among them. However, even in this respect, whether the Prime Minister will have a completely free hand or not, depends upon the following two factors.

The standing of the Prime Minister in the Party. The nature of the Council of Ministers, if one of the parties has a clear majority and has a clearly recognised leader who has an unchallengeable position in the party, he may have relatively a greater freedom in the allocation of portfolios among his colleagues. In the party if there is another leader of equally strong standing who can challenge him, in that case, the freedom of the Prime Minister to that extent will be limited.

For example, between 1947-50. Sardar Patel had this position in the Congress Party and hence, he chose his own portfolio. Patel was keen to get the portfolio of Home and he got it Similarly, in 1967, when Morarji Desai was offered Deputy Prime Ministership, he wanted to get the portfolio of Home Though Mrs. Indira Gandhi did not agree for this yet he was given the option of choosing any other portfolio except Home, and he selected the portfolio of Finance.

This shows the difference in the dimension of the positions occupied by Patel and Desai in the party. It also shows that Paters position as a Deputy Prime Minister vis-a-vis Nehru, the then Prime Minister, was stronger as compared to Desai's position visa vis Mrs. Gandhi. However, Desai's position was not so weak as for him to be completely ignored, because the slightest limitation placed on him in this regard was that except Home he could select any other portfolio. But when there was a rift between Desai and Mrs. Gandhi over the selection of the Presidential candidate in 1969, she deprived him of that portfolio and as a result. Morarji

Desai resigned because he felt humiliated and downgraded— a position which he was not prepared to accept.

It there is a coalition ministry in office, the choice of the Prime Minister in allocating the portfolios among his colleagues will be still more limited because, in that case, it would be decided by agreement among the coalition partners. It will be appropriate to mention in this context that in the Janata Party Government. Charan Singh, who was No. 2 in the Government, selected his own portfolio, that is Home, because of his standing in the Janata Party. The Prime Minister not only allocates portfolios, but he can also reallocate them at any time In this respect too, sometime he may be successful and he may not have his say at another time. For example, in 1963. Nehru wanted to change the portfolio of S.K. Patil. He wanted him to shift from Food to Railways, which he successfully resisted.

Similarly in 1966. Mrs. Indira Gandhi, wanted to take Home from Nanda but he did not budge an inch. She also wanted to change the portfolio of Sachindra Chaudhary (Finance) and Manubhai Shah (Commerce) but she could not do so because of pressure from Atulya Ghosh and Hitendra Desai respectively. In February 1969, Mrs., Indira Gandhi wanted to reorganise her Cabinet but she could not.

But after the split of the Congress Party, she was in complete command of the party, and in 1970, she changed the portfolios of Chauhan. Dinesh Singh and Fakhruddin Ali Ahmed and when Y. B. Chauhan expressed his unwillingness, the Prime Minister is reported to have told Chauhan that "If he refused to move as directed, he might have to quit." This explains the fact that the Prime Minister's position in the party will determine whether she or he will have a free hand in this respect or not. When she acquired complete control over the party after the elections of 1971, she made more frequent changes in the portfolios of ministers and very few could think of resisting it or hardly any could resist it.

While allocating a portfolio, it is not necessary that a minister who is an expert in a particular field should a Sways get that portfolio. Sometimes 'Ministers and departments are treated like so many pieces of cloth in the absent minded tailor's shop, they are cut and recut, sewn together and torn asunder and often stitched into garments without any regard to whatever the texture, colour-scheme or even measurement". Sometimes, it may also happen that a Minister may get the portfolio in which he is an expert. For example, Professor Nurul Hasan—an educationist, got the portfolio of Education in 1971.

Similarly in Desai's Council of Ministers formed in March 1977, Pratap Chandra got Education. Law was given to Shanti Bhushan, a top-ranking Jurist, and H M Patel an expert in financial matters got Finance. In this respect, it may be mentioned that "Ministers should not become unduly attached to a subject or a portfolio, any more than officials should."

It is also important to mention here that even in the matter of ranking in the Cabinet, sometimes, there may be a problem. For example in 1964, after the death of Nehru, when Shastri had taken over as Prime Minister and asked Morarji Desai to join the Cabinet at place number 3 but Desai wanted to be placed as number 2, and when Shastri could not accept this, he refused to join the Cabinet. However, subsequently, in 1967 Jagjivan Ram, who was placed at number 3 in 1966 was placed as number 7, and Fakhruddin Ali Ahmed, who was placed at number 16 in 1966 was placed as number 3 in 1967.

Size of the Ministry

Closely related to the question of the appointment of Ministers, is the question of the size of the Ministry. In England, it may be mentioned that there is a limit of 91 in this respect. However, in India, there is no such limit, though sometimes, it has been suggested that the maximum number of Ministers should not be more than 10 per cent of the total strength of the members of the legislature, if it is bicameral and not more than 11 per cent when it is unicameral.

This matter was also discussed by the Committee on defections but the defection bill, which was introduced on May 16, 1973, had no such provision and the size of the Central Council of Ministers has been constantly fluctuating. For example in 1975, the number of Ministers was 39, in 1962 it was 49, in 1964 it was 51, in 1965, it was 51. It was again 51 in 1966 and in 1971 it was only 36. In May 1975, the strength of the Council of Ministers was 51.

The three-tier council of Minister mentioned above included, besides the Prime Minister, the Minister of Cabinet rank. Minister of State and Deputy Ministers.

Though all the Ministers of the Cabinet rank. Ministers of the State and Deputy Ministers are the members of the Council of Ministers, and all of them are to be sworn in by the President, yet there is some difference among them. The Ministers of Cabinet rank constitute the decision-making or policy-making body of the

Year	*Name of Prime Minister*	*Number of Cabinet Minister*	*Number of Minister of State*	*Number of Deputy Minister*	*Total*
1957	Jawaharlal Nehru	13	14	12	39
1962	Jawaharlal Nehru	16	12	21	49
1964	Lal Bahadur Shastri	15	16	20	51
1966	Mrs. Indira Gandhi	16	18	17	51
1967	Mrs. Indira Gandhi	18	17	15	51
1971	Mrs. Indira Gandhi	13	5	18	36
May, 1971	Mrs. Indira Gandhi	14	20	20	54
July, 1972	Mrs. Indira Gandhi	14	20	20	54
Feb., 1973	Mrs. Indira Gandhi	17	22	27	66
Nov., 1973	Mrs. Indira Gandhi	17	18	23	58
Oct., 1974	Mrs. Indira Gandhi	16	22	22	60
30 Nov., 1975	Mrs. Indira Gandhi	15	22	21	58
20 Oct., 1975	Mrs. Indira Gandhi	15	22	22	59
1976	Mrs. Indira Gandhi	15	22	23	60
1977	Morarji Desai	20	—	—	—

Government

Sometimes, out of the Cabinet even a small committee may also be appointed for this purpose. For example, in 1962 at the time of Chinese aggression. Nehru appointed an Emergency Committee Ministers of state usually hold independent charge of some of the subjects, "which are included within the portfolio of a senior Minister." It is significant to note that ARC had proposed the abolition of the present practice of giving independent portfolios of Ministers of State but the government did not accept this recommendation. The Deputy Ministers are appointed to help the Ministers.

It will not be out of place to mention here, that in 1962 Nehru had appointed 7 Parliamentary Secretaries, besides the Ministers. Parliamentary Secretaries do not come within the definition of a Minister under the Constitution.

The difference between a Parliamentary Secretary and a Minister is that the former is administered oath of secrecy by the Prime Minister, whereas the latter is administered the oath of office by the President The practice of having Parliamentary Secretaries from amongst MPs belonging to the party in office to assist a Minister in dealing with questions and other matters in Parliament, was copied from British practice In that country, a period spent as parliamentary Secretary has been regarded as a training ground and testing period towards possible selection later for full-fledged Ministership.

Though the size of the Council of Ministers has not been fixed and is to be decided by the Prime Minister, yet it should not be unduly large. If it is unduly large, it may be considered as a misuse of the constitutional powers. This type of situation developed in Haryana. For example, while recommending the dismissal of Rao Ministry in 1967. B. N. Chakravarty, the then Governor, wrote to the President.

The Government has also sought to maintain itself precariously in power by creating too many Ministers which is an abuse of its constitutional powers. Such a large number of Ministers and Parliamentary Secretaries numbering at one stage 23 out of ruling party's strength of 41 and 22 now out of total strength of 40 cannot be justified on any ground of administrative requirement The position is even worse, if it is remembered that 10 Jan Sangh members in Samykukta Dal, have not accepted any office as Ministers, so that in reality 22 out of the 30 remaining MLAs are holding office."

Though at the centre so far such a situation has not emerged. Yet if it emerges in future, a possibility which cannot be ruled out, then what would be the attitude of the President, is a matter of speculation. If the President is hostile, he may adopt this attitude and if he is favourable, then he may completely ignore it For example, even in Haryana in 1972, the number of Ministers was 20 and the same person was the Governor (B.N. Chakravarty) who got the Rao Ministry dismissed in 1967. Contrary to this, it is, however, quite interesting and necessary to point out her that in Madhya Pradesh the Governor reported to the President that "due to the acceptance of the resignations of a larger number of Ministers the work of the Government had been suffering." By implication, it means that generally the size of the Council of Ministers should neither be very small nor very large.

Cabinet and the Principle of Collective Responsibility

According to article 75(3) of the Constitution: "The Council of Ministers shall be collectively responsible to the House of the People". Speaking on the Principle of collective responsibility, in the constituent Assembly, B.R. Ambedkar said: 'All the members of the House are very keen that the Cabinet should work on the basis of collective responsibility and all agree that it is a sound Principle. But I do not know how many members of the house realise what exactly is the machinery by which the collective responsibility is enforced'.

Obviously there cannot be a statutory remedy. Supposing a Minister differed from other members of the Cabinet and gave expression to his views which were opposed to the views of the Cabinet, it would be hardly possible for the law to come in and to prosecute him having committed the breach of what might be called collective responsibility.

The only sanction through which collective responsibility is endorsed, is through the Prime Minister Collective responsibility is enforced by the enforcement of two principles. One principle is that no person shall be nominated to the Cabinet except on the advice of the Prime Minister. Secondly, no person shall be retained as a member of the Cabinet if the Prime Minister says that he should be dismissed. It is only when the members of the Cabinet, both in the matter of (her dismissal are placed under the Prime Minister, that it would be possible to realise our ideal of collective responsibility.

But what does the term "collective responsibility" mean? According to V.K Krishna Menon "Whether in England or here, the term collective responsibility covers many sins and also excludes many virtues. Collective responsibility as such does not exist today. It is not even that for the sins of one Minister, the whole Cabinet would resign; if it were so, the resignations of certain members would not have taken place. Collective responsibility regarding decisions on actions which concerned a department (Ministry) do not necessarily come before Cabinet. They would come there if the Prime Minister thought it was necessary, and no doubt, any member could raise it.

But you must appreciate the fact that, while in certain circumstances, through consent of the Prime Minister, one Minister may call for the papers of another Ministry this is not usually done. First of all, each member has his own troubles.

Secondly, he does not want to antagonise his colleagues or create difficulties. So collective responsibility in the sense that a decision once made is everybody's decision is very largely a myth, certainly in the Indian Cabinet Even today, one Cabinet member speaks almost like a Swatantra Party man, another member speaks very much more with emphasis on Gandhi's philosophy, a third one speaks with socialist point of view and so on."

Menon's forthright exposition of the fact that collective responsibility in the sense that a decision once taken is everybody's decision is largely a myth—certainly in the Indian Cabinet—is also supported by Gulzari Lal Nanda who said "It is nothing but the sheerest calumny to attribute to me shortcomings and flaws which are built in some of the policies we have pursued and in the manner in which we have implemented them."

This was exactly the complaint of Gulzari Lal Nanda that the Prime Minister (Mrs. Gandhi) in order to pacify Parliament, was making him the scapegoat for failure of policies which were not his but those of Government as such.

N. V. Gadgil, who was a Minister of the Cabinet rank in Nehru's Council of Ministers from 1947-52, however, did not agree with this view, when he sad A Minister has no individual policy once his opinion or viewpoint is accepted by the Cabinet, it becomes the opinion and viewpoint of all of them. If any one differs, he has either to resign or to accept the majority view.

The convention is that he is not entitled to public protest He has every right to try and get the decision revised, but that too by a resolution in the Cabinet What emerges from discussions in the Cabinet, might not be the original proposal. Hence, its parenthood is joint and not individual." But this principle applies only to those decisions which are taken in the Cabinet meeting. If a particular decision is taken by the Prime Minister without consulting his colleagues, they can oppose it when it is placed before the Cabinet, as it happened in the case of the Nehru Liaquat Pact of 1950.

There are many instances, when the Prime Minister has failed to take the whole Cabinet into confidence. Sometimes the Prime Minister did not take any of his Cabinet Ministers into confidence even while taking some of the most important decisions. For example, this happened when internal emergency was declared on June 25, 1975.

The Prime Minister did not consult any one of her colleagues. The Cabinet was merely informed the next day, i.e. on June 26, 1975. Similarly, when Lok Sabha was dissolved in February, 1977, none of the members of the Cabinet was consulted. Even in England, there are cases where the Prime Minister took decisions without consulting the Cabinet Attlee's decision to make the atom bomb and Anthony Eden's decision to attack the Suez were taken by them without any reference of the Cabinet.

If any Minister feels strongly and is deadly against a decision, he can resign at once. This step was taken by C. D. Deshmukh in 1956 on the reorganisation of Maharashtra. On this burning issue. Nehru did not care to consult the Cabinet, when he announced his decision to keep Bombay a separate state.

Thus, the principle of collective responsibility means that when a decision is taken by the Cabinet and if a particular Minister does not agree with it, he will have only two alternatives, that is, either to reconcile himself with the views of the majority in the Cabinet or quit it. There is a long list of Ministers who resigned on the basis of policy differences.

If there is a coalition Ministry in office then the position in this respect is different For example, "an interim government headed by Nehru was formed on September 2, 1946. It was enlarged into a Congress-League coalition on October 15, 1946. Soon after Patel described the coalition which was functioning without joint responsibility an arena of Party-Politics and intrigue." More or less similar was the situation when there was a coalition Ministry in West Bengal between 1968-69. At that time. Ministers belonging to various parties freely criticised each other, so much so that Ajoy Mukherjee, the then Chief Minister, had to go on fast for few days against the policy of violence followed by CPI (M)—a partner in the government.

The obvious fad is that whenever there are differences of opinion between the Prime Minister and the Minister or the Prime Minister wants to drop somebody from the Council of Ministers then he can ask the latter to resign. This course of action was adopted by Mrs. Gandhi in 1969, when she asked to resign four of her junior ministers in October and, two Cabinet Ministers in November 1969. These ministers submitted their resignations as directed by the Prime Minister.

In Mohan Dharia's case. Mrs. Indira Gandhi, the then Prime Minister, did not have even the courtesy of asking him to resign. She while recommending his dismissal wrote a letter on March 1, 1975 in which she said: "I have been astonished to read newspaper reports of some of your speeches and also your reply to the tetter of the Maharashtra Pradesh Congress Committee. It is obvious that your views on the issue are not in conformity with the thinking of the Congress Party. If you had any doubts, was it not your duty to convey them to me? In these circumstances, it is not proper for you to continue in the Council of Ministers. I am informing the President accordingly. When Mohan Dharia came to know about his virtual dismissal through this letter, he immediately submitted his resignation. It is interesting to note in this case that subsequently the Prime Minister accepted the view that though it might be a mistake to remove Dharia, however, "it was the privilege of the Prime Minister to remove any one from office". "The differences between member became sharper as the time went on. Nehru was not pleased by the action taken in Junagarh by Vallabhbhai. He was equally displeased at the firmness displayed by Vallabhbhai in Hyderabad affair. It was rumoured that Nehru had then given a hint through one of his confidants that he might have to go if he did not behave."

Though there has been no such example at the centre, yet at the State level, there are many instances where the Ministers refused to resign when asked by the Chief Minister. In such circumstances, the Chief Ministers have adopted either of the two courses of action, namely.

- The Chief Minister resigned and reconstituted the Council of Ministers.
- The Chief Minister recommended the dismissal of the recalcitrant Minister.

The Prime Minister can also adopt either of these two courses of action When the Prime Minister recommends the dismissal of a Minister, ordinarily, it is expected that he would be dismissed by the President but if the Prime Minister is heading a coalition Ministry and belongs to a minor party and if the Ministers belonging to the major partner do not resign, they may or may not be dismissed by the President. At the state level, the Governor of U.P. in 1970 in Charan Singh's case, did not dismiss the Ministers on his recommendation Instead of dismissing them, he asked the Chief Minister to resign and when he refused to tender his resignation, the Governor recommended his dismissal to the President under article 356, and he was dismissed.

This action of the Government from the Constitutional point of view was wrong. Agreeing with this view Justice J.L. Kapoor, the former Judge of the Supreme Court, says: "The Prime Minister possesses the right to ask a Minister to resign. The right arises from the necessary pre-eminence of the Prime Minister in his Cabinet. There is a tradition—a kind of public school fiction that no Minister desires office but he is prepared to carry on for the public good—that tradition implies a duty to resign, when a hint is given but in the last resort, the Prime Minister could advise the Queen to dismiss any recalcitrant Minister. Therefore, according to the British practice, the Prime Minister is not only the Sun around whom the planets revolve, he has also the power of designating who the planets should be and then to change the interplanetary position of the various planets or to drop them out of the solar system." It means that no Minister should stay in the Council of Ministers against the advice of the Prime Minister and whatever was done in U.P. in Charan Singh's case was constitutionally wrong Whether the President would also adopt this course of action, if such a situation emerges at the centre, is a matter yet in the realm of speculation, however, its possibility cannot be completely ruled out It should be remembered that in the 19th century in England, the Prime Minister's power to get the Minister dismissed was in some doubt "Gladstone failed in his attempt to drop Lord Carlingford in 1884, when Harcourt said the Prime Minister, was point-blank refused and acquiesced." But the Prime Minister's right in this connection can hardly be questioned today because "a Minister holds office at the Queen's pleasure, and the Queen in such matters traditionally accepts the advice of the Prime Minister."

It will not be out of place to mention here that Nehru, instead of asking his colleagues to resign, used the Kamaraj Plan under which six Cabinet Ministers including four senior ones were dropped Even in England we have examples where the Prime Minister dropped his colleagues in a summary manner. "Under Harold Macmillan who dismissed a third of his Cabinet, including the Chancellor of Exchequer, Setwyn Lloyd in July 1962, the country, as the Times noted in a despatch in early November 1962, 'moved near enough to the Presidential form of Government' This process was still perfected under Harold Wilson (1964-1970) who is said to have functioned 'more like the President in the American system of democracy than Prime Minister in the British Parliamentary system.'

Prime Minister and the Cabinet Committees

The Cabinet Committees are appointed with a view to divide the workload of the Cabinet in a systematic and scientific manner so that it becomes possible to go into the smallest details through the proper collection and processing of the available data on a subject and then to make the pros and cons of a proposal for taking a decision. These committees also help in the quick disposal of business and an expert examination of the issues at hand.

The Prime Minister, for example, may appoint a subcommittee to investigate into a specific question for further use and reference of the Cabinet. The Cabinet Committees are also there to reconcile the conflicting claims of joint responsibility of the Cabinet for scientific investigation and expert analysts of a problem for facilitating a quick decision and its effective implementation for proper coordination in intra-ministerial matters and for a closer and general supervision of the Prime Minister over the functioning of the various ministries and departments.

These Committees are of two types—Standing Committees and Ad-hoc Committees and there may also be Subcommittees under a Committee of the Cabinet At present there are more than a dozen Cabinet Committees functioning for the Indian Cabinet.

The prominent among these are the Committee for Political Affairs (previously known as the PAC), Emergency Committee or ECC, Committees on Foreign Affairs, Policy Planning for External Affairs, Defence, Internal Affairs, Economic Policy, Economic Coordination, Prices, Production and Exports, Trade and Industry, Food and Agriculture, Tourism and Transport, Parliamentary Affairs, Appointments and Family Planning.

Since the Prime Minister himself is the Chairman of a large number of these committees and the Home Minister is represented as member on most of them, it is quite obvious that these committees in several cases are given the authority to make final decisions, although their decisions are placed before the Cabinet for the information of all the members and the Cabinet may review any one of them.

Commenting on the functioning of these committees. Krishna Menon says, 'the Defence Committee of the Cabinet is the Cabinet itself that is to say, it does not include the whole Cabinet Decisions taken by the Defence Committee are tantamount to decisions taken by the Cabinet, unless of course, the Prime Minister, who is Chairman of it, should say that it is a matter which should be considered by or mentioned to all our colleagues. But even so, certain questions are referred to the Defence Committee alone Normally this only happens if the Defence Minister or the Prime Minister desires it.

With the Foreign Affairs Committee usually no issue of policy arises. But when serious matters take place, for example, a very considerable raid by Pakistan, it is necessary to meet. Usually the Prime Minister mentions it to the people concerned, he must carry his colleagues with him and by implication it is a Cabinet decision." In the beginning, the Foreign Affairs Committee consisted of four or five members including the Chairman. But later on this Committee was broad-based to make it a representative body of the Cabinet.

But this is not the case with all committees For example, the Economic Committee which is a subcommittee of the Cabinet, does not make any decision Matters are referred to it or it can take up something and study it if it wants and then formally it comes before the Cabinet. The Foreign Affairs Committee is rather in the same position but in certain matters it is more like the Defence Committee.

The Economic Committee of the Cabinet in the later days of Nehru-era certainly did not have much impact on the government so far as formulation of policies was concerned because Economic affairs were largely considered by the Finance Minister, the Economic Affairs Committee, the Planning Commission and Public discussion and so on Menon holds that by and large these committees did not shape policy although they did at times Next to the Prime Minister and the Home Minister, the special position of the Finance Minister is inherent in his office due to the fact that he controls and checks the expenditure of various ministries He has an important position having a dominant say so far as the Economic Affair Committee of the Cabinet is concerned. Therefore, generally, his rote cannot be minimised in the decision-making process of the Cabinet and in its committees.

But the Committee system of the Cabinet is not without contradictions and has also been responsible for developing, to some extent, cracks in the joint responsibility and unity, thereby creating a sense of heart-burning among the members of the Cabinet, because it creates an imbalance in the sharing of power by the individual Ministers. Hence, it is said: "the Cabinet Committees, organised by the Prime Minister to coordinate the functions of various Ministers have been largely dominated by the same few Ministers. As Prime Minister Nehru himself was the Chairman of 9 to the 10 Committees and the Home Minister was a member of all committees and was Chairman of the tenth.

The Finance Minister was the member of the seven." Secondly, appointments to these Committees have been made "more on personal considerations than on considerations of bringing only the Ministers concerned together". The Emergency Committee of the Cabinet setup in 1962 and composed of six senior Ministers including the Prime Minister, came in Nehru's last years to assume the role of inner Cabinet and took over many of the decision-making responsibilities of the whole Cabinet As Prime Minister.

Nehru exercised a pre-eminent role; his dominance of the Cabinet was overwhelming Under Shastri the Emergency Committee declined in importance. The Cabinet primacy was restored in domestic affairs, as each Minister was given a greater rote of initiative and discretion.

The Emergency Committee in Shastri's regime was enlarged and besides the Prime Minister, the Finance Minister and the Defence Minister, who were already its members, the Foreign Affairs and Information and Broadcasting Ministers were also included Even after the emergency had ended, it continued to be pre-eminent in foreign and defence matters. As seen from the Rann of Kutch dispute in 1965, the Emergency Cabinet Committee was the supreme organ of decision-making in the domain of foreign affairs.

But since Indira Gandhi assumed power, the Emergency Committee had lost much of its authority. Being at the helm of affairs, it was a golden opportunity for Indira to strengthen and consolidate her power and position in the Cabinet. And in this process of capturing the power-base, she created the Political Affairs Committee composed of a small group of senior Cabinet Ministers (Jagjivan Ram, Y. B. Chauhan. Fakhruddin Ali Ahmad,

Swaran Singh) under her Chairmanship. Responsible for the coordination of major Cabinet concerns in domestic and international affairs and in defence, the Committee became "the most important decision-making body in India after the Prime Minister herself." A similarly constituted Economic Policy Committee was at that time reconstituted in February 1972 by Mrs. Gandhi to give direction to India's economic policy. Proposals for setting up a public corporation to take over and manage sick industrial units and Ganga Flood Control Project were considered in its first meeting.

This Committee has the Prime Minister as its Chairman and deals with policy matters alone. The Finance. Planning. Industrial Development and Steel Ministers are its members Another Committee dealing with Inter-ministry economic coordination was renewed during July 1972 Then came the "Ministerial task force" consisting of six key Ministers to solve Inter-ministry problems and to make important economic decisions This task-force consisted of the Industrial Development Minister, the Planning Minister, the Steel Minister, the Railway Minister, the Minister of Petroleum and Chemical and the Foreign Trade Minister This economic group aimed at an action-oriented programme to step up production in the country and the cynics called this 'Dosa Cabinet' after C. Subramaniam instead of the 'Kitchen Cabinet' the express-on used for Mrs. Gandhi's Cabinet in 1966-67.

In fact these Ministers were very close to the Prime Minister and they—C. Subramaniam, Mohan Kumaramangalam, T.A. Pai, H. R. Gokhale, D.P. Dhar and L.N. Mishra—had influenced the formulation of the economic policies of the Indira Government since the 1971-74 period. The cases in point at that time were the despair of the Steel and Mines Minister about how to get the Railway Minister to move the Coal stocks from pitheads in time or the Agriculture Minister about the speedy movement of foodgrains to the scarcity-hit areas.

But there is a sharp criticism against these committees in the sense that two-tier, three-tier or multi-tier committee system purports no improvement in the solution of the pressing problems faced by the masses grilling under the wheels of starvation, shortage, hike in prices and unemployment.

This only suits the Ministers and bureaucrats These committees have not been able so far to cut much ice by taking timely initiative, adopting proper coordinating techniques, and taking effective steps for administrative action But without such committees, which are in fact the operative parts of the Cabinet-Machine the smooth and quick deliberative functioning and effective implementation of policies of the government will be an uphill task.

Bibliography

Arya, M. V.: *Lal Bahadur Shastri : An Era of Transition in Indian Foreign Policy*, MacMillan, 1999.

Bhattacharya, B. K.: *India's Freedom Movement: Legacy of Bipin Chandra Pal*, Deep and Deep, New Delhi, 2007.

Burman, P. L.: *Lal Bahadur Shastri, 'Reflections on Indian Politics'*, Indian Journal of Political Science, 1962.

C.P. Srivastava: *Lal Bahadur Shastri : A Life of Truth in Politics*, Oxford University, 2004.

Chakravarty, Shachi: *Quit India Movement: A Study*, New Century Publication, 2002.

Chandra, Bipan: *India's Struggle For Independence*, Penguin Books India (P) Ltd., New Delhi, 1989.

Chandra, Shailesh: *90 Years of India's Struggle for Independence: 1857-1947*, Alfa Pub, 2008.

Ganjoo, S.: *Muslim Freedom Fighters of India*, Anmol Publication, New Delhi, 2002.

Ghosh, Ratna: *Netaji Subhas Chandra Bose and Indian Freedom Struggle (2 Vols-Set)*, Deep and Deep, 2006.

Goyal, P. K.: *Battle of India's Freedom Movement*, Vista International, 2005.

Gupta, Shantinath: *Great Freedom Fighters of India*, Anmol, 2006.

Hari Hara Das: *The History of Freedom Movement in India (1857-1947)*, National, 1998.

Indu Dave: *Indian Personality in Its Developmental Background*, Himanshu, 1991.

Iyengar, A. S.: *Role of Press and Indian Freedom Struggle: All through the Gandhian Era*, APH, 2001.

John, Noyce: *Lal Bahadur Shastri: an English-language,* Lulu.com, 2002.

Kailash Khanna: *History of Indian Freedom Struggle*, Commonwealth Publication, 2004.

Kaushik, A. S.: *Great Freedom Fighters of India*, Indian Publication, 2007.

Khairul Anam, Md.: *Indian Freedom Movement and Murshidabad District 1905-1947*, Bagchi, K. P., 2008.

Krishan Mohan: *Encyclopaedic History of Indian Freedom Movement (4 Vols-Set)*, Book Enclave, 1999.

Kumar, Prafulla Pattanaik: *The First Indian War of Independence: Freedom Movement in Orissa, 1804-1825*, APH, 2005.

Kumar, Raj: *Essays on Indian Freedom Movement*, History and Culture Series, Discovery, 2003.

Kumar, Ravindra: *Champaran to Quit India Movement*, Mittal, 2002.

Kumar, Sirisa Shadangi: *The Prisons of South Orissa and the Freedom Fighters in Incarceration, 1900 - 1947*, Punthi Pustak, 2005.

L.P. Singh: *Portrait of Lal Bahadur Shastri*, Ravi Dayal Publishers, Delhi, 1996.

Lion Agrawal, M. G.: *Freedom Fighters of India (4 Vols-Set)*, Isha Books, 2008.

Majumdar, R. C.: *History of the Freedom Movement in India (3 Vols-Set)*, Firma KLM, 1997.

Malhotra, Sumiti: *Thoughts of Great Personalities in 20 Century*, Raj Publishing, 2003.

Manju Verma: *The Role of Women in the Freedom Movement in Punjab (1919-1947)*, Abhijeet, 2003.

Maulana Syed Mohammad Mian: *The Prisoners of Malta (Asira'n-E-Malta): The Heart-Rending Tale of Muslim Freedom Fighters in British Period,* Manak, 2005.

Mazhar Kibriya: *Gandhi and Indian Freedom Struggle,* APH, 1999.

Muthaiah, S.: *Women Freedom Fighters,* The Hindu, 2004.

Nanda, S. P.: *Freedom Movement and Constitutional Development in India,* Dominant, 2004.

Om Prakash: *Encyclopaedic History of Indian Freedom Movement (12 to 21 Vols),* Anmol, 2003.

Omesh Saigal: *Shaheed Bhagat Singh: Unique Martyr in Freedom Movement,* Gyan Publication, 2002.

Parashar, Parmanand: *Kashmir and the Freedom Movement,* Sarup, 2004.

Pradhan, K. B.: *Freedom Movement in India,* Arise Pub, 2007.

Prasad, Rajeshwar: *Days with Lal Bahadur Shastri,* Allied, New Delhi, 1991.

Rafiya, Nisar: *Shaikh-Ul-Hind Maulana Mahmud Hasan and Indian Freedom Movement,* Manak Pub, 2008.

Ram Sharma, S.: *Education of Women and Freedom Movement,* Discovery, 1996.

Ram, S. and Kumar, R.: *Encyclopaedia of Indian Freedom Struggle (10 Vols-Set),* Commonwealth Pub, 2008.

————: *Quit India Movement: 1942-1945,* Commonwealth Pub, 2008.

Ramanathan, K. V.: *The Satyamurti Letters, Vol. II: The Indian Freedom Struggle Through the Eyes of a Parliamentarian,* Dorling Kindersley for Pearson Longman an Imprint of Pearson Education, 2008.

Ramu, P. S.: *Azad Hind Fauj (I.N.A.) and The Freedom Movement,* Freedom Movement Memorial Comm, 1998.

Saksena, N.S.: *India: Towards Anarchy, 1967-1992,* Abhinav, New Delhi, 1993.

Sen Gupta, Bhabani: *Communism in Indian Politics,* Columbia University Press, New York, 1972.

Sen, S.P.: *Dictionary of National Biography,* Institute of Historical Studies, Calcutta, 1975.

————: *Sources of the History of India,* Institute of Historical Studies, Calcutta, 1978.

Sharma, S. K.: *Eminent Indian Freedom Fighters (2 Vols-Set),* Anmol Publication, New Delhi, 2004.

Sir, C.P. Srivastava: *Corruption: India's Enemy Within,* MacMillan India, New Delhi, 2001.

————: *Lal Bahadur Shastri: A Life of Truth in Politics,* Oxford University Press, New Delhi, 1995.

————: *Lal Bahadur Shastri, Prime Minister of India, 1964-1966: A Life of Truth in Politics,* Oxford University Press, Delhi, 1995.

Sundaram, V.: *Great Crusader for Women's Emancipation,* News Today, 2005.

Sundararaja, Saroja: *March to Freedom in Madras Presidency, 1916-1947,* Lalitha Publication, Chennai, 1989.

Taneja, Anup: *Gandhi, Women and the National Movement, 1920-47,* Har-Anand Publications, Delhi, 2005.

Index

J

K

L

M

N

P

Q

R

S

T

U

V

W

❑❑❑